Advancing Big Data Analytics for Healthcare Service Delivery

In recent years, there has been steady increase in the interest shown in both big data analytics and the use of information technology (IT) solutions to improve healthcare services. Despite the growing interest, there are limited materials, to addressing the needs and challenges posed by the activities and processes including the use of big data. From IT solutions' perspectives, this book aims to advance the deployment and use of big data analytics to increase patients' big data usefulness and improve healthcare service delivery.

The book provides significant insights and useful guide on how to access and manage big data, in improving healthcare service delivery. The book contributes a fresh perspective, which primarily comes from the complementary use of analytics approach with actor-network theory (ANT), and other techniques, in advancing healthcare service delivery. Accessing and managing healthcare big data have always been a challenging exercise. Due to the sensitivity of the health sector, the focus on patients' big data is from either technical or social perspective. Thus, the book employs sociotechnical theories, ANT and structuration theory (ST) as lenses to examine and explain the factors that enable and constrain the use of patients' big data for health services. By doing so, the book brings a different dimension and advance health service delivery.

Providing a timely and important contribution to this critical area, this book is a valuable, international resource for academics, postgraduate students and researchers in the areas of IT, big data analytics, data management and health informatics.

Tiko Iyamu holds a PhD in information systems from the University of Cape Town, South Africa. Currently, Iyamu is a Research Professor at the Faculty of Informatics and Design, Cape Peninsula University of Technology (CPUT), Cape Town, South Africa. Previously, he was with the Tshwane University of Technology, South Africa, and Namibia University of Science and Technology, Namibia. Iyamu served as a Professor Extraordinaire at the Department of Computer Science, University of the Western Cape, Cape Town, South Africa, from 2006 to 2015. In 2014, he was a Visiting Professor at the Flensburg University of Applied Sciences, Germany. Professor Iyamu's areas of focus include enterprise architecture, health informatics, big data analytics and mobile computing. In addition, he has keen interest in the application of sociotechnical theories, such as actor-network theory, structuration theory and diffusion of innovation for information systems research. He has authored over 160 peer-reviewed research articles in journals, conference proceedings and book chapters. Prof Iyamu has authored seven books, including *Applying theories for information systems research* and *Enterprise Architecture for Strategic Management of Modern IT Solutions*. He has received several awards in research and excellence in supervision of postgraduates.

Routledge Studies in Innovation, Organizations and Technology

The Business Model Innovation Process
Preparation, Organization and Management
Yariv Taran, Harry Boer and Christian Nielsen

Management, Organisations and Artificial Intelligence
Where Theory Meets Practice
Piotr Buła and Bartosz Niedzielski

Disruptive Platforms
Markets, Ecosystems and Monopolists
Edited by Tymoteusz Doligalski, Michał Goliński and Krzysztof Kozłowski

Inclusive Innovation
Robyn Klingler-Vidra, Alex Glennie and Courtney Savie Lawrence

Organizational Change, Innovation and Business Development
The Impact of Non-Technological Innovations
Edited by Magdalena Popowska and Julita E. Wasilczuk

Public Innovation and Digital Transformation
Edited by Hannele Väyrynen, Nina Helander and Harri Jalonen

Innovation and Leadership in the Public Sector
The Australian Experience
Mahmoud Moussa, Leonie Newnham, Adela McMurray and Nuttawuth Muenjohn

Advancing Big Data Analytics for Healthcare Service Delivery
Tiko Iyamu

For more information about this series, please visit: www.routledge.com/Routledge-Studies-in-Innovation-Organizations-and-Technology/book-series/RIOT

Advancing Big Data Analytics for Healthcare Service Delivery

Tiko Iyamu

LONDON AND NEW YORK

First published 2023
by Routledge
4 Park Square, Milton Park, Abingdon, Oxon OX14 4RN

and by Routledge
605 Third Avenue, New York, NY 10158

Routledge is an imprint of the Taylor & Francis Group, an informa business

© 2023 Tiko Iyamu

The right of Tiko Iyamu to be identified as author of this work has been asserted in accordance with sections 77 and 78 of the Copyright, Designs and Patents Act 1988.

All rights reserved. No part of this book may be reprinted or reproduced or utilised in any form or by any electronic, mechanical, or other means, now known or hereafter invented, including photocopying and recording, or in any information storage or retrieval system, without permission in writing from the publishers.

Trademark notice: Product or corporate names may be trademarks or registered trademarks, and are used only for identification and explanation without intent to infringe.

British Library Cataloguing-in-Publication Data
A catalogue record for this book is available from the British Library

ISBN: 978-1-032-16933-0 (hbk)
ISBN: 978-1-032-16934-7 (pbk)
ISBN: 978-1-003-25106-4 (ebk)

DOI: 10.4324/9781003251064

Typeset in Bembo
by codeMantra

Contents

List of Figures ix
List of Tables xi
Acknowledgements xiii
Preface xv

1 Introduction   1

2 A Structuration View in Managing Healthcare Data   14

3 Open Technology Innovation for Healthcare Services   30

4 Interaction with Cloud-Hosted Health Data   46

5 A Framework for Selecting Healthcare Big Data Analytics Tools   58

6 The Interpretivist and Analytics Approaches for Healthcare Big Data Analytics   74

7 A Multi-Level Approach for Analysis of Healthcare Big Data   89

8 Transforming Big Data for Healthcare Service Delivery   106

9 The Integration of Social Media with Healthcare Big Data for Services   126

10 Actor-Network Theory View of Healthcare Big Data   141

11 The Implementation of Big Data Analytics for
Healthcare Services 159

12 The Evaluation of Big Data Analytics Tools for Healthcare
Services 175

Index 189

Figures

2.1	The dimension of duality of structure (Giddens, 1984, p. 128)	18
2.2	Theoretical framework	19
2.3	Data management conceptual framework for healthcare services	21
3.1	Factors influencing open innovation in healthcare	37
3.2	Information flow (Mashilo & Iyamu, 2012, p. 491)	41
4.1	Interaction by healthcare actors	53
5.1	Big data analytics framework	65
6.1	Complementary use of big data analytics and *interpretivist* approach	82
7.1	Four moments of translation (Callon, 1986)	94
7.2	Multi-level analysis of big data	98
7.3	Heterogeneity of big data	101
8.1	Four moments of translation (Callon, 1986)	110
8.2	ANT for analysis of healthcare big data	112
8.3	Big data transformative in healthcare	119
9.1	Factors of influence for social media and healthcare big data	130
9.2	IT integration of social media with healthcare big data	135
10.1	Data analysis framework	151
12.1	Building blocks	182

Tables

5.1	Big data and healthcare	60
5.2	Big data analytics and healthcare	61
6.1	Implications of practice	83
8.1	Implication of practice	121
11.1	Criteria for big data analytics tools	170
11.2	Key indicator for the use of big data analytics tools	171

Acknowledgements

To Department of Information Technology, Cape Peninsula University of Technology, I am thankful for your support.

To the Research Forum at the IT department that I have chaired since its inception, humbly, I thank the current and past members that I have been opportune to work with over the years.

To my good editor, Tony Ekata, I thank you immensely for painstakingly proofreading the manuscript; you are one of a kind.

To my valued friends, Osaro Odemwingie, Olusesan Ibitomi, Eula Mothibi, John Otasowie, Randy Osayande and Innocent Davidson, thank you for your advice and support of many years. Robust discussion with you have made so many experiences joyful and satisfying for me in my journey.

To my cousins, Christopher Osayande and Clement Osayande, gratefully, I offer warmth and profound appreciation to your sincere kindness and support.

To my siblings, I will always feel a deep sense of gratitude for your affectionate interest in my pursuits; and to my mother and late father, the wisdom that you shared with me has been my light and rock.

To my family, I am deeply indebted to my family for their consistent and constant love and care; to my children, Osa and Osagie; and Ruvimbo, thank you for being a trusted confidant, and for your relentless patience and support.

To my late bosom friends, Godwin Iyamu and Emmanuel Irorere, to whom this book is dedicated, I will always miss you.

Above all, I am forever grateful to God, our merciful Lord.

Preface

In recent years, there has been steady increase in the interest shown in both big data analytics and the use of information technology solutions, to improve healthcare services. The interest has been from both practitioners and academics, including students. Despite the growing interest, there are limited materials to address the needs and challenges posed in the areas of big data for healthcare services. The combination of big data analytics and healthcare is a major contribution of this book. Another significant contribution is the complementary use of analytics with actor-network theory (ANT) and other techniques, to advance solutions that can improve healthcare service delivery. Currently, there seems to be limited materials, book or research article where ANT has been complementarily used with big data analytics for healthcare purposes.

The book covers four main and significant areas. First, it focuses on improving the use of big data analytics for services. Second, it explores a mechanism through which healthcare service delivery can be improved using big data analytics. Third, very importantly, it examines a complementary use of big data analytics with other analysis techniques, to improve big data usefulness for healthcare service delivery. Finally, it employs sociotechnical theories, ANT and structuration theory to improve the management of healthcare big data.

It is the guest of many healthcare facilities to improve the use of big data tools but there are challenges, such as know-how. The knowledge derived from the analysis of big data gives healthcare providers clinical insights not otherwise available. The insights enable and guide the healthcare practitioners in decision-making with much more accuracy. This book identifies and addresses some of the challenges which many healthcare facilities encounter. The challenges encounter with data in healthcare are in some areas and facilities considered myriad. The challenges include lack of, or limited access to, data on health facility's outcomes. Other challenges identified in the book include data and big data fragmentation and the lack of uniform digitisation, which impede efficiency and effectiveness. In addition, some patients' data are often overlooked because it is in silos.

Holistically, the book explains how the above challenges, including how risks can be reduced, and effectiveness and efficiency can be improved through an analysis of patients' big data. The primary objectives of analysis of healthcare big data are to transit from a reactive, treatment-based approach to a more integrated, preventive model. Also, the insights from the analysis of health big data can lead to greater patients' engagement, and significantly improve service delivery and increase compliance level with policies relating to health matters. Primarily, this is because analysis of data can shed light on healthcare drivers for different segments of the population and health conditions. As covered in the book, analysis of patients' big data increases evidence level and helps healthcare providers to develop best practices.

The book emphasises on the use of analytics, to unlock better prospects in carrying out healthcare activities and processes, such as applying diagnostic for health conditions and predicting patient's behaviour. The prescriptive and descriptive enable effective ways of managing patients' health conditions, to facilitate precision of care through detection of heterogeneity in patients' big data and responses to treatments. *Big data analytics* help drive towards appropriateness of insights for decision-making.

This book is divided into three main parts in a total of twelve chapters. Chapter 1 is the introduction. Part 1 contains four chapters: Chapters 2 to 5. In Chapter 2, the structuration theory is applied to provide a fresh perspective and increase health data usefulness and improvement. This is followed by Chapters 3 and 4, where open technology innovation and interaction with cloud solutions are holistically discussed, respectively, in the context of accessing healthcare big data. Chapter 5 covers the integration of social media with healthcare bid data for service delivery purposes.

Part 2 consists of three chapters. It begins from Chapter 6, which presents a model to guide the selection of analytics tools for organisational purposes. In the remaining two chapters, Chapters 7 and 8, the implementation and evaluation of healthcare big data analytics in health facilities are examined and models developed. The chapters emphasise the influencing factors that help gain a deeper comprehension in applying the concept of big data analytics, to improve health services.

Four chapters, from Chapters 9 to 12, are covered in Part 3. Chapter 9 presents the interpretivist approach as a dynamic alternative for analysing healthcare big data, in improving service delivery. Next, a multiple-level framework is developed to guide the complementary use of ANT with big data analytics to provide an innovative and holistic analysis of healthcare big data. Chapter 11 discusses how healthcare big data is transformed for service delivery. Finally, an empirical case study is presented in Chapter 12.

1 Introduction

Introduction

The chapter begins by clarifying two sets of concepts that are fundamentally significant to this book: healthcare vs health care; and analysis vs analytics. These are often seen as two distinctive terms or concepts. Notwithstanding, the terms are consistently interchangeably used in both academic and business domains. The interchangeability carries a huge challenge and implication from the perspectives of interpretation and context. The challenge confuses many people, especially students and researchers of information systems (IS), information technology (IT) and health informatics. The implication arises from misunderstanding the attributes associated with the concepts. From the healthcare vs health care front, the confusion increasingly gets silenced because the health profession is not helping enough to clarify the matter. The dictionaries too could only nationalise the terms between the North American and the British.

The concept of 'health care' refers to the actions of providers of health-related services. This includes actions and activities that nurses and other medical practitioners carry out, such as diagnoses and prescriptions of medications. On the contrary, 'healthcare' means the system through which people (or patients) get health care services. Data (and big data) are generated from the actions or efforts and systems used for health-related issues towards restoring well-being. This means that both the actions and services are inseparable. Thus, the term healthcare is adopted in this book.

The other concept, analytics, is often thought of as analysis, which confuses many people. Analytics and analysis are slightly different, although they have much in common than differences. The contrast lies in the emphasis that is associated with each of the concepts. Both concepts refer to an examination of data or information. Analysis is broader of the two concepts primarily because it is more general, while analytics is more specific to task and systematic data examination. Think of *analysis* as the action humans carry out in building a narrative, and *analytics* as a computational process. From a practical front, analytics is a thing, and analysis is an action. In that regard, analytics can be thought of as tools, while analysis is the process of developing scenarios using tools.

DOI: 10.4324/9781003251064-1

Primarily, healthcare provides care to the patients through private or public facilities, which are hospitals and clinics. The need for quality and comprehensive healthcare is increasing across the globe. Thus, IS and IT solutions are employed to enable and support the processes and services that health facilities provide to patients and the community in general. Some of the services are documenting and managing of patients' records for better decision-making, diagnoses, x-rays and prescriptions. Even more important is the accuracy of patients' medical records, which contain various sets of data (or big data) from different sources, gathered at unprecedented times, and in diverse formats.

Health professionals rely on medical history and its corroboration with the current state, to provide quality and life-saving services to patients. On this premise, there has been an increasing emphasis on the quality and usefulness of patients' data through management and governance. However, it becomes challenging as the data grows, its variety increases and the rapidity at which the data is retrieved, accessed and used continues to upsurge at an exponential degree. Subsequently, IT solutions, such as big data and big data analytics, are explored to advance healthcare service delivery in many facilities.

The term big data refers to data that comprises characteristics which include a wide variety, huge volume and increasing velocity (Baig, Shuib, & Yadegaridehkordi, 2019). Big data is a set of data of unprecedented size, complexity, from numerous sources, and which come from structured, semi-structured and unstructured types of data sets (Mikalef, Krogstie, Pappas, & Pavlou, 2020). Big data has size, type or rapidity beyond the comprehension of traditional methods, to capture, store, manage and process the data with low latency. Examples of sources of data types are sensors, video and audio. These require more sophisticated devices and networks for storing and transporting various patients' data sets in real-time. The unprecedented nature of big data makes it difficult or impossible to process using traditional methods. Thus, the analytics technique is employed.

Big data analytics is critical for analysing healthcare big data. It is used for large, diverse and rapidly changing patients' big data, including structured, semi-structured and unstructured data sets. Subsequently, this spun the existence of many big data analytics approaches, of which the most common are descriptive, diagnostic, predictive and prescriptive analytics (Lepenioti, Bousdekis, Apostolou, & Mentzas, 2020). Big data analytics is considered an advanced method of analysis because it uses algorithms to uncover trends and multiplexity of links and heterogeneity of patients' data. The misunderstanding and similarity between the tools within these approaches make their selection, management and use challenging.

In advancing healthcare service delivery, this book presents a solution through which the management of patients' data can be strengthened by applying several techniques, approaches and sociotechnical theories, such as the structuration theory (ST) as a lens. In addition to the analytics technique, the interpretive approach and sociotechnical theory, such as the actor-network theory (ANT), can be used for analysing patients' big data. Also, both the interpretive approach and ANT can be applied separately and singularly or complementarily with analytics techniques to advance health big data analysis, to gain deeper insights for decision making.

The processing entails analyses intended to reveal patterns, relationships and trends related to human actions and interactions with big data. This makes big data analytics a complex process in examining big data to reveal critical health-related information, such as unknown circumstances, why things happen the way they do and unformulaic trends among patients' big data. The complexity influences decisions and becomes terrifying if an emerging or less experienced medical practitioner relies on such inchoate (unclear) information to make decisions that affect human care or life.

The Objective and Focus of the Book

Due to the sensitivity of the healthcare environment, there are many challenges in enabling and supporting health-related activities and processes with IT solutions, such as databases, integration of software and network protocols. This can be attributed to the openness and usage of IT solutions. For many years, literature and case studies have identified many IT-healthcare challenges; yet some of them persist (Dash, Shakyawar, Sharma, & Kaushik, 2019). This is due to focusing too much on technology enablement and less on why things happen how they do (Iyamu, 2021). Some of the challenges are briefly mentioned in the remainder of the chapter and holistically addressed in the remaining chapters of the book.

This book brings a fresh perspective through its contribution. It provides an advanced mechanism by offering methods through models and frameworks that guide applying (1) ST to understand data management and governance; (2) big data analytics selection method; and (3) big data analytics and ANT complementarily for analysis to enhance the usefulness of healthcare big data and improve service delivery. Primarily, this book critically and fundamentally helps to:

i clearly harness the capabilities of big data analytics and analysis to provide compelling benefits for healthcare service delivery;
ii gain deeper insights into the relationships that exist between the actors involved in carrying out big data analytics and analysing healthcare big data for service enhancement.

Problematisation

Within the healthcare environment, there exist increasingly huge patients' big data. Despite the criticality involved, many health professionals lack knowledge about how to make the data more useful for wider purposes; they only know how to access the data for their minimal, specific tasks. The main challenges often encountered in the use of big data analytics are identified in four categories: (1) selecting the most appropriate tools; (2) analysing healthcare big data; (3) managing healthcare big data; and (4) employing IT solutions such as social media and cloud computing. In addition, the challenges experienced from both healthcare and big data perspectives are briefly explained.

Many health facilities (hospitals and clinics) are challenged by not knowing how to select the most appropriate big data analytics to analyse and interpret healthcare big data (Wu, Li, Cheng & Lin, 2016). As a result, healthcare continues to strive and is not close to realising the potentials of big data analytics, which sometimes negatively affects service delivery. In Chapter 5, this book provides a framework to guide the selection of big data analytics for healthcare purposes.

Many healthcare facilities lack appropriate IT solutions, to enable and support their services (Mehta & Pandit, 2018; Wang, Kung & Byrd, 2018). The challenge can be attributed to slowness in transiting from a paper-based approach to automated data processing (Zhang et al., 2015). The resistance by many health professionals, manifest from lack of know-how in applying techniques for the analysis of healthcare big data, is also a challenge. As discussed, in Chapters 5–8, this book presents approaches that can be adopted, to easy analysis.

Essentially, the healthcare environment and the data it generates are sensitive; thus, privacy and confidentiality of patients' data are of utmost importance to the actors involved (such as patients, physicians, policymakers and regulators). Consequently, using IT solutions, such as cloud computing, limits access, understanding and insights, affects service delivery and complicates the sharing of patients' data (Wang, Kung, Wang & Cegielski, 2018). The use of big data analytics encounters challenges such as fragmented data, validation, data standardisation, and data inaccuracy and inconsistency (Rumsfeld, Joynt & Maddox, 2016). These challenges are because of poor or lack of management. The challenges manifest in interoperability, security and privacy complications.

Social media has been used to examine users' predictive power and prescribe the velocity of information (Dewan & Ramaprasad, 2014). For strategic purposes, both analytics tools (Budhiraja, Thomas, Kim & Redline, 2016) and analysis techniques can be employed to strengthen the management, exchange and transportation of healthcare big data obtained from social media and stored and distributed using cloud solutions.

The constant exchanges and flows of data at unprecedented ways and rates present different challenges (Raghupathi & Raghupathi, 2014) to many healthcare facilities. Consequently, by storing, accessing and managing the increasing volume, variety and velocity of data change. This has implications for the security, ownership and governance of big data (Wang, Kung, Wang & Cegielski, 2018). Although incorporating cloud computing into healthcare big data would eliminate cost (Wang, Kung & Byrd, 2018), it imposes challenges from the perspective of accessing and interacting with patients' data.

Chapter 4 focuses on the influencing factors based on which a better understanding can be gained, and solutions developed.

Big data analytics contributes significant value in its use. At the same time, it brings about some challenges. Mehta and Pandit (2018) argued that some big data analytics could be complex, limiting the use of IT solutions in enabling healthcare services. Using big data analytics in healthcare becomes more cumbersome and sometimes leads to errors, which can be detrimental to both patients and service provider (Kruse, Goswamy, Raval & Marawi, 2016; Raghupathi & Raghupathi, 2014). This challenge necessitates further applying sociotechnical theories such as ANT and ST as lenses, to analyse healthcare big data. The approach is intended to increase the usefulness of big data, improve its quality and advance service delivery.

Challenges of Healthcare

Many healthcare facilities suffer from multiple challenges, ranging from data management to selecting analytics tools and analysing patients' big data. The challenges manifest in numerous factors and affect operational efficiency and strategic effectiveness in the areas of scalability and capability (Nambiar, Bhardwaj, Sethi & Vargheese, 2013), integration and security (Pastorino et al., 2019). Some of the challenges include preventable medical errors, lack of transparency, adjusting to rapidly changing clinical data, not understanding digital relationships that should ease physicians' burdens, uncertain forecasting and reshaping health data portfolios.

For one reason or the other, healthcare data sets are rarely standardised. Increasingly, patients' big data is often fragmented (Raghupathi & Raghupathi, 2014). Also, the big data is often incompatible with various formats, such as unstructured and semi-structured. These challenges are critical and need to be always addressed. The size of big data in healthcare periodically rises to petabytes and beyond. Big data is generated from both internal and external sources, such as laboratories, pharmacies, data aggregators and medical journals (Mehta & Pandit, 2018). Heterogeneous data is a challenge for many health facilities and practitioners. Attempts to trace the root cause and transformation of the attributes ultimately affect generating insights for improved services.

Challenges of Big Data

Some of the fundamental challenges of big data analytics are in securing and managing data and processing sensitive, personal health data in high volumes from different sources (Galetsi, Katsaliaki & Kumar, 2019). Some of these challenges are detrimental as they influence erroneous diagnoses and treatments. Big data analytics is required to address or overcome some of the challenges. However, improvement relies on the availability and accuracy of big data quality (Rehman, Naz & Razzak, 2021). Other challenges hinge on complexity, accessibility, compliance and regulation, which require efficient analytics methods (Rehman, Naz & Razzak, 2021).

Types of Big Data Analytics

There are many types of big data analytics techniques. The most common techniques in both academic and business domains are diagnostic analytics, descriptive analytics, predictive analytics and prescriptive analytics (Iyamu & Mgudlwa, 2021). Recently, detective analytics have emerged. These analytics tools are essentially relevant at various levels of degree, to one or more areas of health-related aspects of service delivery.

Diagnostic Analytics

Diagnostic analytics focuses on gaining insights into why things happen or happened in an activity. The technique involves using technologies and applications to conduct exploratory data analysis, to better understand the reason behind outcomes in an activity or episode (Ghani, Hamid, Hashem & Ahmed, 2019). Thus, the use of the techniques begins with the aim or objective based on which relevant data is collected, stored and analysed (Delen & Zolbanin, 2018).

In using diagnostic analytics, the findings discovered that the analytical process could be linked back to the health-related services and objectives. Bendre and Thool (2016) provide a useful explanation of how diagnostic analytics is significant to an organisation that endeavours to identify and value its organisational ecosystem, client base and risks associated with new products and services. Thus, the technique helps to identify the causes of certain outcomes and guide informed decision-making (Duan & Xiong, 2015). For example, the analytics processes can consist of discovering and understanding the effect of organisational factors and policies on performance.

Descriptive Analytics

Descriptive analytics is a technique used to examine and describe a current situation with data relative to context and relevance. Watson (2014) describes descriptive analytics as a technique for narrating what has occurred. It involves summarising knowledge, including patterns and trends, based on analysis. Sivarajah, Kamal, Irani and Weerakkody (2017) explain how the technique can be applied to analyse data sets, define the current state and model past behaviour, and better comprehend business data for organisational goal and objectives. Descriptive analytics is usually employed as a statistical method to search and summarise historical data.

One of the strengths is that it leads to discovering what happened or drawing attention to what can occur. The process helps to identify trends and patterns, which ultimately leads to the meaning being associated. The appropriation of meanings enacts decision-making and aids organisational processes and competitiveness. Various methods, such as clustering, regression analysis and summary statistics, can be used for descriptive analytics. On the downside, descriptive analytics does not necessarily allow generalisation. Also, the results are not always accurate. In addition, the technique only describes the situation and refers to underlying relations but does not allow a conclusion to be drawn.

Predictive Analytics

Predictive analytics helps predict the future based on assessing historical data, discovering patterns and observing trends. It means that the technique focuses on forecasting and modelling, based on which a future state is defined (Joseph & Johnson, 2013; Waller & Fawcett, 2013). In essence, it suggests what can happen in the future by analysing past activity or performance. This involves probing and inferring patterns. Siegel (2013) argues that predictive analytics assists with better planning and mitigation against risks. Essentially, determining what happened and knowing why specific outcomes occurred help to predict what can possibly happen (Khanra, Dhir, Islam & Mäntymäki, 2020). In addition, predictive analytics enables a more accurate prediction of performance that is based on the past.

One of the challenges of predictive analytics is that data often come from different sources and vary in quality and format. Also, data from various sources are usually not compatible. Thus, the data requires major pre-processing before embarking on the analytics process. In addition, the challenges can get worse in usually unforeseen circumstances caused by natural disasters and unprecedented pandemics. Also, human control leading to limited access due to sensitivity of personal data, as in the case of healthcare, can derail the predictive analytics process.

Prescriptive Analytics

Prescriptive analytics prescribes activities like possible situations or scenarios, available resources and what should be done. It guides decision-making in both the short and long terms. Essentially, prescriptive analytics enables the optimisation of process models for goal and objective purposes, based on results from data sets (Bihani & Patil, 2014; Sivarajah, Kamal, Irani & Weerakkody, 2017). In addition, prescriptive analytics can be viewed as a technique that provides insights that help decide or dedicate action that should be taken. Subsequently, it enables improvement towards efficacy and success. On this basis, Lepenioti, Bousdekis, Apostolou and Mentzas (2020) argue that the technique is beyond defining, explaining and forecasting events to proposing options that can be adopted for future efficiency and effectiveness determinations.

Prescriptive analytics can be complex (Frazzetto, Nielsen, Pedersen & Šikšnys, 2019) and, seemingly, can be detrimental to the healthcare environment. Primarily, this is because the results from predictive analytics persuade actors into action, inaction or complacency. Thus, accuracy is critical. However, information is not always accurate, which can lead to false or inaccurate predictions. It gets worse when the predictions are impervious to changes.

Distinctively and collaboratively, big data analytics is used to assist organisations, including healthcare facilities to get insights from data resources. Different tools, including graphical, kurtosis, skewness and Cronbach alpha, are used for descriptive analytics.

Diagnostic analytics is usually carried out by using techniques such as correlation, data mining and drill-down. Belhadi, Zkik, Cherrafi and Sha'ri (2019) state that diagnostic analytics utilises some of the same tools used in descriptive analytics. However, the process differs; it requires making correlations to gain deeper insights. Predictive analytics uses tools such as machine learning, computational modelling and statistical data mining to establish the likelihood of various outcomes (Shah, Steyerberg & Kent, 2018). Tools such as simulations and optimisations are used for prescriptive analytics (Lepenioti, Bousdekis, Apostolou & Mentzas, 2020).

Descriptive analytics points to the occurrence, while diagnostic analytics helps understand why certain things happened in the past. Predictive analytics goes beyond the past and predicts what is likely to happen. Prescriptive analytics recommends actions taken to affect those outcomes. However, the usefulness of healthcare big data can be better gained by expanding the analytics into analysis.

Types of Analysis

There is a need to employ approaches beyond big data analytics to enable a holistic analysis and enhance the usefulness of patients' data, to improve and advance service delivery. Mehta and Pandit (2018) explain that despite the value brought by using big data analytical tools, challenges in healthcare persist. Multiple levels of analysis are required to improve the usefulness of big data for healthcare service delivery. Thus, both the interpretive and ANT approaches are considered the most suitable (Walsham & Han, 1993) for analysing healthcare big data. The approaches deepen an understanding and help gain new insights and knowledge.

Interpretive

Interpretivism is a suitable approach for insight into reality in natural settings' activities (Kwayu, Lal & Abubakre, 2018) that can shape the description (descriptive), diagnosis (diagnostic), prediction (predictive) and prescription (prescriptive) of big data usefulness in healthcare. Long before now, Hirschheim, Smithson and Whitehouse (1988) argued that treating phenomena from only a technical perspective could lead to meaningless conclusions that undermine involving social facets. Healthcare is human-centric as it focuses on health-related care and well-being.

The interpretive approach is significant in uncovering factors that influence values within context and content. This is done by using attributes such as what, why, who, how and when to assess healthcare big data for better conclusive and more accurate ends. The interpretive approach recognises both social and technical entities of phenomena (Sarker, Xiao, Beaulieu & Lee, 2018). Stockdale and Standing (2006) argue that the power and strength of interpretivism lie in sense-making and account for multiple views from subjectivism. The interpretive approach encompasses sociotechnical theories such as ANT that hold perspectives of reality as socially constructed to enhance the understanding of events through shifting negotiation.

Actor-Network Theory

ANT is a sociotechnical theory that focuses on shifting negotiation by actors within networks (Callon, 1986). The negotiation influences human and non-human actors' action, technology change (Heeks & Stanforth, 2015), network formation and relationships between entities (Iyamu, 2021). ANT's analytic dimensions provide useful understandings of both human and non-human's actions and processes (Andrade & Urquhart, 2010). Also, ANT's translation concept provides an insight into how process might play out.

The theory is increasingly applied for analysing phenomena, including studies about healthcare (Iyamu, 2021). Altabaibeh, Caldwell and Volante (2020) employed ANT to examine the interplay between actors, including agency and the resources in a health organisation. ANT has been used to underpin many studies that focus on healthcare big data, such as Mgudlwa and Iyamu (2021), Greenhalgh and Stones (2010) and Cresswell, Worth and Sheikh (2010).

Contribution of the Book

This book aims to technologically advance the deployment and advance the use of big data analytics to increase patients' big data usefulness and improve healthcare service delivery. This is a critical area that has received immense attention but with limited research studies.

Key points and concepts to be learnt from the book include but are not limited to the following:

i   Understand how big data analysis can drive learning and decision for healthcare service delivery.
ii Learn how to employ different types of big data analysis: the complementary use of big data analytics with interpretivist approach and ANT for analysing healthcare big data.
iii How to employ analysis, to associate various meanings and usefulness with healthcare big data, in improving the services delivered to patients.

10 *Introduction*

The use of big data analytics is helpful to health facilities to address some of their challenges at the point of services and care (Nambiar, Bhardwaj, Sethi & Vargheese, 2013). In addition, big data analytics enables and supports better and faster decision-making. It entails data-driven decisions to improve operational efficiency and is an effective strategy in providing healthcare services. The use of analytics techniques helps create value that exposes the power relationship between medical personnel and patients (Galetsi, Katsaliaki & Kumar, 2019). This helps reshape a platform for negotiation and interaction between the actors, based on which many patients can express themselves more freely than before.

Summary

This chapter introduces the content and focus of the book. It began by clarifying terms, such as health care and healthcare, and analytics and analysis that are essentially useful to the book. Thereafter, it problematises the book's aim and provides valuable synopses about big data analytics techniques and analysis approaches. Furthermore, the chapter briefly explains challenges from healthcare and big data perspectives. In the chapter, it is clear how the book inversely combines academic rigour with professional practice. This combination includes using the ANT for analysing healthcare big data and ST to underpin aspects of big healthcare data. This permeates rigour from an academic perspective. It emphasises the criticality of improving healthcare service delivery by employing different approaches to examining and managing big data patients. Thus, the book advances the concept of big data analytics for healthcare service delivery from both academic and health sector perspectives.

Postgraduates, researchers, academics and professionals in IS, IT, health informatics, data management, information management and health professionals are the audience of this book. The audience extends to private and public sectors, including government administration. The book can be prescribed for postgraduate programmes as material in the fields of IS and health informatics for research and classroom teaching. Globally, there is an increasing need to improve healthcare services, which makes this book an international material that fits academic libraries.

References

Altabaibeh, A., Caldwell, K. A., & Volante, M. A. (2020). Tracing healthcare organisation integration in the UK using actor–network theory. *Journal of Health Organisation and Management, 34*(2), 192–206.
Andrade, A. D., & Urquhart, C. (2010). The affordances of actor network theory in ICT for development research. *Information Technology & People, 23*(4), 352–374.
Baig, M. I., Shuib, L., & Yadegaridehkordi, E. (2019). Big data adoption: State of the art and research challenges. *Information Processing & Management, 56*(6), 102095. https://doi.org/10.1016/j.ipm.2019.102095

Belhadi, A., Zkik, K., Cherrafi, A., & Sha'ri, M. Y. (2019). Understanding big data analytics for manufacturing processes: Insights from literature review and multiple case studies. *Computers & Industrial Engineering, 137*, 106099. https://doi.org/10.1016/j.cie.2019.106099.

Bendre, M. R., & Thool, V. R. (2016). Analytics, challenges and applications in big data environment: A survey. *Journal of Management Analytics, 3*(3), 206–239. https://doi.org/10.1080/23270012.2016.1186578.

Bihani, P., & Patil, S. T. (2014). A comparative study of data analysis techniques. *International Journal of Emerging Trends & Technology in Computer Science, 3*(2), 95–101. https://doi.org/10.1080/23270012.2016.1186578.

Budhiraja, R., Thomas, R., Kim, M., & Redline, S. (2016). The role of big data in the management of sleep-disordered breathing. *Sleep Medicine Clinics, 11*(2), 241–255. https://doi.org/10.1016/jsmc_2016.01.009.

Callon, M. (1986). Some elements of the sociology of translation: Domestication of scallops and the fishermen of St Brieuc Bay. In Law, J. (ed.), *Power, action and belief* (pp. 196–233). London: Routledge & Kegan Paul.

Cresswell, K. M., Worth, A., & Sheikh, A. (2010). Actor-network theory and its role in understanding the implementation of information technology developments in healthcare. *BMC Medical Informatics and Decision Making, 10*(1), 1–11. https://doi.org/10.1186/1472-6947-10-67.

Dash, S., Shakyawar, S. K., Sharma, M., & Kaushik, S. (2019). Big data in healthcare: management, analysis and future prospects. *Journal of Big Data, 6*(1), 1-25.

Delen, D., & Zolbanin, H. M. (2018). The analytics paradigm in business research. *Journal of Business Research, 90*, 186–195. https://doi.org/10.1016/j.jbusres.2018.05.013.

Dewan, S., & Ramaprasad, J. (2014). Social media, traditional media, and music sales. *Management Information Systems Quarterly, 38*(1), 101–121.

Duan, L., & Xiong, Y. (2015). Big data analytics and business analytics. *Journal of Management Analytics, 2*(1), 1–21. https://doi.org/10.1080/23270012.2015.1020891.

Frazzetto, D., Nielsen, T. D., Pedersen, T. B., & Šikšnys, L. (2019). Prescriptive analytics: A survey of emerging trends and technologies. *The VLDB Journal, 28*(4), 575–595. https://doi.org/10.1007/s00778-019-00539-y.

Galetsi, P., Katsaliaki, K., & Kumar, S. (2019). Values, challenges and future directions of big data analytics in healthcare: A systematic review. *Social Science & Medicine, 241*, 112533. https://doi.org/10.1016/j.socscimed.2019.112533.

Ghani, N. A., Hamid, S., Hashem, I. A. T., & Ahmed, E. (2019). Social media big data analytics: A survey. *Computers in Human Behavior, 101*, 417–428. https://doi.org/10.1016/j.chb.2018.08.039.

Greenhalgh, T., & Stones, R. (2010). Theorising big IT programmes in healthcare: Strong structuration theory meets actor-network theory. *Social Science & Medicine, 70*(9), 1285–1294. https://doi.org/10.1016/j.socscimed.2009.12.034

Heeks, R., & Stanforth, C. (2015). Technological change in developing countries: Opening the black box of process using actor–network theory. *Development Studies Research, 2*(1), 33–50. https://doi.org/10.1080/21665095.2015.1026610.

Hirschheim, R. A., Smithson, S. C., & Whitehouse, D. E. (1988). A survey of microcomputer use in the humanities and social sciences: A UK university study. *Education and Computing, 4*(2), 77–89. https://doi.org/10.1016/S0167-9287(88)90548-1.

Iyamu, T. (2021). *Applying Theories for Information Systems Research*. London: Routledge. https://doi.org/10.4324/9781003184119

Iyamu, T., & Mgudlwa, S. (2021). ANT perspective of healthcare big data for service delivery in South Africa. *Journal of Cases on Information Technology (JCIT), 23*(1), 65–81. https://doi.org/10.4018/JCIT.2021010104.

Joseph, R. C., & Johnson, N. A. (2013). Big data and transformational government. *IT Professional, 15*(6), 43–48. https://doi.org/10.1109/MITP.2013.61.

Khanra, S., Dhir, A., Islam, A. N., & Mäntymäki, M. (2020). Big data analytics in healthcare: A systematic literature review. *Enterprise Information Systems, 14*(7), 878–912. https://doi.org/10.1080/17517575.2020.1812005.

Kruse, C. S., Goswamy, R., Raval, Y. J., & Marawi, S. (2016). Challenges and opportunities of big data in health care: A systematic review. *JMIR Medical Informatics, 4*(4), e38. https://doi.org/10.2196/medinform.5359.

Kwayu, S., Lal, B., & Abubakre, M. (2018). Enhancing organisational competitiveness via social media—A strategy as practice perspective. *Information Systems Frontiers, 20*(3), 439–456. https://doi.org/10.1007/s10796-017-9816-5

Lepenioti, K., Bousdekis, A., Apostolou, D., & Mentzas, G. (2020). Prescriptive analytics: Literature review and research challenges. *International Journal of Information Management, 50*, 57–70. https://doi.org/10.1016/j.ijinfomgt.2019.04.003

Mehta, N., & Pandit, A. (2018). Concurrence of big data analytics and healthcare: A systematic review. *International Journal of Medical Informatics, 114*, 57–65.

Mgudlwa, S., & Iyamu, T. (2021). A framework for accessing patient Big Data: ANT view of a South African health facility. *The African Journal of Information Systems, 13*(2), 225–240.

Mikalef, P., Krogstie, J., Pappas, I. O., & Pavlou, P. (2020). Exploring the relationship between big data analytics capability and competitive performance: The mediating roles of dynamic and operational capabilities. *Information & Management, 57*(2), 103169. https://doi.org/10.1016/j.im.2019.05.004

Nambiar, R., Bhardwaj, R., Sethi, A., & Vargheese, R. (2013, October). A look at challenges and opportunities of big data analytics in healthcare. In: *2013 IEEE international conference on Big Data* (pp. 17–22). IEEE. https://doi.org/10.1109/BigData.2013.6691753

Pastorino, R., De Vito, C., Migliara, G., Glocker, K., Binenbaum, I., Ricciardi, W., & Boccia, S. (2019). Benefits and challenges of Big Data in healthcare: An overview of the European initiatives. *European Journal of Public Health, 29* (Supplement_3), 23–27. https://doi.org/10.1093/eurpub/ckz168

Raghupathi, W., & Raghupathi, V. (2014). Big data analytics in healthcare: Promise and potential. *Health Information Science and Systems, 2*(1), 1–10. https://doi.org/10.1186/2047-2501-2-3.

Rehman, A., Naz, S., & Razzak, I. (2021). Leveraging big data analytics in healthcare enhancement: Trends, challenges and opportunities. *Multimedia Systems*, 1–33. https://doi.org/10.1007/s00530-020-00736-8.

Rumsfeld, J. S., Joynt, K. E., & Maddox, T. M. (2016). Big data analytics to improve cardiovascular care: Promise and challenges. *Nature Reviews Cardiology, 13*(6), 350–359. https://doi.org/10.1038/nrcardio.2016.42.

Sarker, S., Xiao, X., Beaulieu, T., & Lee, A. S. (2018). Learning from first-generation qualitative approaches in the IS discipline: An evolutionary view and some implications for authors and evaluators (PART 1/2). *Journal of the Association for Information Systems, 19*(8), 752–774.

Shah, N. D., Steyerberg, E. W., & Kent, D. M. (2018). Big data and predictive analytics: Recalibrating expectations. *JAMA, 320*(1), 27–28. https://doi.org/10.1001/jama.2018.5602.

Siegel, E. (2013). *Predictive analytics: The power to predict who will click, buy, lie, or die*. New York: John Wiley & Sons.

Sivarajah, U., Kamal, M. M., Irani, Z., & Weerakkody, V. (2017). Critical analysis of Big Data challenges and analytical methods. *Journal of Business Research, 70*, 263–286. https://doi.org/10.1016/j.jbusres.2016.08.001.

Stockdale, R., & Standing, C. (2006). An interpretive approach to evaluating information systems: A content, context, process framework. *European Journal of Operational Research, 173*(3), 1090–1102. https://doi.org/10.1016/j.ejor.2005.07.006.

Waller, M. A., & Fawcett, S. E. (2013). Data science, predictive analytics, and big data: A revolution that will transform supply chain design and management. *Journal of Business Logistics, 34*(2), 77–84. https://doi.org/10.1111/jbl.12010.

Walsham, G., & Han, C. K. (1993). Information systems strategy formation and implementation: The case of a central government agency. *Accounting, Management and Information Technologies, 3*(3), 191–209. https://doi.org/10.1016/0959-8022(93)90016-Y.

Wang, Y., Kung, L., & Byrd, T. A. (2018). Big data analytics: Understanding its capabilities and potential benefits for healthcare organisations. *Technological Forecasting and Social Change, 126*, 3–13. https://doi.org/10.1016/j.techfore.2015.12.019.

Wang, Y., Kung, L., Wang, W. Y. C., & Cegielski, C. G. (2018). An integrated big data analytics-enabled transformation model: Application to health care. *Information & Management, 55*(1), 64–79. https://doi.org/10.1016/j.im.2017.04.001.

Watson, H. J. (2014). Tutorial: Big data analytics: Concepts, technologies, and applications. *Communications of the Association for Information Systems, 34*(1), 1247–1268. https://doi.org/10.17705/1CAIS.03462.

Wu, J., Li, H., Cheng, S., & Lin, Z. (2016). The promising future of healthcare services: When big data analytics meets wearable technology. *Information & Management, 53*(8), 1020–1033. https://doi.org/10.1016/j.im.2016.07.003.

Zhang, F., Cao, J., Khan, S. U., Li, K., & Hwang, K. (2015). A task-level adaptive MapReduce framework for real-time streaming data in healthcare applications. *Future Generation Computer Systems, 43*, 149–160. https://doi.org/10.1016/j.future.2014.06.009.

2 A Structuration View in Managing Healthcare Data

Introduction

Healthcare data are generated from different sources, including consultations, diagnoses, follow-up on medications and x-ray reports (Archenaa & Anita, 2015). According to Kaur and Rani (2015), a significant amount of data is generated from patients' medical records, treatments and financial billings. The data are stored, retrieved and managed differently by the various agencies and medical personnel (stakeholders) within the health sector (Bernardi, 2017). Ethically, healthcare service providers and receivers, including the regulators, are duty-bound to act according to their roles, affiliations and in association with the professional bodies and health facilities that hold the right of the data. The use and management of patients' data require uniqueness because of the confidentiality, security and privacy of the health environment (Banerjee, Hemphill & Longstreet, 2018).

Physicians and other practitioners associated with medical services in healthcare facilities encounter various challenges related to data management in their quest to provide care for patients. Some of the challenges begin at the points where patients' biodata is collected, retrieved or shared between practitioners, without involving or using information systems (IS) or information technology (IT) (Yue et al., 2016). Also, many health and IS or IT solutions are often not integrated, which affects information sharing, retrieval and efficiency of operations, and impedes decision-making (Assem & Pabbi, 2016). This is associated with various factors of significance, legitimacy and the power to enable services. According to Viceconti, Hunter and Hose (2015), healthcare data is a sensitive matter that affects shareability and, if not managed well, can cause deficiencies in services such as wrong diagnosis or incorrect medication. Therefore, it is important for healthcare practitioners to protect the privacy, security and confidentiality of patients' data while carrying out services within a regulatory framework (Fabian, Ermakova & Junghanns, 2015).

Constitutionally, the governments of many countries are the main stakeholders of healthcare services to the communities (Coovadia et al., 2009). This mandates the government of some countries to promulgate rules through

DOI: 10.4324/9781003251064-2

legislation and policies that guide the operations and activities of agencies in the health sector (Greer, Wismar & Figuras, 2016). Based on the privacy, security, ease of use and usefulness that the healthcare data require and deserve, there is a high and consistent need for rules, regulations and resources within which patients' data can be stored, retrieved, used and managed by facilities over some time (Andreu-Perez et al., 2015). Also, there is a consistent increase in the volume, types and speed at which patients' data are created or retrieved and used, making constant improvement of the managerial aspect of the patients' data critical. Essentially, this includes the differentiation of data types, an understanding of significance levels and legitimation of applying various resources, rules and regulations to patients' data management.

In this chapter, structuration theory (ST) is employed as a lens to gain a deeper insight into managing patients' data. The theory is selected for two primary reasons: (1) essentiality of significance and (2) duality of rules and events, which edify useful and valuable constructs in the creation or retrieval, management and use of patients' data. The theory focuses on agents (or agencies) and structure, and in duality, how they consciously and unconsciously enable and, at the same time, constrain activities within a social system (Giddens, 1979, 1984). Structure in ST means rules and resources (Roberts, 2014). This point is highlighted so that it is not mistaken for its literal meaning in the English language, where structure means organised hierarchy.

Consciousness implies that agencies act with awareness and knowledge, which is significant in healthcare service delivery, due to implications for human lives. McPhee and Canary (2014) suggest that for agents to make a difference, they must consciously use their powers. In ST, structures and agencies are both implicated in the production and reproduction of activities, events or actions within a social system (Bernardi, 2017) and ensure interdependency (Giddens, 1984).

In a social system such as the healthcare environment, the agents (medical personnel, patients and government representatives) consciously employ structure (rules and resources) to guide their interactions and operations in providing and receiving healthcare services. Indeje and Zheng (2010) explain how structures are the medium of human activities as well as the outcome of those activities. Therefore, when agents interact to produce and reproduce social systems, they are not only enabled by the structures in place but are also constrained by them (Vyas, Chisalita & Dix, 2017; Walsham, 1993). In Giddens' (1984) explanation, systems are patterns of relations categorised into groupings within which relationships exist and interactions are carried out to produce and reproduce actions towards achieving specific goals. As a social system, healthcare is influenced by agents' interactions, carried out within rules, using available resources such as IT solutions (e.g., mobile and database technologies). The influence shapes healthcare service delivery, relative to time and space (geographical locations), public and private facilities.

The question posed in this chapter is how can healthcare data be better managed to improve the services that health facilities provide to communities? Based on the question, Giddens' (1984) duality of structure from ST is employed as a lens to have deeper view in the management of patients' data. A framework is constructed from the outcome of the view and discussion guided by the duality of structure. The framework can be used for data management to ease its usefulness towards improving healthcare services by health facilities.

For logical flow and better understanding, this chapter is divided into five main sections. An introduction is provided in the first section, which is followed by a review of literature that mainly covers healthcare and ST. The third and fourth sections present the theoretical and conceptual frameworks for healthcare services, respectively. The conclusion of the chapter is drawn in the last section.

Healthcare data and Structuration theory

A review of literature is conducted. It is based on the focus of the chapter. Hence, it covers two areas, healthcare data and ST, considered central to the chapter's objective.

Healthcare Data

From one sector to another, data are generally rapidly increasing across the world (Zyskind, Pentland & Nathan, 2015). This is highly likely to be the trend for a long time to come. Matthias, Fouweather, Gregory and Vernon (2017) noted that in the year 2010, enterprises and individuals collectively generated and stored an estimated 13 exabytes of data from the use of the internet and mobile technologies. This was projected to increase to 40 exabytes in 2020 (Zyskind, Pentland & Nathan, 2015) and 90 exabytes by 2030. The outbreak of the COVID-19 pandemic has accelerated unprecedented data volumes (Ciotti et al., 2020). As data sets increase, so do their complexity, which makes it more difficult to manage. Data management influences its use in decision-making during operational or strategic activities. Such difficulty and challenges have affected decision-making during healthcare service provision in some countries' health facilities over the years (Miotto, Wang, Wang, Jiang & Dudley, 2018; Gotz & Borland, 2016; Sultan, 2014). For example, data collected about HIV/AIDS patients from some facilities were considered unreliable and lacked usefulness (Mate et al., 2009).

Healthcare data provides many benefits, including insights into pandemics, diagnoses of viruses and laboratory research (Ciotti et al., 2020; Fabian, Ermakova & Junghanns, 2015). According to Castiglione et al. (2015), healthcare data are imperative for ensuring proper diagnoses, assessments and treatment procedures. Gebremeskel, Yi, He and Haile (2016) add that healthcare data are essential for identifying disease patterns in patients' records. The governments of some countries and other healthcare stakeholders use healthcare data to resolve challenges such as procuring equipment, implementing appropriate treatments for patients, supporting clinical improvements and monitoring the safety of healthcare systems (Jee & Kim, 2013). Therefore, due to the criticality of healthcare data, organisations should ensure accurate and efficient flows and exchanges of patients' data for improved healthcare services. Srinivas, Rani and Govrdhan (2010) advised that timely flow of healthcare data can be improved through the support and enablement of IT solutions such as data warehouses.

Data retrieved and used for healthcare services, often encounter challenges that impede healthcare service efficiency. In Smith, Nachtmann and Pohl's (2012) explanation, healthcare stakeholders encounter many problems due to poor data quality, and this has a negative impact on the healthcare supply chain and service delivery that a health facility undertakes. Due to patients' privacy concerns, sharing data for healthcare services among different providers is a challenge (Groves, Kayyali, Knott & Van Kuiken, 2013). Data sharing becomes even more challenging when the supporting systems are not integrated. Data for healthcare services are categorised as either structured or unstructured data. Kaul, Kaul and Verma (2015) argued that most patients' data are unstructured and, consequently, difficult to analyse. For example, due to the large size of 3D medical images, hospitals are challenged with storage capacity, processing power and slow network access (Castiglione et al., 2015). Jee and Kim's (2013) assessment was that selecting and implementing the most appropriate technologies, and finding competent staff are some of the challenges which healthcare organisations encounter in their quests to manage and extract value from patients' data.

Structuration Theory

ST is a sociotechnical theory that focuses on agent, structure, social system and relationship. In ST, agents and structure are the two core constructs (Iyamu, 2021). From the interaction between structure and agents, actions are conditioned and routinised through processes that create and recreate structures (Pozzebon & Pinsonneault, 2005). Giddens (1984) refers to such occurrence as a reproductive system. The theory is regarded as a continual transformation of structure through the production and reproduction of social systems (Iyamu, 2013). Giddens (1984) describes structure as resources and guidelines and agents as technical and non-technical entities existing within a structure.

The interaction between agent and structure constitutes the duality of structure (Iyamu, 2021). In essence, the duality of structure means that social structure is reproduced by repeated human actions, while structure enables and constrains human action (van Veenstra, Melin & Axelsson, 2014). The three dimensions of the duality of structure are signification, legitimation and domination (Lamsal, 2012). These dimensions seek to illustrate the links between the structure and the interaction system.

one of the reasons ST is considered a social theory is based on the notion of structure and agents together with the idea of a duality of structure through which the relationship between agents and structure is described (Englund & Gerdin, 2016). The theory is seen as an endeavour to reconcile the dualism that existed for a long time between structure and actions (Bracker, Schuhknecht & Altmeppen, 2017). Therefore, ST helps to clearly gain an understanding of how social systems are created and how both social structures and agencies reproduce these systems (Vyas, Chisalita & Dix, 2017). Thus, ST has been used by scholars in many fields, including IS, to understand how the interactions between users (non-technical agents) and IT (technical agents) develop gradually, the consequences and how to deal with them (Bernardi, 2017) (Figure 2.1).

The three fundamental elements of structure are signification, domination and legitimation (Lamsal, 2012). The interaction between the agents and structure is highlighted through the modalities (McPhee & Canary, 2014). Humans based signification of events on the interpretive schemes, which is determined by the type and nature of communication, and thus gain the ability to make sense of their own and others' actions (Englund & Gerdin, 2014). Human agents utilise power by their ability to allocate facilities such as materials, resources and human capital, thereby creating, reinforcing or changing structures of domination (Gao & Li, 2010). Legitimation applies norms, values and standards that sanction certain forms of conduct and behaviours (Feeney & Pierce, 2016). Sanction means approval in ST (Giddens, 1984).

The ST is a social theory that has been applied in IS studies as a lens to interrogate and understand technical and non-technical agents in computing environments (Bernardi, 2017; Jones & Karsten, 2008). As technical agents of structures, IS enables and constrains people as they perform their business processes (Rose & Scheepers, 2001). Indeje and Zheng (2010) suggest that IS cannot be understood if it is not through the study of people, their social relationships and work practices that they are engaged in, daily. Therefore, through the tenets of the duality of structure, ST provides a good foundation for IS scholars to investigate both technical and non-technical agents and their reproductive actions as they consciously and continuously communicate

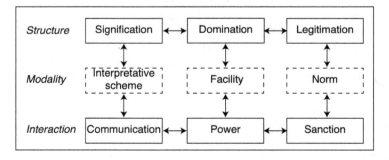

Figure 2.1 The dimension of duality of structure (Giddens, 1984, p. 128)

and apply their skills and knowledge to select, develop, implement and use IT solutions (Iyamu, 2021). Walsham (1993) argues that the power of ST is the emphasis on the inter-linked nature of the interaction between structure and its operations through the linking modalities. The ST enables researchers to study agents' intentionality and how their intended and unintended outcomes transform agencies and IS.

Theoretical Framework

Based on the use of ST to underpin the phenomenon, Figure 2.2 shows a theoretical framework. This means that the framework can be used to guide data management. For example, it steers the discussion and an understanding of the interaction between agents and structures in using data to provide healthcare services to various communities in different facilities and countries. As shown in Figure 2.1, the three dimensions of the duality of structure from the perspective of ST, namely structure, modality and interaction, can guide the management and use of healthcare data towards providing services as a reproductive system. Vyas, Chisalita and Dix (2017) explain how ST is used to understand the ways in which human agents create and reproduce social systems through social structures.

Within structure (rules and resources), some countries' governments or their representing agency formulate and legitimise policies employed to manage and use patients' data (Jack, Singh & Ncama, 2015). Aspects of the policies are intended to maintain and uphold the privacy of patients' data in providing and receiving healthcare (Stellenberg & Dorse, 2014). As shown in Figure 2.2, there are different data types of data from various sources (Archenaa & Anita, 2015). This sometimes makes it difficult or affects how various medical personnel and other stakeholders interpret the policies.

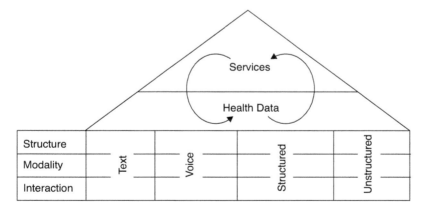

Figure 2.2 Theoretical framework

Within the healthcare sector, data are generated from text, voice, images and audio, either structured or unstructured, or both. Through the dimension of structure, data are categorised into levels of signification, which guides decision-making at various healthcare facilities, for services. This is critical in that some conditions are more serious than others. Services are result-oriented, which comes from patients' care. This process requires interactions that are often influenced by interpretations and the facility employed in categorising the required data. The purpose of employing data, and its usefulness, requires harnessing its capabilities from both technical and human agents. Harnessing health data capabilities is guided and determined by many factors, such as the availability of facilities, interpretation of policies and an understanding of the data relative to patients' condition at the time.

The provision of health services entails a duality between data and services in that they depend on and influence each other towards patients' care (Luthuli & Kalusopa, 2018). As shown in Figure 2.2, the interaction between health data and services is iterative in reproducing patients' care. This means that data, interaction and the other facilities are used to enable, and at the same time, they constrain the processes and activities of patients' care (Mosadeghrad, 2014).

In organisations, data are an important resource that organisations use to execute business processes, make informed decisions and gain competitive advantages. ST helps unpack the significance of data to organise activities and how people's skills and knowledge influence its application. In the context of ST, data can be categorised as either a non-technical agent or an allocative resource. In addition, ST brings a fresh perspective to how data is implicated in an organisation's processes as an agent and a resource. As an allocative resource, agents cognitively access, retrieve, process and manage data to gain dominion over others.

Data can constrain or enable activities in the process of providing services to the community. For example, when the specific data required to make products and services are not immediately available, it negatively affects its time to respond or decide. The application of ST for data enables an understanding of how data can constrain or enable agents in performing their activities.

Conceptual Framework for Healthcare Services

ST is useful in understanding how technical and non-technical agents interact (Iyamu, 2021). This is illuminated by the relationships and interdependence between the agents. Chang (2014) argues that this interaction occurs between the agents through which activities are reproduced. From the same viewpoint, Englund and Gerdin (2014) state that agents and structures do not consequently constitute independent sets of phenomena (a dualism) but represent two sides of the same coin. Thus, agencies such as health professionals and medical associations exist through the rules they created. As a result, neither agency nor structure can exist without the other. In the process, both agency and structure reproduce their activities as they evolve.

A conceptual framework was developed based on subjective understanding, guided by the duality of structure from ST. As shown in Figure 2.3, the framework is intended to contribute to advancing the healthcare services that the patients receive. The framework consists of four main components, namely, structure, agency, facility and agent. The components are interrelated in providing and receiving healthcare services, through which huge volumes and various types of data are generated and managed. The data are often reused in the course of service delivery, over a period.

However, the reuse and management of patients' data have always been, and highly likely, will continue to be challenging to healthcare service providers in many countries. This is attributed to the fact that many health professionals do not fully understand how the factors (components) that underpin their services connect and relate to each other. The conceptual framework that is proposed in this chapter reveals and explains the underpinning factors. The components enable and at the same time constrain the healthcare service delivery in many health facilities across the globe.

In some countries, healthcare workers must register with the Health Professional Council or various related regulatory bodies to practise or work in the healthcare sector (Siagian, Wandasari, Sahputra, & Kusumaningrum 2019; Stagg, Jones, Bickler, & Abubakar, 2012). If a professional is not registered, regardless of whether qualification, he or she cannot practise or provide health services to the community. This rule determines whether an individual can be allowed or prevented from practising.

Resources enable and at the same time constrain healthcare services offered to the patients. For example, (i) the operations (such as surgical) of patients with various medical conditions are either enabled or constrained by the availability of medical specialists and devices. This alludes to the fact that some

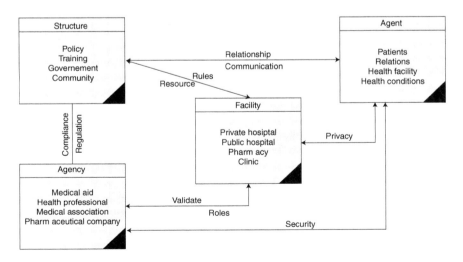

Figure 2.3 Data management conceptual framework for healthcare services

hospitals do not have sufficient medical expertise in all disciplines. Also, some policies can be constraining owing to the sensitive nature, needing extra care and highly experienced personnel; (ii) patients have the right to refuse medical treatment, and for this reason, healthcare workers may not force any medication or procedure on them even if this may result in loss of life. Healthcare workers are required to accede to the wishes of the patient regardless of their professional opinion. If the patient is unable to decide on their own, the healthcare workers apply the professional know-how and proficiency in the course of duty. The interrelationship and interconnection between the components, as shown in the figure, are discussed and presented below.

Structure

As shown in Figure 2.3, on the one hand, the structure interacts with the agencies. On the other hand, the same structure has a relationship with human agents. The structure consists of policy, training, government, community and health professionals. These structures are used to liaise with the agency, including medical aid professionals, medical associations and pharmaceutical companies to provide services to the patients. The interactions between the two entities, structure and agency, are enclaved in rules and compliance and regulate the functioning and activities of stakeholders in the healthcare sector. Valuably, governments of some countries publish legislation and policy frameworks through which operations of agencies such as non-governmental organisations, pharmaceutical companies and medical facilities are sanctioned and legitimised. The sanctioning of policies, rules and resources primarily communicates legitimacy, thus promoting transparency between the agencies and agents.

Government and policymakers such as the legislators also sought to improve the interaction between themselves and the patients by integrating community-based healthcare programmes into the various universal health programmes. Some universal health programmes are intended to facilitate the interaction and communication between the healthcare service providers and the healthcare beneficiaries in the country.

Agency

The agencies within the healthcare environment include medical aid organisations, medical associations, healthcare professionals and pharmaceutical companies. These groups are the core instruments in the provision of healthcare services. The agencies are not independent of agents and available facilities. As already highlighted, the agencies are interrelated and interconnected with the existing structure. The agencies employ various tools and means, such as non-government organisations and ambulance services, to provide individuals and groups with services (Crush & Chikanda, 2015; Mash et al., 2015).

The agencies are conscious of their actions from a confidentiality and security viewpoints. The roles and responsibilities of the agencies are also well guided by laws and policies owing to the sensitivity of the healthcare environment. Thus, the agencies' actions and activities are always validated against various facilities. The validation process, including roles and responsibilities, is legitimated through government accreditation procedures, as promulgated by the policies. The agencies operate under the guidance and watchful eye of the existing authorities, such as the government and policymakers (Bernardi, 2017).

Facility

Healthcare services are sought and provided through clinics, pharmacies, public and private hospitals. Figure 2.3 shows the facility being somewhat integral through its interaction with parts of the framework, which are structure, agency and agents. As explained above, these facilities are some of the important features of the healthcare sector because services are provided through them, whether private or public. Evidently, the interaction between structure and facility is through the application of rules and resources. To address inequality and access to healthcare services, some countries seek to strengthen primary healthcare services (the first level of the public healthcare system) by channelling resources to provide free services such as antenatal care, immunisations and chronic treatment (Vearey et al., 2018). A government can also have an interest in the distribution of resources for the benefit of the citizens. For example, as a result of the apartheid legacy in South Africa, where private healthcare was far better resourced than the public health sector, after the democratic shift, the government embarked on programmes to promote universal health coverage, seeking to facilitate fair redistribution of resources between the private and public health sectors for all citizens (Niekerk, Surender & Alfers, 2015).

Facility and agent interaction are characterised by the need to keep data private. Patients' records held by healthcare facilities contain sensitive and personal information. The healthcare data also hold huge potential for medical research and shaping public health policy, but if there is a perception of misuse and disregard of patient privacy, it may lead to distrust by the public. For this reason, the privacy of healthcare data should be safeguarded to ensure that negative perception about the handling of healthcare data does not arise. The misuse and breach of privacy may also lead to stigmatisation and discrimination of patients by the healthcare workers and the public, such as those diagnosed with leprosy, HIV and other chronic diseases (Arrey et al., 2017).

In using data for healthcare service delivery, the actions of practitioners are centred around patients' care. The people employed or contracted at medical facilities are often associated or affiliated with different professional associations of health and medical personnel (Mayosi & Benatar, 2014). This means that even though the roles of individuals are critical to human lives, their actions are consciously or unconsciously guided and influenced by the code of conduct, ethics of the associations to which they are affiliated or of which they are members.

Agent

This chapter explains that agents are differentiated as technical and non-technical (Bernardi, 2017, p. 939). This concept is demonstrated in Figure 2.3, where the non-technical agents are the patients, their relatives and their health conditions, whilst the technical agent include the health facility, patients' data, and IT solutions. Both the technical and non-technical agents work together to ensure that healthcare services are offered effectively and efficiently. However, agents do not operate independently; therefore, there is a dual interaction between agents and facilities. For instance, patients seek healthcare services provided and accessed through various means, including personal visitation to the health facilities, emails or telephonic communication (Ebrahimian, Seyedin, Jamshidi-Orak & Masoumi, 2014).

Due to the sensitivity of healthcare data, privacy must be considered during the interaction between agents and facilities. This is a two-way interaction in that the non-technical agents, such as patients and their relatives, are responsible for their data privacy. Also, each facility, such as a private hospital, public hospital, pharmacy or clinic, must apply practical measures to maintain the privacy of patients' data. In the same way, during the interaction between facilities, the patients' data privacy should be protected.

The healthcare service providers consider the well-being and safety of patients in their care to be of great significance (El-Jardali et al., 2014). Because of this significance, patient education programmes have been introduced to facilitate interaction, communication and greater awareness of patient health and privacy by the different agencies (Hill et al., 2015). The agents' interaction with agencies is based on ensuring the security of agents in a more general sense. For example, when a health practitioner performs an unethical act, the agencies are the ones that determine the punishment of the health practitioner for the security of the patient. In extreme situations, it may cancel the licence that allows the health practitioner to practise in the profession. However, there can be situations where the agents interact or communicate directly with the structures, including the government.

These relationships or interactions between agents and structure involve reproducing social systems such as practices or a specific pattern of behaviour by the agents (Giddens, 1984). This constitutes the duality of structure, focusing specifically on how structure and agents influence each other in enabling or constraining events (Roberts, 2014). This influence happens through a cycle consisting of how rules and resources are created through actions from the interaction between agents, and how agents base their behaviour on those rules and resources (Iyamu, 2021).

As agents' actions reproduce themselves, they occur iteratively so that agents can perform certain activities repeatedly without knowing how to explain what they are doing (Iyamu, 2017, p. 3). Therefore, the social structures produced through the interaction between agents and structure are products of the reproduction of human actions (Englund, Gerdin & Burns, 2017).

Summary

Healthcare services are delicate services provided to citizens by their government, together with their health facilities. This can be attributed to the fact that poor healthcare service delivery can result in loss and/or damage to lives. Therefore, the goal of any healthcare facility is to provide quality services to its patients. However, poor management of healthcare data hinders the process and goals of achieving quality services. Thus, the duality of structure of the ST is employed in the chapter as a lens to understand how different agencies use structures to improve healthcare services. As a result, a conceptual framework was developed to guide how data could improve healthcare service delivery. The conceptual framework provides a view of how structure may influence the interactions between the role players in the healthcare sector and the government representatives. Thus, healthcare facilities and government representatives can benefit from this chapter by using it to facilitate policy formulation. The chapter also contributes to the body of knowledge by adding to existing literature.

Although the chapter comprehensively covers the objective, there is still room for further research on this topic. This includes the implementation of the framework and measurement assessment model. Also, different theories, such as actor-network theory and activity theory, should be used in similar studies to ascertain if different outcomes can be reached.

References

Andreu-Perez, J., Poon, C. C. Y., Merrifield, R. D., Wong, S. T. C., & Yang, G.-Z. (2015). Big data for health. *IEEE Journal of Biomedical and Health Informatics, 19*(4), 1193–1208. https://doi.org/10.1109/JBHI.2015.2450362.

Archenaa, J., & Anita, E. M. (2015). A survey of big data analytics in healthcare and government. *Procedia Computer Science, 50*(1), 408–413. https://doi.org/10.1016/j.procs.2015.04.021.

Arrey, A. E., Bilsen, J., Lacor, P., & Deschepper, R. (2017). Perceptions of stigma and discrimination in health care settings towards Sub-Saharan African migrant women living with HIV/AIDS in Belgium: A qualitative study. *Journal of Biosocial Science, 49*(5), 578–596. https://doi.org/10.1017/S0021932016000468.

Assem, P. B., & Pabbi, K. A. (2016). Knowledge sharing among healthcare professionals in Ghana. *VINE Journal of Information and Knowledge Management Systems, 46*(4), 479–491. https://doi.org/10.1108/VJIKMS-08-2015-0048.

Banerjee, S., Hemphill, T., & Longstreet, P. (2018). Wearable devices and healthcare: Data sharing and privacy. *The Information Society, 34*(1), 49–57. https://doi.org/10.1080/01972243.2017.1391912.

Bernardi, R. (2017). Health information systems and accountability in Kenya: A structuration theory perspective. *Journal of the Association for Information Systems, 18*(12), 931–957. https://doi.org/10.17705/1jais.00475.

Bracker, I., Schuhkecht, S., & Altmeppen, K. D. (2017). Managing values: Analysing corporate social responsibility in media companies from a structuration theory perspective. In: Altmeppen, K. D., Hollifield, C., & van Loon, J. (eds), *Value-oriented media management. Media business and innovation* (pp. 159–172). Cham: Springer. https://doi.org/10.1007/978-3-319-51008-8_13.

Castiglione, A., Pizzolante, R., De Santis, A., Carpentieri, B., Castiglione, A., & Palmieri, F. (2015). Cloud-based adaptive compression and secure management services for 3D healthcare data. *Future Generation Computer Systems, 43*(44), 120–134. https://doi.org/10.1016/j.future.2014.07.001.

Chang, C. L. (2014). The interaction of political behaviours in information systems implementation processes – Structuration theory. *Computers in Human Behavior, 33*(21), 79–91. https://doi.org/10.1016/j.chb.2013.12.029.

Ciotti, M., Ciccozzi, M., Terrinoni, A., Jiang, W. C., Wang, C. B., & Bernardini, S. (2020). The COVID-19 pandemic. *Critical Reviews in Clinical Laboratory Sciences, 57*(6), 365–388. https://doi.org/10.1080/10408363.2020.1783198.

Coovadia, H., Jewkes, R., Barron, P., Sanders, D., & McIntyre, D. (2009). The health and health system of South Africa: Historical roots of current public health challenges. *The Lancet, 374*(9692), 817–834. https://doi.org/10.1016/S0140-6736(09)60951-X.

Crush, J., & Chikanda, A. (2015). South-South medical tourism and the quest for health in Southern Africa. *Social Science and Medicine, 124*, 313–320. https://doi.org/10.1016/j.socscimed.2014.06.025.

Ebrahimian, A., Seyedin, H., Jamshidi-Orak, R., & Masoumi, G. (2014). Exploring factors affecting emergency medical services staffs' decision about transporting medical patients to medical facilities. *Emergency Medicine international, 1*, 1–8. https://doi.org/10.1155/2014/215329.

El-Jardali, F., Sheikh, F., Garcia, N. A., Jamal, D., & Abdo, A. (2014). Patient safety culture in a large teaching hospital in Riyadh: Baseline assessment, comparative analysis and opportunities for improvement. *BMC Health Services Research, 14*(1), 1–15. https://doi.org/10.1186/1472-6963-14-122.

Englund, H., & Gerdin, J. (2014). Structuration theory in accounting research: Applications and applicability. *Critical Perspectives on Accounting, 25*(2), 162–180. https://doi.org/10.1016/j.cpa.2012.10.001.

Englund, H., & Gerdin, J. (2016). What can (not) a flat and local structuration ontology do for management accounting research? A comment on Coad, Jack and Kholeif. *Qualitative Research in Accounting & Management, 13*(2), 252–263. https://doi.org/10.1108/QRAM-02-2016-0012.

Englund, H., Gerdin, J., & Burns, J. (2017). A structuration theory perspective on the interplay between strategy and accounting: Unpacking social continuity and transformation. *Critical Perspectives on Accounting, 30*(3), 1–15. https://doi.org/10.1016/j.cpa.2017.03.007.

Fabian, B., Ermakova, T., & Junghanns, P. (2015). Collaborative and secure sharing of healthcare data in multi-clouds. *Information Systems, 48*(1), 132–150. https://doi.org/10.1016/j.is.2014.05.004.

Feeney, O., & Pierce, B. (2016). Strong structuration theory and accounting information: An empirical study. *Accounting, Auditing & Accountability Journal, 29*(7), 1152–1176. https://doi.org/10.1108/AAAJ-07-2015-2130.

Gao, P., & Li, J. H. (2010). Applying structuration theory to the benchmarking analysis. *Benchmarking: An International Journal, 17*(2), 253–268. https://doi.org/10.1108/14635771011036339.

Gebremeskel, G., Yi, C., He, Z., & Haile, D. (2016). Combined data mining techniques based patient data outlier detection for healthcare safety. *International Journal of Intelligent Computing and Cybernetics, 9*(1), 42–68. https://doi.org/10.1108/IJICC-07-2015-0024.

Giddens, A. (1979). *Central problems in social theory: Action, structure and contradiction in social analysis*. Berkeley: University of California Press.

Giddens, A. (1984). *The constitution of society: Outline of the theory of structuration*. Berkeley: University of California Press.

Gotz, D., & Borland, D. (2016). Data-driven healthcare: challenges and opportunities for interactive visualization. *IEEE computer graphics and applications, 36*(3), 90-96. https://doi.org/10.1109/MCG.2016.59.

Greer, S. L., Wismar, M., & Figueras, J. (2016). Policy lessons for health governance. In: Greer, S. L., Wismar, M., & Figueras, J. (eds), *Strengthening health system governance* (pp. 105–125). Berkshire: Open University Press.

Groves, P., Kayyali, B., Knott, D., & Van Kuiken, S. (2013). The 'big data' revolution in healthcare. *McKinsey Quarterly, 2*(1), 1-19.

Hill, A.-M., McPhail, S. M., Waldron, N., Etherton-Beer, C., Ingram, K., Flicker, L., & Haines, T. P. (2015). Fall rates in hospital rehabilitation units after individualised patient and staff education programmes: A pragmatic stepped-wedge cluster randomised controlled trial. *The Lancet, 385*(9987), 2592–2599. https://doi.org/10.1016/S0140-6736(14)61945-0

Indeje, W., & Zheng, Q. (2010). Organisational culture and information systems implementation: A structuration theory perspective. *Sprouts: Working Papers on Information Systems, 10*(27), 10–27.

Iyamu, T. (2013). Underpinning theories: Order-of-use in information systems research. *Journal of Systems and Information Technology, 25*(3), 224–238. https://doi.org/10.1108/JSIT-11-2012-0064.

Iyamu, T. (2017). Improvising information technology projects through the duality of structure. *South African Journal of Information Management, 19*(1), 1–9.

Iyamu, T. (2021). *Applying theories for information systems research*. London: Routledge. https://doi.org/10.4324/9781003184119.

Jack, C. L., Singh, Y., & Ncama, B. P. (2015). A South African perspective to medical law and ethics in nursing: Getting basic principles right. *Africa Journal of Nursing and Midwifery, 17*(2), 120–131.

Jee, K., & Kim, G. H. (2013). Potentiality of big data in the medical sector: Focus on how to reshape the healthcare system. *Healthcare Informatics Research, 19*(2), 79–85. https://doi.org/10.4258/hir.2013.19.2.79.

Jones, M., & Karsten, H. (2008). Giddens structuration theory and information systems research. *Management Information Systems Quarterly, 32*(1), 127–157. https://doi.org/10.2307/25148831.

Kaul, C., Kaul, A., & Verma, S. (2015). Comparative study on healthcare prediction systems using big data. In: *International conference on innovations in information, embedded and communication systems (ICIIECS)* (pp. 1–7). https://doi.org/10.1109/ICIIECS.2015.7193095.

Kaur, K., & Rani, R. (2015). Managing data in healthcare information systems: Many models, one solution. *Computer, 48*(3), 52–59. https://doi.org/10.1109/MC.2015.77.

Lamsal, M. (2012). The structuration approach of Anthony Giddens. *Himalayan Journal of Sociology & Anthropology, V*, 111–122.

Luthuli, L. P., & Kalusopa, T. (2018). The management of medical records in the context of service delivery in the public sector in KwaZulu-Natal, South Africa: The case of Ngwelezana hospital. *South African Journal of Libraries and Information Science, 83*(2), 1–11.

Mash, R., Almeida, M., Wong, W. C. W., Kumar, R., & von Pressentin, K. B. (2015). The roles and training of primary care doctors: China, India, Brazil and South Africa. *Human Resources for Health, 13*(1), 1–9. https://doi.org/10.1186/s12960-015-0090-7.

Mate, K. S., Bennett, B., Mphatswe, W., Barker, P., & Rollins, N. (2009). Challenges for routine health system data management in a large public programme to prevent mother-to-child HIV transmission in South Africa. *PLoS One, 4*(5), 5483. https://doi.org/10.1371/journal.pone.0005483.

Matthias, O., Fouweather, I., Gregory, I., & Vernon, A. (2017). Making sense of Big Data—Can it transform operations management? *International Journal of Operations & Production Management, 37*(1), 37–55. https://doi.org/10.1108/IJOPM-02-2015-0084.

Mayosi, B. M., & Benatar, S. R. (2014). Health and health care in South Africa: 20 years after Mandela. *New England Journal of Medicine, 371*(14), 1344–1353. https://doi.org/10.1056/NEJMsr1405012.

McPhee, R.D. & Canary, H.E. (2014). Structuration theory. *The International Encyclopedia of Communication Theory and Philosophy, III*, 2–15.

Miotto, R., Wang, F., Wang, S., Jiang, X., & Dudley, J. T. (2018). Deep learning for healthcare: review, opportunities and challenges. *Briefings in bioinformatics, 19*(6), 1236–1246. https://doi.org/10.1093/bib/bbx044.

Mosadeghrad, A. M. (2014). Factors influencing healthcare service quality. *International Journal of Health Policy and Management, 3*(2), 77–89. https://doi.10.15171/ijhpm.2014.65.

Niekerk, V. R., Surender, R., & Alfers, L. (2015). Moving towards universal health coverage in South Africa: The role of private sector GPs. *Public Health Association of South Africa, 3*, 1–4.

Pozzebon, M., & Pinsonneault, A. (2005). Challenges in conducting empirical work using structuration theory: Learning from IT research. *Organisation Studies, 26*(9), 1353–1376. https://doi.org/10.1177/0170840605054621.

Roberts, J. (2014). Testing the limits of structuration theory in accounting research. *Critical Perspective on Accounting, 25*(2), 135–141. https://doi.org/10.1016/j.cpa.2012.12.002.

Rose, J., & Scheepers, R. (2001). Structuration theory and information system development-frameworks for practice. In: *9th European conference on information systems* (pp. 217–231), 27–29 June, Bled, Slovenia.

Siagian, C., Wandasari, W., Sahputra, F., & Kusumaningrum, S. (2019). Strategic yet delicate: the dilemma of involving health workers in facilitating birth registration in Indonesia. *BMC Health Services Research, 19*(1), 1–2. https://doi.org/10.1186/s12913-019-4594-z

Smith, B., Nachtmann, H., & Pohl, E. (2012). Improving healthcare supply chain processes via data standardization. *Engineering Management Journal, 24*(1), 3–10. https://doi.org/10.1080/10429247.2012.11431924.

Srinivas, K., Rani, K., & Govrdhan, A. (2010). Applications of data mining techniques in healthcare and prediction of heart attacks. *International Journal on Computer Science and Engineering (IJCSE), 2*(2), 250–255.

Stagg, H. R., Jones, J., Bickler, G., & Abubakar, I. (2012). Poor uptake of primary healthcare registration among recent entrants to the UK: a retrospective cohort study. *BMJ Open, 2*(4), e001453. http://dx.doi.org/10.1136/bmjopen-2012-001453.

Stellenberg, E. L., & Dorse, A. J. (2014). Ethical issues that confront nurses in private hospitals in the Western Cape Metropolitan area. *Curationis, 37*(1), 01–09.

Sultan, N. (2014). Making use of cloud computing for healthcare provision: Opportunities and challenges. *International Journal of Information Management, 34*(2), 177–184. https://doi.org/10.1016/j.ijinfomgt.2013.12.011.

van Veenstra, A. F., Melin, U., & Axelsson, K. (2014). Structuration theory in public sector information systems research. In: *Proceedings of the European conference on information systems (ECIS)* (pp. 1–12). Tel Aviv.

Vearey, J., de Gruchy, T., Kamndaya, M., Walls, H. L., Chetty-Makkan, C. M., & Hanefeld, J. (2018). Exploring the migration profiles of primary healthcare users in South Africa. *Journal of Immigrant and Minority Health, 20*(1), 91–100. https://doi.org/10.1007/s10903-016-0535-7.

Viceconti, M., Hunter, P., & Hose, R. (2015). Big data, big knowledge: Big data for personalised healthcare. *IEEE Journal of Biomedical and Health Informatics, 19*(4), 1209–1215. https://doi.org/10.1109/JBHI.2015.2406883.

Vyas, D., Chisalita, C. M., & Dix, A. (2017). Organisational affordances: A structuration theory approach to affordances. *Interacting with Computers, 29*(2), 117–131. https://doi.org/10.1093/iwc/iww008.

Walsham, G. (1993). *Interpreting information systems in organisations.* John Wiley & Sons, Inc. https://doi.org/10.1111/j.1365-2575.1995.tb00101.x.

Williams, H., Spencer, K., Sanders, C., Lund, D., Whitley, E. A., Kaye, J., & Dixon, W. G. (2015). Dynamic consent: A possible solution to improve patient confidence and trust in how electronic patient records are used in medical research. *JMIR Medical Informatics, 3*(1), e3. https://doi.org/10.2196/medinform.3525.

Yue, X., Wang, H., Jin, D., Li, M., & Jiang, W. (2016). Healthcare data gateways: Found healthcare intelligence on blockchain with novel privacy risk control. *Journal of Medical Systems, 40*(10), 1–8. https://doi.org/10.1007/s10916-016-0574-6.

Zyskind, G., Pentland, A. S., & Nathan, O. (2015). Decentralising privacy: Using blockchain to protect personal data. In: *Conference of the IEEE security and privacy workshops (SPW)* (pp. 180–184), 21–22 May, San Jose, CA, USA.

3 Open Technology Innovation for Healthcare Services

Introduction

Globally, particularly in developing countries, there are consistently increasing demands for better and quality healthcare service delivery (Iyamu, 2020). To this extent, technology innovations are being employed to respond to the demands in many quarters. Even though the deployment of technologies enhances and enables service delivery, it also creates challenges for many healthcare facilities at the same time. It is worse with the open technology innovation (OTI) because of the flexibility associated with the concept (Savory & Fortune, 2015). Also, many healthcare facilities in both developed and developing countries continue to experience challenges in deploying technologies such as Open Health and mHealth, by following the OTI concept.

The OTI emerged from the open innovation concept, which Mashilo and Iyamu (2012:2) defined as 'the use of purposive inflows and outflows of knowledge to accelerate internal innovation and expand the markets for external use of innovation respectively'. OTI and open innovation are interchangeably used throughout this chapter, with a specific focus on its influence on healthcare service delivery. Groen and Linton (2010) viewed the concept of open innovation from two perspectives: (1) it focuses on the creation of new ideas, which include products, services and processes; and (2) it is inclusive in nature, which means that more stakeholders, including patients, health practitioners, IT specialists and government representatives that can add value, are involved in developing and using products (innovation) for health services through the open innovation concept.

In the drive to improving service quality and maintain the privacy of patients' information, many healthcare facilities expect innovation to be tested, often through proof of concepts (PoCs) before deployment. This is to gain better understanding of how technological innovation can enable and support efficiency and effectiveness in an environment (Cui, Ye, Teo & Li, 2015). This approach creates inclusiveness, promotes openness and encourages engagement, allowing the stakeholders to contribute (Savory & Fortune, 2015). However, such a contributory approach exposes the internal logic of

DOI: 10.4324/9781003251064-3

the system or technology to vulnerability, which takes away confidentiality and serviceability associated with competitive edge.

Some health facilities in many countries enrol in the concept of open innovation for different reasons. For some organisations, it allows them to access the experiences and knowledge of experts, which, in return, contributes to their knowledge 'bank'. This approach frees the organisation from employment responsibility and financial implications (Gassmann, Enkel & Chesbrough, 2010). This is not surprising, as Bogers et al. (2017) explain the rationale for focusing on the cost implication perspective in the interest and adoption of the open innovation concept. This does not take away the emphasis on the rapid advances in IT, which continue to influence the healthcare sector to increase its reliance on open innovation (Cui, Ye, Teo & Li, 2015). Also, the concept of open innovation affirms and promotes collaboration within which both external and internal ideas can be shared freely towards advancing technologies for healthcare purposes (Mashilo & Iyamu, 2012).

The essential advancement of innovation in healthcare is seen more from the integration perspective (Bullinger et al., 2012). Through such essentiality, the creative building of healthcare services in many countries, particularly developing countries, has improved tremendously in the last decade. However, there remain many challenges, which technological innovation itself brings to the fore of healthcare. This is attributed to the uniqueness and sensitive type of data used within the healthcare environment. IT challenges include insufficient data storage capacity, which requires creative technology solutions to accommodate more influx and rapidity of healthcare data experienced with the COVID-19 spread. Despite the high volumes of patient data, it is essential to be guided by a country's security and privacy laws (Raghupathi & Raghupathi, 2014). Thus, the OTI concept cannot readily be transferred to the public health sector, particularly in countries where governance is consistently a challenge (Mergel & Desouza, 2013).

In the concept of OTI, ideas and knowledge are used as both inputs and outputs in an innovation process (Reinhardt, Bullinger & Gurtner, 2015). One of the challenges is exploiting the concept to creatively enhance processes without compromising patients' medical (or personal) information. This brings about the criticality of the human-centric approach, to which many studies have paid less attention to the OTI (Pikkarainen, Hyrkäs & Martin, 2020). This is attributed to the OTI's challenges in employing the concept to proactively detect and prevent diseases, including health promotion because it is constrained by a regulatory oversight policy.

This chapter undertakes to explore and clarify the factors that influence the OTI concept for healthcare services as employed and experienced in the environments of many countries. This includes understanding the implications of the factors as they manifest themselves during the process. The chapter primarily intends to share explicit knowledge about the OTI concept for healthcare services, particularly from a developing country perspective.

The chapter is divided into six main sections. The first section introduces the focus. In the second section, the literature review is presented in which the gap this chapter tries to bridge, is discussed. The third section covers OTI from a healthcare service perspective. The implications of the OTI for health services are discussed in the fourth section. The influencing factors are presented and discussed in the fifth section. Finally, a conclusion is drawn in the summary section. It includes suggestions for further studies.

Literature Review

The concept of OTI is intended to accelerate processes within an environment, actively. Some of the processes that can be employed through the open innovation concept are (1) the outside-in process, (2) the inside-out process and (3) the coupled process (Enkel, Gassmann & Chesbrough, 2009). The outside-in process seems to be more commonly practised than the other two processes (Gassmann, Enkel & Chesbrough, 2010). The processes promote knowledge sharing, which helps to build a culture of openness. Such culture encourages stakeholders and beneficiaries to contribute to advancing an innovative process, enriching innovativeness in an environment (Cui, Ye, Teo & Li, 2015).

The necessity of the OTI also arises from the fact that health practitioners capture, store and instantly share or update patients' data in real-time, in a centralised area, by using several open innovation technologies (Ventola, 2014). From a different angle, the benefits of OTI expose patients' information to increased risk and vulnerability through the services they provide (Wikhamn & Styhre, 2020). As a result, OTI requires a thorough understanding by health practitioners and other contributing actors before adopting the concept.

In many health facilities, healthcare services are often inefficient and ineffective. Some of the problems are known to have triggered increasingly enormous investments in innovation in the last decade. However, too many efforts fail, and ingenious solutions are required, particularly in applying the concept of OTI for healthcare service delivery. Reinhardt, Bullinger and Gurtner (2015) explain the peculiarities that influence and constrain the concept of OTI in healthcare. Wass and Vimarlund (2016) identified some of the constraining factors for open innovation in healthcare, including complexity, policies and regulations, and routinisation for capturing ideas and knowledge relating to patients' data.

Therefore, it is not surprising that there has been a significant increase in the awareness of the open innovation concept over the last decade. This helps an environment better understand how to build or facilitate the open innovation concept (Enkel, Gassmann & Chesbrough, 2009). Although open innovation creates opportunities for technological advancement and economic growth for individuals and healthcare facilities, the concept has challenges. Davies, Roderick and Huxtable-Thomas (2019) argue that healthcare organisations or facilities employ the open innovation concept to collectively encourage and empower citizens to create knowledge to improve healthcare service quality.

However, there have been challenges in the areas of security and confidentiality. The use of patients' data or personal information to conduct PoC for OTIs is a prevalence challenge. According to Davies, Ronan, Bowman and Clement (2018), this type of challenge sometimes hampers the concept of openness within the healthcare environment. Beginners of the practice of the OTI are more affected because they sometimes struggle to draw the line between where and when openness starts and stops when carrying out PoCs on innovation. This type of challenge necessitates policy formulation to guide the application of the open innovation process (Davies, Roderick & Huxtable-Thomas, 2019).

Over the years, the health sector has promulgated various laws to protect its activities and processes in their sensitive nature. The laws cover activities such as encryption, which sometimes threaten the use of technology to access and manage patients' data (Kumar & Aldrich, 2010). Another aspect of the challenge is to prevent patients' data losses, which can potentially lead to life-threatening incidents. According to Murphy (2015), such challenges occur during deployment of the open innovation, which breaches security relating to patients' data.

Despite the increasing attention that the concept of open innovation has gained, the focus seems to remain on theorising rather than practising the concept. This can be attributable to the focus on commercialising products and ideas (Mashilo & Iyamu, 2012). Enkel, Gassmann and Chesbrough (2009) suggested that the commercialisation approach can influence the goals and objectives of research & development (R&D). One of the ironic effects is that when technology is the primary focus, many healthcare facilities struggle to practise the innovation concept.

The concept of the OTI allows individuals and organisations to contribute to the development of an idea or service (Groen & Linton, 2010), which can be a risk to healthcare activities and processes because of the sensitive nature of the environment (Mashilo & Iyamu, 2012). This explains why even though there is a steadily increasing interest in the concept of OTI in countries across the globe, its application has been in the area of business only (Krause, Schutte & Du Preez, 2012; Wikhamn & Styhre, 2020). As a result of the many challenges, fears associated risk, which prevent some health facilities from taking advantage or exploring the OTI benefits (Kankanhalli, Zuiderwijk & Tayi, 2017). The scepticism is rooted in a lack of stiff governance and an understanding of the factors that influence OTI adoption (Fascia & Brodie, 2017). Yun et al. (2016) suggest that the challenges get worse in employing the concept of artificial intelligence (AI) to practise OTI. AI has not been easy in the concept of open innovation in areas such as healthcare.

It is emphatically clear that users have a critical role in an open innovation process, and requirements must be well understood for quality purposes

(Mashilo & Iyamu, 2012). The emphasis was based on the premise that open innovation can enable and support organisations in their pursuits for sustainability and competitiveness. The premise has hardly reflected in individuals and organisations' enrolment in the concept, particularly in delivering health services. This triggered a fundamental question by Mashilo and Iyamu (2012): 'how open is open innovation'? Even though this question was posed over a decade ago, the situation has really not changed. This means that the question is as crucial as it was then, primarily because OTI adoption has implications for, and it influences the delivery of health services to the needy.

In some circumstances, innovation determines the integration of external knowledge with the internal knowledge drive services (Wass & Vimarlund, 2016). This enables and supports healthcare facilities in creating more value in the usefulness of patients' data. Consolidation of ideas and knowledge is intended to address unprecedented patient-related challenges through innovation-based management of data (Ciasullo, Carli, Lim, & Palumbo, 2021). This chapter identifies and discusses some of the fundamental challenges for healthcare in applying the concept of OTI towards managing patients' data and general workable solutions to advance solution that improves service delivery.

Open Technology Innovation for Healthcare Service

Through such extensive learning, a stock of knowledge is acquired, and meanings are shared to understand the factors that influence OTI adoption for healthcare services. This section focuses on gaining comprehension about the factors that influence OTI deployment, in attempts to advance healthcare services delivery by health facilities in many environments.

The focus is threefold. First, to establish the current OTI solutions, as in some public hospitals and private hospitals or clinics, respectively. Second, to reveal the factors that influence the deployment of the OTIs. Third, to provide insights into the implications of influence by several factors. Epistemologically, new knowledge relating to using open innovation for healthcare services is gained from the interaction between stakeholders, including patients, service providers (health practitioners) and service enablers (IT specialists). Innovation of healthcare technology solutions can be broad and complex, partly rooted in the wide range of actors' actions (Savory & Fortune, 2015). The involvement of various actors from outside of health practitioners is a paradigmatic shift from the old traditional approach in which healthcare practitioners solely developed and disseminated solutions for services (Bullinger et al., 2012).

Healthcare facilities in many countries work towards an innovative paradigm for different reasons, such as responding to rapid technology change and employing technology advancement to address health services and societal needs. In some hospitals, solutions are developed through the OTI approach to enhance communication between healthcare providers and patients. Many health facilities, public and private hospitals, or clinics employ OTI-based solutions to manage processes and activities relating to patients' care, including monitoring the CD4 count of patients infected by human immunodeficiency virus (HIV). The view of some medical practitioners which many IT specialists often echo is that an open innovation platform is necessary to enable actors to have a more collaborative interaction for continuous improvement of the quality of healthcare services. In providing healthcare solutions, health facilities abide by the policies of privacy and confidentiality of patients' information.

The innovation concept can be considered a set of activities that lead to creating or introducing a fresh perspective, which results in an innovative approach for a company's competitive advantage (Fascia & Brodie, 2017). Conceptually, innovation can be employed to produce new or fresh ideas or reengineer existing phenomenon, to aid competitiveness. Open innovation is commonly seen as a concept that enables an individual or organisation or both to own an idea. Davies, Ronan, Bowman and Clement (2018) argue that innovation (fresh idea) allows further development from more contributors, extends and widens the scope and defines pathways.

Generally, the open innovation concept solves some challenges in providing IT solutions for healthcare services (Biancone, Secinaro, Brescia & Calandra, 2019), particularly in developing countries. However, using open innovation is not enough to fulfil the requirements of health services (Pikkarainen, Hyrkäs & Martin, 2020). Hence, it is critical to understand the influencing factors and how they manifest, to produce and reproduce results. This is to avoid a complete disregard for the concept. Some medical personnel and IT specialists seldom view the concept as a solution to promote synergy and improve performance in providing service to the community. The challenge is understanding the users' knowledge and useability of the innovation.

This is a challenge for an hospital and other health facilities that deploy the OTI concept in that there seem to be no clear guidelines on success factors (Durst & Ståhle, 2013). In addition, one of the challenges in developing a useful and secure innovation for healthcare services involves continuous translation and negotiation of activities with relevant actors. Lundberg et al. (2013) argue that one of the challenges of the OTI is how to standardise terminologies for healthcare services. Another concern in the deployment of the OTI for healthcare services is the capability to transform knowledge into value and usefulness towards efficiency and effectiveness (Biancone, Secinaro, Brescia & Calandra, 2019).

The open innovation practices and activities are expected to allow and enable inflow and outflow of knowledge to integrate solution and technology transfer (Pikkarainen, Hyrkäs & Martin, 2020). However, this is not always the case in a correlation between hospitals and clinics in different countries, for two simultaneous reasons: (1) privacy and confidentiality policies; and (2) cultural affiliation of the patients and environment effect. Some of the factors influencing OTI for health technologies are the different regulations whose implications are not often known (Savory & Fortune, 2015). In many health facilities in some countries, IT specialists readily share their experiences in developing OTI-based solutions. Despite the traditional health IT tradition, which is usually a closed process to physicians, IT specialists are allowed to contribute their ideas and knowledge from the beginning to the release of the solution.

The innovation of health technology is intrinsically linked to the innovation of healthcare services (Savory & Fortune, 2015). Lundberg et al. (2013) emphasised the centredness of open innovation for healthcare, which should involve collaboration between the relevant actors about patients' care process. Also, some medical personnel in public and private hospitals and clinics endeavour to have a process of OTI that improves the quality of healthcare service. This entails internal and external medical practitioners, government representatives, IT specialists and patients partake in the requirements gathering and solution development. In such an inclusive approach, the concept can be widely used to advance generally acceptable solutions, irrespective of cultural belief, affiliation and economic status.

The OTI provides actors with a platform for inclusive control and responsibility to secure and advance integrated healthcare solutions for public and private hospitals or clinics. According to Bullinger et al. (2012), some results from the open innovation concept are acceptable practices in the health environment.

Factors Influencing Open Technology Innovation

This chapter reveals five main factors that influence OTI in advancing health services in public and private hospitals and clinics in many countries across the world. The factors are information security, health economy, technology solution, cultural affiliation and social context. The factors are depicted in Figure 3.1, to show the relationship between the factors diagrammatically. The discussion that follows should be read with the figure to understand better how the factors influence or can be used to influence open innovation for healthcare services.

As shown in Figure 3.1, different actors contribute to the concept of OTI from various perspectives, such as health economy, cultural affiliation and social context. The actors contribute through a single channel. However, some actors explore alternative channels, which can induce gap and pose security challenges.

Social Context

Social context refers to a specific activity with boundaries that only exists for a purpose and fades away with time. In many health facilities, practitioners do not always rely, in totality, on their inbound knowledge and expertise to carry out specific tasks or operations. This is despite the high levels of

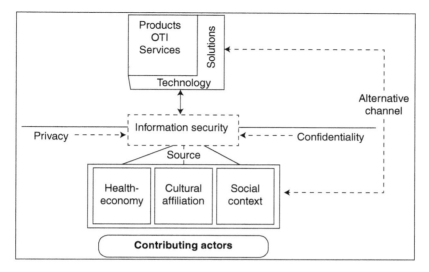

Figure 3.1 Factors influencing open innovation in healthcare

specialised expertise of the employed practitioners. According to Secundo, Toma, Schiuma and Passiante (2019), the outbound approach helps leverage IT solutions and the discoveries of new ones, including transferability. According to Mashilo and Iyamu (2012), actors can demonstrate and depict realities within an environment through the social construction of IT solutions' profoundness and creative inductions or deductions.

Innovation produced based on social context is often challenging when applied in a sensitive environment such as healthcare. Therefore, it requires an assessment by groups or a network of specialists. This is to ensure that the innovation is open and that it can add value to healthcare services.

Also, through the networks, the openness of the innovation helps to create ideas, to advance health services. Innovations within a social context, including healthcare, continue for various reasons and interests, such as the mobility for services (Mashilo & Iyamu, 2012). Innovative initiatives are intended to enable and support activities. However, some innovations are constraints, which sometimes result from the practical unconsciousness of either the innovator or the user. For example, social media has been used to cause damage and pain to individuals, groups and families over the years. This is one of the primary reasons the OTI has been challenged in sensitive environments such as the healthcare.

Technology Solution

Technologies are employed in OTI to innovate or discover other IT solutions through actors' actions, produced and reproduced over a period. Technology is the main driver of the OTI primarily because it enables healthcare facilities and practitioners to collaborate and interact (Bughin, Chui & Johnson, 2008). Collaborative effort facilitates knowledge sharing, including R&D among organisations, and ultimately promotes efficiency.

Individuals and groups employ various ways to adopt technology solutions, which increase levels of innovation in an environment. In healthcare, such a multidimensional approach is limited, owing to restrictive access to information and the generally sensitive nature of the environment. However, this does not retard innovative efforts. By enabling and supporting innovative efforts, healthcare has improved over the years. This includes integration and mobility of services. Lasers are used to record events and documented in a centralised repository through scanning (Davies, Roderick & Huxtable-Thomas, 2019). Technology solutions are adopted to improve effectiveness and efficiency in the process, creating opportunities and challenges.

By enabling technology, concepts are published on public domains, such as the website, for inputs from both internal and external experts. For example, technology enables an organisation to connect with higher institutions and be competitive by advertising its services. However, the openness of these innovations has attracted some individuals to be inquisitive, thereby innovatively intruding into the activities of others. Services supported by innovative technology attract more consumers and enrol various individuals without geographical barriers. Hence, there is a particular focus on environmental influences when it comes to open innovation.

Cultural Affiliation

Each environment constitutes attributes, agents (or agency) and actors, often referred to as factors or determinants of factors. This is primarily because they influence or are influenced by situations within and environment. The healthcare environments are influenced by patients, technology, people and processes. An environment such as healthcare has an impact on creating innovative opportunities (Mashilo & Iyamu, 2012). Thus, health facilities need to understand the external and internal factors required to complement innovative efforts towards improving services. This makes the need for a relationship between entities critical, such as the agencies and actors managing the enablement of technology solutions.

As the need for improved services continues, innovations become even more critical, particularly when it is open to all interested parties. The interest and goal begin to diversify, which bears both positive and negative consequences, manifesting from actors' deliberate and unconscious actions. Incrementally, the actions produced and reproduced from innovations have impact on, and influence the patients in a health facility, and ultimately affect society and the economy in general. The OTI approach in the public sectors, such as healthcare, is not straightforward and will continue to pose challenges. Some of the challenges are attributable to factors of mandates and legislation.

Health Economy

Innovation is significant and essential to the health economy. This makes the OTI critical as the approach allows contributions towards the enrichment of initiatives and efforts. The provision of alternatives through the OTI promotes the reliability of technology solutions. Lack of alternatives is detrimental to the growth of the health economy. On this front, the health economy requires more innovative efforts and initiatives. Also, innovation increases performances that leverage the growth of the economy. This entails the commercialisation of new ideas and approaches (Chesbrough, 2011). However, the openness of innovation in this context could be of huge concern in the areas of privacy, ownership and profitability.

Knowledgeable external counterparts enact knowledgeable internal practitioners; together, they form networks of innovation for healthcare services (Wass & Vimarlund, 2016). In the context of the United Kingdom's National Health Systems (NHS), Fascia and Brodie (2017) consider open innovation as a tool for optimisation and strategic development in addressing barriers and inconsistencies in providing services.

However, the economy can sometimes be very sensitive to the surrounding where innovation happens or occurs or lacks presence. This brings about accidental discovery due to the openness, from the viewpoint of critical OTI, and can be of high risk. The varying and conflicting interests from technologists and non-technologists make the health economy vulnerable, cause uncertainty and weaken innovative determinations. The OTI approach within the health economy space can be analysed or seen as free trade with little or no satisfactory security strength. It is more challenging when an OTI solution is used to provide healthcare services. Technology, in its conservatism, has always been a sceptical subject for many people, particularly in an unfamiliar circumstance such as the health environment.

Information Security

It is well understood that the concept of OTI encourages productivity, collective knowledge and networking collaboration (dos Santos et al., 2015). However, there are security challenges from confidentiality and patients' information privacy angles. Salter, Criscuolo and Ter Wal (2014) argue that academic research and managerial practice have focused less on the challenges associated with open innovation. This includes how the challenges of privacy and patients' confidentiality manifest to influence objectives and healthcare service delivery. Şimşek and Yıldırım (2016) found confidentiality as a constraint to open innovation.

Policies and legislative acts are promulgated to protect the confidentiality and privacy of patients' information owing to the sensitive nature of the healthcare environment. Increasingly, countries are exploring stricter measures to protect patients' information. In the United Kingdom, the

Data Protection Act regulates the use of personal information by businesses, organisations or the government. The Australian government refers to it as the Privacy and Personal Information Protection Act (PPIPA), while the Taiwanese government as the Personal Data Protection Act (PDPA). The act is enacted to control the collection, dissemination and use of personal data. In South Africa, it is the Protection of Personal Information Act (PoPIA). The PoPIA is one of the legislative acts used to protect individual information. These laws limit actors' contributions to the healthcare open innovation concept, and influence knowledge sharing and transfer. As a result of the security constraints, some contributors explore alternative channels to contribute to ongoing innovation, as shown in Figure 3.1. Some of the actors engage in such practices consciously, while others are unconscious in their actions. This impacts the type of innovation produced and ultimately influences the services that healthcare offers.

Implications of the Open Technology Innovation

Some healthcare facilities invest in the adoption of technology solutions with the intent to improve service delivery. This is despite the complexities in managing the activities, processes and contributions of the involving actors. Some of the complexities emanate from both inside and outside processes that were applied. This includes the discrepancy in the activities of developing initiatives that can influence and impact a facility's services, reputation and revenues.

It is critical for health facilities to find relevant collaborative partners in executing an open innovation initiative for trust, ethics and professional alignment purposes. Academic and other R&D institutions also form a formidable collaborative partnership in enhancing and boosting the execution of open innovation ideas and initiatives. Thus, it is necessary to formulate criteria for partnership and collaboration. Mashilo and Iyamu (2012) cautioned against such a view that criteria for new ideas might be a hampering factor. This could be attributed to the fact that the healthcare sector already has many policies, laws, by-laws and constitutional mandates that govern its operations, processes and activities.

One of the challenges of OTI is that it is disruptive to development in an integrated health economy owing to its flexibility (Davies, Roderick & Huxtable-Thomas, 2019). It is worse in the healthcare environment in that the factors that influence the OTI are not well understood, including the motivation for innovation and the knowledge transfer processes (Secundo, Toma, Schiuma & Passiante, 2019).

External actors have unlimited access to the internet, which is a challenge to many health facilities, particularly in developing countries. This is primarily because of the ease to request the contribution of new ideas to technology solutions. Figure 3.2 depicts information flow about technology solutions through the internet platform.

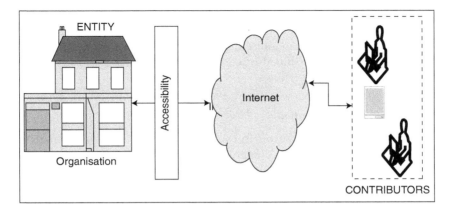

Figure 3.2 Information flow (Mashilo & Iyamu, 2012, p. 491)

Based on the above discussion, there are many unresolved implications of the openness of the open innovation concept within the healthcare sector. The implications could be viewed and understood from different perspectives of the benefits and challenges discussed as follows:

Benefits of Open Innovation

The benefits of open innovation are many, depending on the angle, technology solutions, patients or services from which they are viewed and assessed. In the context of this chapter and book, the following three factors are of crucial benefit to the healthcare industry: availability of resources, timeline and cost. According to Mashilo and Iyamu (2012), the benefits of the factors can hardly be separated in executing the open innovation concept. The factors influence and have impact on each other in enabling or constraining the materialism of the open innovation concept. Some of the attributes of the factors are reuse and knowledge sharing, which promote development enhancement. The benefits can be associated with individuals' growth and advancing service delivery in health facilities.

Over the last decade, the execution of the OTI concept has managed to improve efficiency and productivity in some health-related research institutions through access to technology solutions and skilled personnel. Increasingly, the open innovation approach assists health facilities in improving innovation capacity and structures towards better management services (Fascia & Brodie, 2017). Secundo, Toma, Schiuma and Passiante (2019) argue that the open innovation structure can be complex due to the composition of inter-organisational structures entailing various players that support the processes through collaboration and interaction in an environment such as healthcare.

Despite its openness, facilities or institutions that problematised an initiative have the right to the intellectual property (IP). However, the IP can be shared, and ownership is maintained. This helps to manage privacy and security policies in the implementation and use of such technology solutions. In addition, tracing and tracking of other facilities that enrol to the use of tools, to construct innovation and enhance services can be made easier. An understanding of IP ownership also assists in distinguishing the formation of alliances in a collaborative effort.

Challenges of Open Innovation

Presented in this chapter, the openness of the OTI concept is an enabler (benefit) and a constraint (challenge), which are both of technical and non-technical nature. The challenges are consequences of actors' deliberate or unconscious actions. Some of the challenges negatively impact healthcare processes and activities on medium-term and long-term service strategies. Some of the examples of the challenges are (1) compromise of patient's data integrity during pilots of technology solutions, (2) use of untested solutions in rendering service to patients, which can sometimes be detrimental, (3) difficulty in creating a balance between innovative ideas and the daily routine of providing services and (4) it is a grim task to control the limit of innovative contributions from both internal and external actors.

One of the challenges of OTI is in managing how citizens access their personal and collective health information. Otherwise, it can be disruptive to the health economy (Davies, Roderick & Huxtable-Thomas, 2019). Wass and Vimarlund (2016) identified some constraining factors in the open innovation approach for healthcare as, health regulations, data laws and patient's empowerment. Some of these challenges can be associated with experts continuing emergence and prohibitive contributions.

Contribution to a technology solution can be made heterogeneous, which enforces duplication. It is difficult to control and manage the dissemination of contributing artefacts by interested and enrolled actors. This, therefore, requires quality control measures and an information flow strategy. Otherwise, contributions will continue to be hampered or lose value. Also, organisations' management attempts to identify, clarify and validate what is needed from external ideas should be enforced through policy (Hastbacka, 2004). These challenges make it near impossible for some health facilities to adopt the OTI concept in their environments.

Summary

This chapter can be of interest to both academics and business domains as in the original study. In addition, healthcare practitioners are likely to show interest in exploring how the concept can advance service delivery. As revealed in the chapter, this is primarily because the concept of open innovation allows the integration of inputs from both internal and external contributing actors in an organisation. From a business viewpoint, one of the values of OTI is that an organisation can leverage its sustainability, profits and competitiveness through free access to other stakeholders' IP allowed by the concept of open. This type of contribution of the chapter should be more important to developing countries. The chapter's contribution to the academic domains should be seen from its addition to the literature in the areas of emerging technology concepts, health informatics and information systems perspectives. The contributions of the chapter should therefore be of significance to researchers in both academic and business domains.

This chapter is intended to encourage healthcare facilities, particularly in developing countries, to build networks in advancing the concept of open innovation in their environments. This is to accelerate and leverage their service delivery through the concept of open innovation. This chapter lays a foundation for further research in OTI and privacy in healthcare service delivery and open innovation and AI for organisations' purposes. Such studies will assist in the advancement of technology innovation and business competitiveness.

References

Biancone, P., Secinaro, S., Brescia, V., & Calandra, D. (2019). Management of open innovation in healthcare for cost accounting using EHR. *Journal of Open Innovation: Technology, Market, and Complexity*, 5(4), 2–16. https://doi.org/10.3390/joitmc5040099.

Bogers, M., Zobel, A. K., Afuah, A., Almirall, E., Brunswicker, S., Dahlander, L., ... & Hagedoorn, J. (2017). The open innovation research landscape: Established perspectives and emerging themes across different levels of analysis. *Industry and Innovation*, 24(1), 8–40. https://doi.org/10.1080/13662716.2016.1240068.

Bughin, J. R., Chui, M., & Johnson, B. (2008). The next step in open innovation. *McKinsey Quarterly*, 4(4), 112–122.

Bullinger, A. C., Rass, M., Adamczyk, S., Moeslein, K. M., & Sohn, S. (2012). Open innovation in health care: Analysis of an open health platform. *Health Policy*, 105(2), 165–175. https://doi.org/10.1016/j.healthpol.2012.02.009.

Chesbrough, H. W. (2011). Bringing open innovation to services. *Massachusetts Institute of Technology Sloan Management Review*, 52(2), 85–90.

Ciasullo, M. V., Carli, M., Lim, W. M., & Palumbo, R. (2021). An open innovation approach to co-produce scientific knowledge: An examination of citizen science in the healthcare ecosystem. *European Journal of Innovation Management*. https://doi.org/10.1108/EJIM-02-2021-0109.

Cui, T., Ye, H. J., Teo, H. H., & Li, J. (2015). Information technology and open innovation: A strategic alignment perspective. *Information & Management*, 52(3), 348–358. https://doi.org/10.1016/j.im.2014.12.005.

Davies, G. H., Roderick, S., & Huxtable-Thomas, L. (2019). Social commerce Open Innovation in healthcare management: An exploration from a novel technology transfer approach. *Journal of Strategic Marketing*, 27(4), 356–367. https://doi.org/10.1080/0965254X.2018.1448882.

Davies, G., Ronan, G., Bowman, M., & Clement, M. (2018). Life sciences & health: Open access open innovation in South West Wales. In: *13th European conference on innovation and entrepreneurship* (pp. 227–XIV). Academic Conferences International Limited, 20–21 September, Aveiro, Portugal.

dos Santos, A. C., Zambalde, A. L., Veroneze, R. B., Botelho, G. A., & de Souza Bermejo, P. H. (2015). Open innovation and social participation: A case study in public security in Brazil. In: Kő, A. & Francesconi, E. (eds), *Electronic government and the information systems perspective*. EGOVIS 2015. Lecture Notes in Computer Science, Vol. 9265. Cham: Springer. https://doi.org/10.1007/978-3-319-22389-6_12.

Durst, S., & Ståhle, P. (2013). Success factors of open innovation—A literature review. *International Journal Business Research Management, 4*, 111–131.

Enkel, E., Gassmann, O., & Chesbrough, H. W. (2009). Open R&D and open innovation: Exploring the phenomenon. *R&D Management, 39*(4), 311–316. https://doi.org/10.1111/j.1467-9310.2009.00570.x.

Fascia, M., & Brodie, J. (2017). Structural barriers to implementing open innovation in healthcare. *British Journal of Healthcare Management, 23*(7), 338–343. https://doi.org/10.12968/bjhc.2017.23.7.338.

Gassmann, O. T., Enkel, E., & Chesbrough, H. (2010). The future of open innovation. *R&D Management, 40*(3), 213–221. https://doi.org/10.1111/j.1467-9310.2010.00605.x.

Groen, A. J., & Linton, J. D. (2010). Is open innovation a field of study or a communication barrier to theory development? *Technovation, 30*(11–12), 554.

Hastbacka, M. A. (2004). Open innovation: What is mine is mine what if yours could be mine, too? *Technology Management Journal, 12*(3), 1–4.

Iyamu, T. (2020). Examining e-government enabling of e-health service through the lens of structuration theory. *International Journal of Sociotechnology and Knowledge Development (IJSKD), 12*(3), 26–40. https://doi.10.4018/IJSKD.2020070102.

Kankanhalli, A., Zuiderwijk, A., & Tayi, G. K. (2017). Open innovation in the public sector: A research agenda. *Government Information Quarterly, 34*(1), 84–89. https://doi.org/10.1016/j.giq.2016.12.002.

Krause, W., Schutte, C., & Du Preez, N. (2012, July). Open innovation in South African small and medium-sized enterprises. In: *Proceedings of international conference on computers & industrial engineering*, 15–18 July, Cape Town, South Africa.

Kumar, S., & Aldrich, K. (2010). Overcoming barriers to electronic medical record (EMR) implementation in the US healthcare system: A comparative study. *Health Informatics Journal, 16*(4), 306–318. https://doi.org/10.1177/1460458210380523

Lundberg, N., Koch, S., Hägglund, M., Bolin, P., Davoody, N., Eltes, J., ... & Winsnes, C. (2013). My care pathways-creating open innovation in healthcare. *Studies in Health Technology and Informatics, 192*, 687–691.

Mashilo, M., & Iyamu, T. (2012). The openness of the concept of technology open innovation. In: *2012 IEEE international conference on management of innovation & technology (ICMIT)* (pp. 487–492), 11–13 June, Bali, Indonesia. IEEE. https://doi.org/10.1109/ICMIT.2012.6225854.

Mergel, I., & Desouza, K. C. (2013). Implementing open innovation in the public sector: The case of Challenge.gov. *Public Administration Review, 73*(6), 882–890. https://doi.org/10.1111/puar.12141.

Murphy, S. (2015). Is cybersecurity possible in healthcare. *National Cybersecurity Institute Journal, 1*(3), 49–63.

Pikkarainen, M., Hyrkäs, E., & Martin, M. (2020). Success factors of demand-driven open innovation as a policy instrument in the case of the healthcare industry.

Journal of Open Innovation: Technology, Market, and Complexity, 6(2), 39–55. https://doi.org/10.3390/joitmc6020039.

Raghupathi, W., & Raghupathi, V. (2014). Big data analytics in healthcare: Promise and potential. *Health Information Science and Systems, 2*(1), 1–10. https://doi.org/10.1186/2047-2501-2-3.

Reinhardt, R., Bullinger, A. C., & Gurtner, S. (2015). Open innovation in health care. In: Gurtner, S. & Soyez, K. (eds), *Challenges and opportunities in health care management* (pp. 237–246). Cham: Springer.

Salter, A., Criscuolo, P., & Ter Wal, A. L. (2014). Coping with open innovation: Responding to the challenges of external engagement in R&D. *California Management Review, 56*(2), 77–94. https://doi.org/10.1525/cmr.2014.56.2.77.

Savory, C., & Fortune, J. (2015). From translational research to open technology innovation systems. *Journal of Health Organization and Management, 29*(2), 200–220. https://doi.org/10.1108/JHOM-01-2013-0021.

Secundo, G., Toma, A., Schiuma, G., & Passiante, G. (2019). Knowledge transfer in open innovation. *Business Process Management Journal, 25*(1), 144–163. https://doi.org/10.1108/BPMJ-06-2017-0173.

Şimşek, K., & Yıldırım, N. (2016). Constraints to open innovation in science and technology parks. *Procedia-Social and Behavioral Sciences, 235*, 719–728. https://doi.org/10.1016/j.sbspro.2016.11.073.

Slam, A. M. (2012). Methods of open innovation knowledge sharing risk reduction: A case study. *International Journal of e-Education, e-Business, e-Management and e-Learning, 2*(4), 294–297.

Ventola, C. L. (2014). Mobile devices and apps for health care professionals: Uses and benefits. *Pharmacy and Therapeutics, 39*(5), 356–264.

Wass, S., & Vimarlund, V. (2016). Healthcare in the age of open innovation—A literature review. *Health Information Management Journal, 45*(3), 121–133. https://doi.org/10.1177/1833358316639458

Wikhamn, B. R., & Styhre, A. (2020). Open innovation groundwork. *International Journal of Innovation Management, 24*(2), 2050013. https://doi.org/10.1142/S1363919620500139.

Yun, J. J., Lee, D., Ahn, H., Park, K., & Yigitcanlar, T. (2016). Not deep learning but autonomous learning of open innovation for sustainable artificial intelligence. *Sustainability, 8*(8), 797–817. https://doi.org/10.3390/su8080797.

4 Interaction with Cloud-Hosted Health Data

Introduction

Increasingly, patients and society in general in many countries are demanding improved healthcare services. This clarion call is louder in some countries than others, in both developed and developing countries (Horner & Coleman, 2016; Iyamu & Mgudlwa, 2018). Despite the essentiality of healthcare, patients continue to experience discomforting services, which can be ascribed to ailing infrastructure and the slow advancement of enabling information technology (IT) solutions. This affects the storing, managing and interaction with patients' data to improve services. As a result of these critical challenges, many countries began to seek alternatives to their current solutions. Thus, mobile systems and cloud computing have been progressively employed as solutions for accessing and storing, respectively (Dick, O'Connor & Heavin, 2020; Ganiga, Pai, Manohara Pai & Sinha, 2020).

Mobile System is a computing system with mobile entities, which can be either software or hardware. Mobile systems are mostly used to facilitate communication, including storing data in the forms of image, text and audio. Cloud computing for healthcare describes the practice of implementing remote servers accessed via the internet to store, retrieve, manage and process healthcare-related data. Additionally, cloud computing constitutes solutions and services. The most common cloud computing solutions include private clouds, public clouds, hybrid clouds and multi-clouds. This chapter focuses neither on a specific mobile system nor on a particular solution or service. It emphasises actors' interaction with patients' data that is hosted in the cloud.

Cloud as a solution facilitates technologies used to enable and support healthcare activities and services such as electronic patients' medical records, mobile applications, patient portals and big data analytics. It provides ease of use through the integration, scalability and flexibility of systems and activities, as well as the interaction, communication and accessing of patients' data. Subsequently, the decision-making process and response time are improved. Thus, the solution increases the efficiency of healthcare, not without challenges, such as privacy and confidentiality, which manifest from interactions.

DOI: 10.4324/9781003251064-4

The essentiality of healthcare requires controls of access to patients' data, which means that interaction must be guided by policy (Al Nuaimi, AlShamsi, Mohamed & Al-Jaroodi, 2015). Thus, the use of mobile systems to reinforce interactive actions between stakeholders in providing services to patients must be enhanced to improve practitioners' service deliverables (Iyamu & Shaanika, 2020). According to Galetsi, Katsaliaki and Kumar (2020), the data-intensive nature of the health environment makes it significant to employ innovative technologies for interactive dynamics to advance patient care and services.

Seamlessly, the use of mobile systems to interact can trace and manage patients' health conditions through data stored, using IT solutions such as cloud. According to Iyamu and Shaanika (2020), mobile solutions can be used to access patients' big data in the form of videos, images and texts, which comes from various sources, such as x-ray diagnoses. However, interaction is a major challenge (Shropshire, Gowan & Guo, 2016) because of the slowness caused by enabling IT solutions (Shaanika & Iyamu, 2019).

Using mobile systems to interact with patients' data hosted in the cloud increases challenges in the health sector. This type of challenge could compromise security and privacy issues and negatively affect efficient and effective data sharing. Despite these compromises and challenges, there is rarely a discussion about the consequence of such interaction among the actors during service delivery. Based on these challenges, this chapter sets out to address two main objectives. First, to examine and understand the factors that influence interaction in accessing patients' data using mobile systems in a healthcare facility. Second, to gain insight about the factors that have impact on the sharing of patients' information stored, using the cloud solution. To this end, a deep analysis of the use of mobile systems for interaction with patients' data stored using the cloud solution is provided.

The chapter is sequentially arranged into five main sections as follows. The first section introduces the chapter. It clearly states the chapter's objectives and structure. In the section that follows, a literature review is presented. It covers key aspects of the chapter, which are mobile systems and cloud solutions for providing healthcare services to the needy. In the third section, an analytical discussion is presented. It focuses on using mobile systems to conduct interactions between the actors, using patients' data stored in the cloud. The factors revealed from the chapter are covered in the fourth section, and finally, a conclusion is drawn.

Literature Review

The combination of rapid growth, sophisticated technologies and patients' need, to improve care generates a high volume of data (Rajabion et al., 2019). Consequently, the handling and processing of high data volumes increase the interaction rate between humans, technologies and humans-to-technologies. To facilitate these activities, cloud computing solutions are increasingly being employed. Iyamu and Shaanika (2020) explain how mobile systems can enable and support interaction and information sharing between healthcare practitioners and patients, to advance services. Also, the diverse nature of interaction draws on the framework designed by Xu et al. (2017). Memos, Psannis, Goudos and Kyriazakos (2021) explain the usefulness of cloud services for healthcare delivery from the angles of two factors: storage and real-time response. These factors enhance interaction between physicians in providing health services to patients. The factors can be viewed and used from both human and technology standpoints.

From the technology perspective, data hosted in the cloud can provide real-time opportunities from an innovative solutions perspective in addressing healthcare challenges (Chen, Lin & Wu, 2020). Also, a cloud antivirus is used as a client for communication between the cloud servers and front-end applications (Memos, Psannis, Goudos & Kyriazakos, 2021). This type of interaction entails different layers built within the security. The advancement of cloud technologies enables physicians and other health facilities staff to access patients' data with flexibility and at low costs, thus encouraging ease of interaction between the actors (Gautam, Ansari & Sharma, 2019).

However, some security challenges need to be addressed for those who decide to implement e-health on the cloud (Al Nuaimi, AlShamsi, Mohamed & Al-Jaroodi, 2015). Mittal (2020) argues that the use of cloud technology for healthcare service delivery could give rise to emerging threats and challenges, which include vulnerability and breach of data privacy. Such challenges could complicate legal and policy aspects of access and interaction between actors in using health data (Zandesh, Ghazisaeedi, Devarakonda & Haghighi, 2019). Thus, more than ever before, there is a need for highly skilled personnel or experts in the use, governance and management of the technology in interacting with patients' data for service delivery (Galetsi, Katsaliaki & Kumar, 2020). Among other things, this is primarily to ensure the confidentiality of diagnostic data (Zhang et al., 2020).

With the advent of mobile systems in health service delivery, concerns such as security, privacy and usability have been raised in many quarters (Lin, Xu, He & Zhang, 2021). Despite the challenges, the usability of mobile systems for healthcare services increases. Choi, Park, Kwon and Kim (2020) explain how many health facilities provide mobile applications to patients, purposely to take responsibility, ownership, access own health information and communicate with healthcare providers. Mobile systems have improved the speed and quality of care in many ways in many health facilities. However, Nwankpa and Datta (2021) argue that, in practice, there is little understanding of how mobile systems influence healthcare service quality.

Another significant aspect of mobile systems is that it enables healthcare workers to connect with patients' records and simplify the workflow for accessing specimens. This enhances accuracy and reduces the need for manual access (Rahman, Khalil & Yi, 2019; Shah et al., 2019). Amid these benefits, Meshram et al. (2020) highlight that clients' personal information and sensitive data can easily be poached by intruders or any malicious party, causing serious security problems and confidentiality issues.

To achieve high-quality health, the use of technologies, such as mobile systems and cloud computing, is critical (Xu et al., 2017). Some organisations have begun implementing pervasive health monitoring systems to improve service delivery (Rajabion et al., 2019). Despite the attractive benefits, some challenges come with the cloud solution. Zandesh, Ghazisaeedi, Devarakonda and Haghighi (2019) point out that current laws do not completely address the challenges of deploying cloud solutions in many countries. Thus, attempts to innovate various mechanisms for interaction could pose a more serious challenge for the healthcare environment that is already fragile to sensitivity. According to Al Nuaimi, AlShamsi, Mohamed and Al-Jaroodi (2015), there are security issues with data stored using cloud solutions, ranging from data encryption, authentication, authorisation and fraud detection to prevention of potential attacks.

Communication between the Actors

In the context of this book, this section provides a guide to gain both theoretical and practical understanding of humans' reproductive actions in carrying out communication to access healthcare data using technology such as mobile systems. Thus, it helps to gain insights into the factors that influence interaction and information sharing between actors for healthcare service delivery. This was done along with the objectives of the chapter: (1) factors influencing humans' interaction using mobile healthcare systems; and (2) how the factors impact the sharing of healthcare information stored using a cloud solution.

The approach employed in this chapter guides sense-making to (1) understand the communicative scheme, that is, how mobile systems are used within context, to interact; and (2) reflexively interpret and understand the implications of sharing information related to patients' health situations. These help to gain a deeper insight into the phenomenon of real-world characteristics and dimensions.

Factors Influencing Humans' Interaction Using Mobile Healthcare Systems

The chapter reveals factors that influence accessing patients' data stored in the cloud by using mobile systems for interaction. The focus on accessing patients' data is from both healthcare practitioners' and stakeholders' (patients and policymakers) perspectives for service delivery. The factors are illustrated in Figure 4.1. As depicted in the figures, there are both technical (IT solutions) and non-technical (such as process, procedure and people) factors.

The factors influence how actors (such as policymakers, health practitioners and IT specialists) collect, store, access and manage patients' data in many health facilities across the world. The factors include policy, communication, synchronisation and IT solutions. The type of information collected from patients and the approach used in the process are guided by policies, as promulgated by policymakers. In many instances, healthcare practitioners rely on or draw from each other's knowledge and expertise to resolve challenges or provide services to patients (Mgudlwa & Iyamu, 2021). Consequent to storing patients' data in the cloud, healthcare practitioners can interact with it from any location and at any time. Therefore, it enables the sharing of information in real-time. However, the use of IT solutions (cloud solutions) to execute such a collaborative service is often limited, owing to the security and privacy of patients' data. Zandesh, Ghazisaeedi, Devarakonda and Haghighi (2019) highlighted security and privacy as challenging aspects of cloud solutions in the healthcare environment.

Thus, the legitimacy of information shared about patients' health and the services provided are of utmost importance to patients and policymakers. As a result, policymakers place emphasis and strictness on the development and implementation of policies. For reliability and consistent manageability, policies are used to govern the operations of healthcare facilities. However, compliance in the health sector has been challenging in some facilities in some countries. This is attributed to the complexity and bureaucracy, which are often synonymous in nature, to some policies. Critically, this determines adherence to policies in an environment. Thus, non-compliance of policies creates disparities in the use of mobile systems to interact or share information in providing healthcare services to the patients.

The type of tools used in interacting with data stored in the cloud is critical. Three groups engage in the use of patients' data for communication; they are: (1) between health practitioners and the data in the cloud, (2) between the health practitioners and (3) between health practitioners and patients. The approaches used for communication include electronic mail (email), telephone and computer software. As revealed in the chapter, not all employees apply electronic communication tools for healthcare service delivery. The non-use of electronic communication tools by some employees poses data management challenges. For example, it is often difficult to trace and retrieve patients' data because of excessive policy control.

Primarily, by applying certain tools, communication can be influenced by two factors: skill and specialisation. Some individuals rely on their skills and knowledge in using the available tools to communicate, which might not necessarily be the most appropriate means or approach. This is attributed to technical know-how in connecting to the cloud and using mobile health systems. Hence, it is critical to train both the health practitioners and other stakeholders.

The cloud solution closes the gap and challenges posed by data backups and recovery processes. The challenges negatively impact the recovery and retrieval of healthcare data when the system fails. This could be attributed to technology monopoly. Due to technology monopolistic approach within some facilities, flexibility is a challenge the cloud solution addresses. Another challenge is that some IT specialists often have their preferences of cloud solutions, sometimes making it difficult for the technical support unit to provide services to healthcare practitioners and administrative staff. Additionally, the preferences negatively affect the IT unit's capability to develop and implement mobile systems according to healthcare needs.

Currently, there are no interactive systems in many health facilities, particularly in developing countries. The lack of interactive systems has impacts on how healthcare data are retrieved, shared and used for interaction in delivering of services to the community. This means manual processes and physical presence for all services and requests including seeking appointment for consultation. Through mobile systems, patients can access and interact with healthcare services anytime and from anywhere. However, mobile systems require integrated systems to enable interaction and information sharing between the actors. Also, the mobile systems support integration for healthcare service delivery by the facility used in this chapter. Otherwise, access to data in the cloud to track patients' medical histories can be difficult. In some cases, where medical histories could not be traced, medical procedures would be re-conducted.

Additionally, unintegrated systems (mobile systems with cloud solutions) impact interaction, collaboration and information sharing between the actors (healthcare practitioners, patients and other stakeholders). Effective collaborations require practitioners to interact and share information to improve and provide quality health services. Thus, the need for systems connectivity is critical. Through interaction, practitioners share medical expertise and information required to provide improved healthcare services.

Factors Impacting Sharing Health Information Stored in the Cloud

Interaction and information sharing are both critical for healthcare service delivery. The factors that impact interaction and information sharing in using mobile systems to access healthcare data for service delivery include security and privacy, communicative tools (Com, 1, 2, 3, etc.) and IT solutions (databases and cloud), as illustrated in Figure 4.1. Also, the actors from both service providers' and recipients' perspectives rely on interaction for healthcare service delivery. Consequently, information sharing between actors is essential for update and record purposes. This facilitates and fortifies the enablement and support of access to patients' data in the cloud.

The connectivity (interaction) between healthcare mobile systems and healthcare data enables a seamless flow of information across the units, thus improving accessibility. Also, the interaction between mobile systems and healthcare data requires enablement by IT solutions. In this context, prevalence IT solutions are cloud solutions, the synchronisation of databases and security tools for patients' data. Some of the rationales are to enable uncompromised interaction and ensure that the privacy of patients' information is protected in providing healthcare services.

Many IT solutions are outdated in some health facilities and cannot be easily integrated with newer solutions such as the cloud. This is somehow understandable because the focus is on health and medical apparatus rather than the sophistication of IT solutions. Ironically, the enablement and support of IT solutions improve the quality of services that health practitioners provide. Also, IT solutions organise and comprehensively tender the processes and activities of healthcare administration, such as filing and distributing medical bills.

As already established in this chapter and book, in healthcare, IT aims to support healthcare processes by using solutions such as mobile and cloud systems. However, to improve the usefulness of mobile systems, the selection of IT must be appropriate and specific to the needs of the facility. This includes mobile systems' flexibility and scalability in enabling interaction between the actors. The flexibility of mobile systems requires policy guidance in its use for interaction and information sharing. Also, the manageability of IT solutions is influenced by users' skills and knowledge. Users are comfortable in managing resources that they are knowledgeable about as they perceive them to be useful.

IT solutions management depends on the governance structures of the environment. Policymakers provide requirements that help guide the selection of cloud solutions, database configuration and levels of security (or authorisation) of access for interaction and information sharing purposes. Thus, integration between the components (cloud solution, database and security tools) is critical. In addition, it is difficult to integrate mobile systems and gain the desirables benefits without governance, which include policies, standards and principles (Iyamu, 2014). Also, governance guides and promotes process uniformity to control and manage unprecedented information sharing between actors using mobile systems to access patients' data. Hence, standards of cloud solutions, security policies and principles on information sharing should be integrated into the development of mobile systems. Subsequently, it becomes a control mechanism as the use of mobile systems for interaction and information sharing for health services grows.

The use of mobile systems to interact with data on the cloud allows for better and improved collaboration on health matters between the main actors: health practitioner-to-health practitioner; and health practitioner-to-patient. This is a drive towards effective interaction, which requires access to vital information and databases interconnectivity. The integration of mobile systems with databases enables ease of patient's medical history traceability and access. Thus, the databases must be always available, which the cloud solution enables and supports.

In addition, databases are configured and structured in the cloud to store and manage diverse types of healthcare data, including text, voice, images and videos, to smoothen the interaction between actors. The use of databases in the cloud provides systematic data entry, storage and retrieval, and reduces the complexity in sharing information on patients' health conditions. This promotes consistency in data management and improves the quality of services provided to patients. Another significant factor is that the cloud solution provides and integrates backup structures to enable healthcare data recovery during systems maintenance or failure.

Interaction and Information Sharing between Actors

The objectives of the chapter, as presented in the introduction, are examined from an interpretivist perspective. From examining the two objectives presented above, three factors are considered fundamental to the interaction between actors in providing and receiving healthcare services in many facilities. The factors are cloud solutions, availability of data and communicative tools. As shown in Figure 4.1, a diagrammatical representation by arrows is used to demonstrate the relationship between the factors: cloud solution; data availability = data #1, #2 and #3; and communicative tools = Com1, Com2, Com3.

Cloud Solution

Cloud solution is an IT service increasingly used to provide services over the internet, as simply shown in Figure 4.1. One of its benefits is flexibility, which enables and supports interaction between the users (actors). According to Al Nuaimi, AlShamsi, Mohamed and Al-Jaroodi (2015), in attempts to increase the useability of information, it is crucial to allow cloud solution users to expand access to the actors. In doing so, control, security and privacy take focal points. Thus, Gautam, Ansari and Sharma (2019) emphasise the security properties of various tools in their scalable use to access and interact with data stored using the cloud solution.

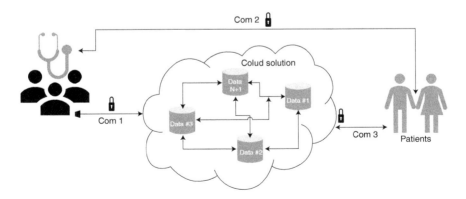

Figure 4.1 Interaction by healthcare actors

Although IT solutions have many benefits, they also bring challenges, directly impacting healthcare data security and privacy. Cloud-based solutions can assist in addressing some challenges of patient's data privacy leakage in the health sector (Sajid & Abbas, 2016). Furthermore, cloud solutions bring about distinct types of benefits for healthcare (Sultan, 2014). However, Zandesh, Ghazisaeedi, Devarakonda and Haghighi (2019) highlighted security and privacy as challenging aspects of cloud computing in the healthcare environment. The cloud solution is patient-centric by processing complexity in terms of speed, variety and latency (Chen, Lin & Wu, 2020).

Availability of Data

The cloud solution has technological advancements, such as storing and structuring huge sizes, velocity and variety of patients' data, which have been problematic for many years. This challenge hampered the availability of data. As a result, many health facilities struggle to provide quality services. Interaction and information sharing between actors rely on the availability of patients' data. The cloud solution gains popularity because it promises efficiency and engrosses the availability of patients' data around the clock. The availability of data stored using cloud solutions is a challenge that requires tighter authorisation, which impedes the smooth use of mobile systems to access and interact with patients' data (Hashem et al., 2015).

Despite the availability, cloud-hosted data is opened to vulnerabilities and needs to be secured (Mittal, 2020). This need is critical to health facilities as they strive to secure and protect patients' privacy. Data availability helps timeliness and reliability of data for interaction purposes. This enables and improves the quality of information and services that are provided to patients significantly. Also, availability aids continuity of information, particularly mission-critical data required for patients' health conditions. In addition, data availability reduces the latency and communication cost (Pitchai, Babu, Supraja & Anjanayya, 2019).

Communicative Tools

Communicative tools combine content, context and technology in conducting interactions between actors (Jin, Zhou & Yu, 2019). For interaction and information sharing purposes, policies can guide and streamline the selection and use of communicative tools. According to Georgio and Lambrinoudakis (2020), compliance with policies protects sensitive personal data hosted by cloud for healthcare service delivery.

Several factors affect the interactions between actors in the process of healthcare service delivery, making it mandatory to have a comprehensive understanding to ensure the quality of patients' healthcare (Kawamoto et al., 2020). Barrett (2021) suggests that the use of communicative tools requires compliance. Therefore, it is fair to argue that interaction is influenced by the way and format in which the communicative tool is used.

Summary

This chapter reveals the factors that influence interaction and information sharing between health practitioners and patients to facilitate and improve the quality of services delivered to the patients. Thus, the chapter can be of use to the administration of health facilities. Also, improved interaction and information sharing boost patients' confidence about the services that they receive. In addition, the factors revealed in the chapter can assist IT specialists to plan and develop solutions for enabling and supporting human interaction and secure information sharing within the healthcare space. This includes a design of architecture that defines data synchronisation, software integration and hardware deployment. Subsequently, this can ease the manageability and governance of the IT solutions that enable humans (health practitioners and patients) to improve interaction and increase the quality of service. Significantly, the factors revealed in the chapter can be used to guide an identity-based interaction between the actors.

References

Al Nuaimi, N., AlShamsi, A., Mohamed, N., & Al-Jaroodi, J. (2015). e-Health cloud implementation issues and efforts. In: *Proceedings of international conference on industrial engineering and operations management (IEOM)* (pp. 1–10), 3–5 March, Dubai, United Arab Emirates. IEEE. https://doi.org/10.1109/IEOM.2015.7093757.

Barrett, A. K. (2021). Healthcare workers' communicative constitution of health information technology (HIT) resilience. *Information Technology & People*. https://doi.org/10.1108/ITP-07-2019-0329.

Chen, P. T., Lin, C. L., & Wu, W. N. (2020). Big data management in healthcare: Adoption challenges and implications. *International Journal of Information Management, 53*, 102078. https://doi.org/10.1016/j.ijinfomgt.2020.102078.

Choi, B. K., Park, Y. T., Kwon, L. S., & Kim, Y. S. (2020). Analysis of platforms and functions of mobile-based personal health record systems. *Healthcare Informatics Research, 26*(4), 311–320. https://doi.org/10.4258/hir.2020.26.4.311.

Dick, S., O'Connor, Y., & Heavin, C. (2020). Approaches to mobile health evaluation: A comparative study. *Information Systems Management, 37*(1), 75–92. https://doi.org/10.1080/10580530.2020.1696550.

Galetsi, P., Katsaliaki, K., & Kumar, S. (2020). Big data analytics in health sector: Theoretical framework, techniques and prospects. *International Journal of Information Management, 50*, 206–216. https://doi.org/10.1016/j.ijinfomgt.2019.05.003.

Ganiga, R., Pai, R. M., Manohara Pai, M. M., & Sinha, R. K. (2020). Security framework for cloud based electronic health record (EHR) system. *International Journal of Electrical and Computer Engineering, 10*(1), 455–466. https://doi.org/10.11591/ijece.v10i1.

Gautam, P., Ansari, M. D., & Sharma, S. K. (2019). Enhanced security for electronic health care information using obfuscation and RSA algorithm in cloud computing. *International Journal of Information Security and Privacy (IJISP), 13*(1), 59–69. https://doi.org/10.4018/IJISP.2019010105.

Georgiou, D., & Lambrinoudakis, C. (2020). Compatibility of a security policy for a cloud-based healthcare system with the EU General Data Protection Regulation (GDPR). *Information, 11*(12), 1–19. https://doi.org/10.3390/info11120586.

Hashem, I. A. T., Yaqoob, I., Anuar, N. B., Mokhtar, S., Gani, A., & Khan, S. U. (2015). The rise of "big data" on cloud computing: Review and open research issues. *Information Systems*, 47, 98–115. https://doi.org/10.1016/j.is.2014.07.006.

Horner, V., & Coleman, A. (2016). Strengthening implementation of guidelines at primary healthcare. In: Iyamu, T. & Tatnall, A. (eds), *Maximising healthcare delivery and management through technology integration* (pp. 133–151). IGI Global. https://doi.org/10.4018/978-1-4666-9446-0.ch009.

Iyamu, T. (2014). *Information technology enterprise architecture: From concept to practice* (2nd ed.). Australia: Heidelberg Press.

Iyamu, T., & Mgudlwa, S. (2018). Transformation of healthcare big data through the lens of actor network theory. *International Journal of Healthcare Management*, 11(3), 182–192. https://doi.org/10.1080/20479700.2017.1397340.

Iyamu, T., & Shaanika, I. (2020). Factors influencing the use of mobile systems to access healthcare big data in a Namibian public hospital. *Information Resources Management Journal (IRMJ)*, 33(3), 81–99. https://doi.org/10.4018/IRMJ.2020070104.

Jin, X. L., Zhou, Z., & Yu, X. (2019). Predicting users' willingness to diffuse healthcare knowledge in social media: A communicative ecology perspective? *Information Technology & People*, 32(4), 1044–1064. https://doi.org/10.1108/ITP-03-2018-0143.

Kawamoto, E., Ito-Masui, A., Esumi, R., Imai, H., & Shimaoka, M. (2020). How ICU patient severity affects communicative interactions between healthcare professionals: A study utilising wearable sociometric badges. *Frontiers in Medicine*, 7, 1–8. https://doi.org/10.3389/fmed.2020.606987.

Lin, W., Xu, M., He, J., & Zhang, W. (2021). Privacy, security and resilience in mobile healthcare applications. *Enterprise Information Systems*, 1–15. https://doi.org/10.1080/17517575.2021.1939896.

Memos, V. A., Psannis, K. E., Goudos, S. K., & Kyriazakos, S. (2021). An enhanced and secure cloud infrastructure for e-health data transmission. *Wireless Personal Communications*, 117(1), 109–127. https://doi.org/10.1007/s11277-019-06874-1.

Meshram, C., Lee, C. C., Meshram, S. G., Ramteke, R. J., & Meshram, A. (2020). An efficient mobile-healthcare emergency framework. *Journal of Medical Systems*, 44(3), 1–14. https://doi.org/10.1007/s10916-019-1458-3.

Mgudlwa, S., & Iyamu, T. (2021). A framework for accessing patient big data: ANT view of a South African health facility. *The African Journal of Information Systems*, 13(2), 225–240.

Mittal, A. (2020). Digital health: Data privacy and security with cloud computing. *Issues in Information Systems*, 21(1), 227–238.

Nwankpa, J. K., & Datta, P. (2021). Leapfrogging healthcare service quality in Sub-Saharan Africa: The utility-trust rationale of mobile payment platforms. *European Journal of Information Systems*, 1–17. https://doi.org/10.1080/0960085X.2021.1978339.

Pitchai, R., Babu, S., Supraja, P., & Anjanayya, S. (2019). Prediction of availability and integrity of cloud data using soft computing technique. *Soft Computing*, 23(18), 8555–8562. https://doi.org/10.1007/s00500-019-04008-0.

Rahman, M. S., Khalil, I., & Yi, X. (2019). A lossless DNA data hiding approach for data authenticity in mobile cloud based healthcare systems. *International Journal of Information Management*, 45, 276–288. https://doi.org/10.1016/j.ijinfomgt.2018.08.011.

Rajabion, L., Shaltooki, A. A., Taghikhah, M., Ghasemi, A., & Badfar, A. (2019). Healthcare big data processing mechanisms: The role of cloud computing. *International Journal of Information Management*, *49*, 271–289. https://doi.org/10.1016/j.ijinfomgt.2019.05.017.

Sajid, A., & Abbas, H. (2016). Data privacy in cloud-assisted healthcare systems: State of the art and future challenges. *Journal of Medical Systems*, *40*(6), 1–16. https://doi.org/10.1007/s10916-016-0509-2.

Shaanika, I., & Iyamu, T. (2019). The use of mobile systems to access health care big data in the Namibian environment. *The Electronic Journal of Information Systems in Developing Countries*, *86*(2), 1–15. e12120. https://doi.org/10.1002/isd2.12120

Shah, N., Martin, G., Archer, S., Arora, S., King, D., & Darzi, A. (2019). Exploring mobile working in healthcare: Clinical perspectives on transitioning to a mobile first culture of work. *International Journal of Medical Informatics*, *125*, 96–101. https://doi.org/10.1016/j.ijmedinf.2019.03.003.

Shropshire, J., Gowan, A., & Guo, C. (2016). Defining audience awareness for information systems research. In: *Proceedings of the ACM SIGMIS conference on computers and people research* (pp. 77–82), 02–04 June, Alexandria, Virginia, USA. ACM.

Sultan, N. (2014). Making use of cloud computing for healthcare provision: Opportunities and challenges. *International Journal of Information Management*, *34*(2), 177–184. https://doi.org/10.1016/j.ijinfomgt.2013.12.011.

Xu, B., Xu, L., Cai, H., Jiang, L., Luo, Y., & Gu, Y. (2017). The design of an m-Health monitoring system based on a cloud computing platform. *Enterprise Information Systems*, *11*(1), 17–36. https://doi.org/10.1080/17517575.2015.1053416.

Zandesh, Z., Ghazisaeedi, M., Devarakonda, M. V., & Haghighi, M. S. (2019). Legal framework for health cloud: A systematic review. *International Journal of Medical Informatics*, *132*, 103953. https://doi.org/10.1016/j.ijmedinf.2019.103953.

Zhang, X., Tang, Y., Cao, S., Huang, C., & Zheng, S. (2020). Enabling identity-based authorised encrypted diagnostic data sharing for cloud-assisted E-health information systems. *Journal of Information Security and Applications*, *54*, 102568. https://doi.org/10.1016/j.jisa.2020.102568.

5 A Framework for Selecting Healthcare Big Data Analytics Tools

Introduction

Information technology (IT) solutions are enabler, as well as the platform for technological activities, such as the transmission of data, which makes it necessary to briefly discuss it prior to focusing on big data (Yu, Lin & Liao, 2017). Also, IT as a unit offer tools and technology solutions that improve the quality of healthcare services (Busagala & Kawono, 2013). However, it is important to highlight that it also has some challenges despite its many benefits. The use of IT solutions and big data, to advance healthcare services has encountered challenges regarding integration and the unavailability of sufficient infrastructure to maximise the benefits of big data (Abouzahra, 2011; Mishra, Kalra & Choudary, 2013).

As discussed in previous chapters, big data refers to data sets obtained from various related or unrelated resources and characterised by volume, velocity and variety, also known as 3Vs (Gandomi & Haider, 2015; Schüll & Maslan, 2018). Belle et al. (2015) deem healthcare to be the prime example of how the 3Vs are an essential aspect of the data it produces. Big data is known to create value, states Watson (2014). However, that can only happen once it is analysed by using data analytics tools. According to Elgendy and Elragal (2014), a simpler description of big data analytics is applying analytics techniques to big data.

In addition to the Vs, the science of big data focuses on heterogeneity, which includes levels of granularity, media formats and complexity. In exploring the value and usefulness of big data, heterogeneity poses a challenge in its analysis (Jagadish et al., 2014). Heterogeneity of the types of devices used and the nature of data generated are risks associated with big data (Marjani et al., 2017). Labrinidis and Jagadish (2012) argue that heterogeneity hinders progress in the creation of value from big data. This makes heterogeneity an important aspect of big data, especially its integration with other systems (Micheni, 2015).

The first specific objective of this chapter is to determine the factors that determine the application of big data analytics by health facilities, to improve service that they provide to the patients. In fulfilling the objective, it is necessary to examine and recognise the determinant factors of data analytics, from

DOI: 10.4324/9781003251064-5

human and big data perspectives. Comprehension of the results lead to the development of Figure 5.1, where factors of influence are depicted.

This chapter is divided into eight main sections. It starts with the introduction. Next, the objective of the chapter is problematised, followed by a literature review. In conducting the review, the chapter's core, big data, big data analytic and healthcare, are combined. Next, big data analytics tools for healthcare are discussed. A framework to guide the selection of big data tools is presented and discussed in the following section. Subsequently, framework validation and the implication of practice are explained. Lastly, the chapter is summarised.

Problematising Big Data for Healthcare Services

The main motivation of this chapter is twofold: (1) majority of previous studies focus on the importance, challenges and opportunities of big data analytics (Shahbaz et al., 2019); and (2) very few studies focus on healthcare big data in practice (Luna et al., 2014; Malaka & Brown, 2015). Purkayastha and Braa (2013) explain how reliable diagnosis is increasingly challenging, and sometimes medical practitioners re-order tests, which can be attributed to lagging analytics (or analysis) of healthcare big data.

In some health facilities of many countries, it is a challenge to bring patients' big data together within a facility or from different health programmes (Luna et al., 2014; Malaka & Brown, 2015). This challenge is caused by the integration and analysis of various healthcare big data to address impending problems (Kankanhalli, Hahn, Tan & Gao, 2016). Thus, scalability is a fundamental challenge for big data analytics and ontological extraction and semantic inference to support innovative processes for patient care. The analytics tools also pose challenges to both scientists and IS/IT specialists in different ways (Nativi et al., 2015). From the academic front, big data analytics is a disruptive innovation that reconfigures how research is conducted and has epistemological implications for data revolution (Kitchin, 2014). From both empirical and experimental perspectives, big data presents technical challenges to analytics tools due to its volume, variety and velocity.

The relationships formed while providing medical services contribute to big data. Therefore, it is important to employ the most appropriate analytics tools in examining the relationship between humans, that is, medical personnel and patients on the one hand, and humans and non-humans (data and medical apparatus in providing and receiving healthcare services) on the other. Exploring these relationships brings out the issues that can contribute to big data analytics. Gaining clarity on these issues helps in proposing a solution that would be suitable for healthcare. Most importantly, it helps develop a solution that considers healthcare needs within context and relevance in both developed and developing countries. One of the critical technical challenges associated with big data analytics is the lack of capability to manage large-scale transactions from non-standard medical terminology in patients' records (Purkayastha & Braa, 2013).

As presented in Tables 5.1 and 5.2, scope, benefits, challenges and gaps are briefly described in the context of this chapter and book. The use of big data in providing healthcare services is influenced by its premise, on the one hand (Luna et al., 2014). On the other hand, the use of the analytics tools manifests into some of the challenges experienced in providing care to patients (Shao et al., 2014). From the perspective of service delivery, big data and big data analytics within healthcare are briefly described in Tables 5.1 and 5.2.

Apparently, using big data analytics for patients' data, to advance healthcare services in many countries has become synonymous with numerous problems, challenges, obstacles and pitfalls, which has prompted this chapter, book and other studies. The practice of healthcare relies heavily on patients' data sets to facilitate the services that practitioners provide (Mathew & Pillai, 2015). These trigger phenomena being studied in big data and healthcare, as briefly described in Table 5.1.

Table 5.2 specifies the scope and briefly describes the disparities and challenges or gaps in the adoption and use of big data analytics tools for healthcare services. The focuses are classified into three categories, as shown in the table.

Thus, it is necessary to identify the factors that influence the use of big data analytics, to advance services that health facilities provide. Another crucial factor is that the meanings humans associated with things and entities are often not expressed directly but embedded in artefacts by their creators, which can only be known through interpretation (Yanow & Schwart-Shea, 2015). Thus, to deeper understanding of the different meanings associated with the data, a close relationship with the data is required.

Table 5.1 Big data and healthcare

Object of focus	Description
Scope and benefits	The focus has been on big data in health informatics, new epistemologies and paradigm shifts based on its potential benefits. Big data is employed to secure healthcare systems, including conceptual design and big data as an e-health service. Increasingly, big data is employed for healthcare services, such as a divided latent class analysis for big data. Research directions on the adoption, usage and impact of the Internet of Things (IoTs) using big data analytics. Predictive methodology for diseases such as diabetic data analysis in big data.
Challenges and gaps	There are challenges in using big data for healthcare services, including integration, scalability and complexity of heterogeneous patients' data. Big data analytics is a disruptive innovation that reshapes research focuses and challenges in a semantic way, to support continuous innovative activities and processes in advancing patient care. Other challenges in using big data in biomedicine and health come from data sources, infrastructure and analytics tools.

Table 5.2 Big data analytics and healthcare

Object of focus	Description
Scope and benefits	The concept of big data analytics is gaining presence in both academic (health informatics and information systems) and business (healthcare) domains. Health informatics combines health and information technology academic courses. Healthcare consists of private and public health facilities.
	Beyond the hypes, promises and potentials, the concept of big data analytics has been used to focus on the analysis of risks and integration of data sets within the healthcare environment. Big data analytics has been explored from various angles , such as cloud-based solutions and innovation diffusion.
	The most common analytics tools, diagnostic, descriptive, predictive and prescriptive, are adopted for healthcare services. Tutorial: big data analytics; concepts, technologies and applications.
Challenges and gaps	The adoption of big data analytics tools to provide healthcare services in some countries has been challenging, particularly in integration and cloud-based innovation. Using systems integration to access healthcare big data is attributable to the lack of architecture that is specific to healthcare big data
	Lack of understanding of the pros and cons of big data analytics in its adoption and use for healthcare services. The challenges are influenced by the uniqueness of health-related tasks, such as cardiovascular care.
	Another set of challenges in using big data analytics in healthcare includes the moderating role of resistance to change. When writing this chapter, there were very few studies that focused on big data analytics for healthcare services, particularly from the developing countries perspective. This gap makes many facilities and developing countries sceptical in their attempts to adopt the concept.

As problematised above, this chapter focuses on the premise that humans' knowledge of reality and actions are socially constructed (Walsham, 2015). Based on this assertion, the selection of big data analytics tools for healthcare purposes is problematised from three angles: (1) it shares a belief that the world is socially constructed and these constructions are possible only because of humans' ability to associate meanings with objects, events and interactions (Prasad, 2017); (2) from the interpretivist approach, there is no objective reality to be discovered by researchers and replicated by others, in contrast to the assumptions of positivist science injunction (Walsham, 2015); and (3) in interpretivism, reality is individually constructed, and there are as many realities as individuals study a phenomenon (Scotland, 2012). The belief in these reasons helps to gain insights into the factors that influence big data analytics for healthcare services.

Literature Review

Big data are collected from various sources, such as healthcare (Song & Ryu, 2015), national geographic conditions monitoring data and earth observation data (Li, Yao & Shao, 2014). Big data is increasingly useful to scientists, including health practitioners and society in general (Shu, 2016). Its usefulness is therefore understandable. However, there is always need for improvement. Thus, improving big data usefulness for healthcare services requires analytics (Abarda, Bentaleb & Mharzi, 2017). Big data analytics refers to a collection of analytic techniques and technologies specifically designed to analyse big data, to inform decision-making (Kwon, Lee & Shin, 2014). Shahbaz et al. (2019) explain that many healthcare facilities lag in the sophisticated use of big data analytics, even though the sector generates one of the highest volumes, and at a high pace. Big data analytics engineers transform data sets from raw to refinement stages (Shu, 2016), a level at which the data become meaningful to the users. Innovation of big data from the perspective of health facilities can be understood from both science and social structure levels, to empower and advance healthcare activities (Micheni, 2015).

Big data analytics is often considered the process of examining copious amounts of data from different sources and in different variations to gain insight that can enable decision-making in real or near future. According to Kwon, Lee and Shin (2014), big data analytics are the technologies and techniques employed to analyse large-scale and complex data, to improve a firm's performance. However, the employment of data analytics cannot be limited to only the business domain; other sectors should be considered for growth purposes. Big data analytics can be further described as a means of helping discover valuable decisions through appreciation of data patterns and their relationships using machine-learning algorithms (Archenaa & Mary Anita, 2015).

Big data analytics enable capturing insights from data gathered from research, clinical care settings and operational settings to build evidence for improved care delivery, as stated by Nambiar, Bhardwaj, Sethi and Vargheese (2013). According to Bottles, Begoli and Worley (2014), studies have proven that the analysis of big data can help uncover patterns and relations in healthcare that are often new to health specialists. Earlier studies, such as that of Raghupathi and Raghupathi (2014), suggest that digitising big data by integrating sources within a hospital network can help with accountability within an organisation, and lead to realisation of its benefits. In Eswari, Sampath and Levanya's (2015) preposition, big data analysis helps discover patterns and helps predict outcomes.

Big data analytics enables a systematic review of existing medical information, informs sound decision-making and improves the efficiency of health professionals and the facilities in general (Kavitha, Kannan & Kotteswaran, 2016). From the patients' perspective, big data analytics can assist in providing patients with more accurate information that can help in decision-making through the analysis of their data (Sarkar, 2017). The patient also benefits from analytics, based on care supported by a timelier diagnosis and a more appropriate medication (Ganjir, Sakar & Kumar, 2016).

In the health sector, many non-technical (IT) oriented employees resist change. This manifests from misunderstanding and lack of training. which are key challenges affecting big data analytics, especially in developing countries (Shahbaz et al., 2019). From a technical viewpoint, the integration of multiple sources of data sets brings about the challenge of increased volumes, amplified velocity and increased variety of data (Purkayastha & Braa, 2013). Some of the challenges encounter with big data analytics limit it benefits since the only way to yield its value is through a thorough analysis (Sarkar, 2017). Also, the slow progress in developing technology that supports big data, especially in developing countries, is not encouraging because earlier warning, predictions stated that the application of big data would be inevitable (Lee & Yoon, 2017).

Big Data Analytics Tools for Healthcare

Big data analytics are used as solutions for healthcare systems in many countries (Song & Ryu, 2015). The four most common big data analytics tools are predictive analytics, prescriptive analytics, descriptive analytics and diagnostic analytics (Shao et al., 2014). In the context of healthcare, Raghupathi and Raghupathi (2014) argue that predictive analytics are used to anticipate risk through the analysis of historical health data and patterns. According to Rumsfeld, Joynt and Maddox (2016), prescriptive analytics support medical decisions on individual cases by assessing the risks and benefits of the available solutions. The descriptive analytics provide a summary of past and present data, which can be used to inform healthcare decisions (Mathew & Pillai, 2015), while the diagnostic analytics focuses on finding solutions or answers as to why certain occurrences happen in the way that they do (Shao et al., 2014).

In the context of healthcare, big data analytics can be used to solve the complexities which reside within information systems used, to host and manage patients' data sets (Hermon & Williams, 2014; Zaman et al., 2017). Micheni (2015) explains how analytics can enhance the provision of quality treatment, better surveying of public health and improve responses to, and mitigation against diseases that may affect patients. Despite these identified challenges, the use of analytics for patients' data is not a one-way affair; it has its challenges. In healthcare, lack of integration is listed as a challenge brought on by the different types and sources of data sets (Abouzahra, 2011; Lee & Yoon, 2017). However, there are no specific challenges that are of standard type. There are often different challenges in many countries; hence, unique solutions are required (Alaboudi et al., 2016).

Other challenges of big data analytics include creating efficient and strong analytics methods essential for healthcare services (Peek, Holmes & Sun, 2014). According to Kumar and Singh (2017), the challenges start from the choice of big data analytics platforms and the functionalities in terms of criteria such as scalability. The integration of big data analytics with current healthcare processes and practices is another challenge highlighted by Lee and Yoon (2017), in that it is not easy to get the entities to co-exist and function appropriately within health facilities. The traditional systems no longer suffice for big data, as stated by Zaman et al. (2017), and this has resulted in issues such as the inability to conduct decision-making in real-time, which challenges predictive analytics. Thus, the challenges in big data analytics limit the potential of healthcare big data in providing services. This is because the analytics tools seem to be the only way to maximise value and usefulness from patients' big data through its use for analysis (Sarkar, 2017).

The outcomes from the analytics tools lie in their applications. This makes the selection and use of the analytics critical if it is to help in addressing functions such as clinical decision support, personalisation of healthcare of activities, public health, operationalisation of processes and policies implementation. The criticality of these functions makes it even more crucial to be more detailed in assessing existing systems because many of them focus on the same or similar solutions, which include storing, finding, analysing, visualising and securing data sets. Some of the most common analytics tools are MapReduce, Hadoop, STORM, Tableau, Apache Hadoop, Apache Hive, Memcached, Cloudera, Hue and Splunk (Chang et al., 2016; Liu & Park, 2014). Even though the existing solutions hold some promise, big data still encounter challenges in healthcare (Rumsfeld, Joynt & Maddox, 2016).

Heterogeneity extends to the network within which big data exist. According to Law (1992), networks are materially heterogeneous, and agents, texts and devices that are subsequently generated form part of a network. It became crucial in examining relationships in which actors participate and influence the shape of the heterogeneous networks (Dwiartama & Rosin, 2014). Heterogeneous entities such as people and data contribute to forming networks (Horowitz, 2012). Devices (Materials) join to generate data and reproduce themselves in the process (Law, 1992). Examples of reproduction of big data include digital closed-circuit television (CCTV); recording of retail purchases and healthcare historical records (Micheni, 2015).

During health activities, the networks become heterogeneous and increase the levels of security, making it more difficult for analytics tools to produce useful and purposeful data sets from analysis (Archenaa & Mary Anita, 2015). In addition, data heterogeneity imposes new requirements from the source viewpoint (Marjani et al., 2017), which can also be challenging as the practitioners attempt to trace the origins.

Framework for Selecting Big Data Analytics

Following the hermeneutics approach, integration, structure, skill, data availability, requirements, data sets, appropriate apparatus, external organisations, integrity and translation were identified as the main entities (actors) that influence healthcare big data usefulness for service delivery. The identification of the actors (or factors) results from two primary qualifications: (a) the frequency of each factor based on the number of articles in which the factor has appeared at the time of this chapter; and (b) which of the factors co-occur. As shown in Figure 5.1, the actors are interrelated and interconnected. The actors are influenced by types and sources of big data, classified as networks. Based on the networks, analytics tools can be appropriately selected to enhance healthcare big data usefulness. The actors, networks and tools are grouped into categories (levels) A, B and C, respectively, and together form the Framework as shown in Figure 5.1.

The Framework is proposed to solve big data challenges in healthcare service delivery in a health facility. The Framework is a bottom-up approach. This means that from the actors (A1 and A2), data are generated and grouped into categories of networks (B). Based on the networks (groupings), analytics tools (C) are selected and applied.

The first, level 'A', consists of the main factors determining big data usefulness. The factors (actors) are divided into two parts, A1 (technical) and

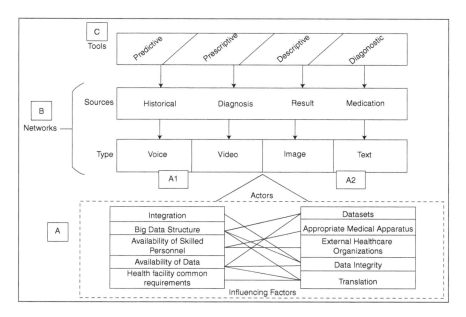

Figure 5.1 Big data analytics framework

A2 (non-technical). This level is intended to assist healthcare practitioners in gaining knowledge and understanding the importance of (1) factors of influence and (2) how the factors are interrelated or interconnected. Level 'B' helps identify, examine and understand the networks, consisting of historical records, diagnoses, results and medications. This level enables the identification of the factors that influence the selection of analytics tools and the analysis of patients' big data. The last, level 'C', comprises of analytics tools from which selection can be made for healthcare big data analysis. The discussion that follows should be read within the Framework (Figure 5.1) to gain deeper comprehension of how it can be applied.

Influencing Factors (Level 'A')

The factors that influence big data analytics for healthcare services are revealed in level 'A' of Figure 5.1. The factors are classified as actors. In this chapter, actors are anything that can make a difference (Callon, 1986). The factors are grouped into two categories, A1 and A2, which are data science/IT (technical) and health facility (non-technical), respectively. The influencing factors are both human and non-human actors because each of them can make a difference. The factors in category 'A1' are mapped against those in 'A2'. This is purposely to establish the relationship between factors and understand how the actors directly or indirectly influence healthcare service delivery. By indication, this means that the factors influence both healthcare practitioners and IT specialists in conducting activities, which necessitates their relationship and the alignment between the two units. On the one hand, the health practitioners solicit support and enablement of their activities from the IT unit. On the other hand, the unit requires information through interaction to provide support and enable healthcare processes and activities.

The mapping helps because many medical practitioners are usually limited in terms of the insights they can gain from the classification of patients' big data, which guides their analysis of the data sets towards providing services. This chapter reveals that many medical practitioners continue to employ traditional analysis methods, which do not necessarily categorise the patients' big data and require a manual application. This is even though the traditional methods are time-consuming, less effective and produce less accurate results, significantly contributing to fatality in some healthcare facilities in many countries.

The existence of these factors holds both negative and positive connotations and effects. This is primarily because each factor can make a difference in either enabling or constraining the use of big data, to provide healthcare services. However, acknowledging these factors as determinants, could drive health facilities to select and use big data analytics tools properly. As presented in Figure 5.1, the factors can potentially support and enable the health facilities towards many benefits, through the following three main ways: (1) put the types of data into perspective; (2) shape their sources of data and (3) select the most suitable data analytics tools.

Considering these influencing factors, health facilities would be able to identify the types of data they accumulate daily and help put them into perspectives. This way, health facilities could identify the structured and unstructured types of data towards grouping them into big data. Moreover, instead of disregarding unstructured data sets in the analysis, unstructured data sets would also have a role in patients' treatment and enhance the standard of health provision. Also, health facilities can shape the data sources through which knowledge is gained by putting the data types into perspectives. The knowledge enables traceability of the sources or origins of patients' data sets. This helps to have a standardised source of reference, to govern health activities including analysis of its data, in caring for patients' health conditions. Knowledge gained about data types and sources would be useful to advise health facilities on the choice and suitability of analytics tools. Thus, the decision can be substantiated in that data types and their sources are known and traceable. Traceability assists in formulating requirements and providing clarity in selecting and using big data analytics tools for healthcare service delivery purposes.

Networks (Level 'B')

As shown in the Framework (Figure 5.1), there are two main categories of networks, namely source of data and type of data. The networks are discussed as follows:

Source of Data

The source of big data within healthcare facilities is a part of the different networks that exist in the environment. From the perspective of healthcare facilities, each source of patients' big data consists of actors with aligned interests. The big data sources proposed in the Framework include historical data, diagnoses, results and medications. Each of these sources of big data has groups of interested actors, purposely, to better patients' care. For instance, historical data is used to inform decisions made on a patient's health condition. This means that diagnoses, results from tests and medications are influenced by a patient's medical history. By analysing each patient's medical history, health practitioners can gain insight distinctly into an individual's case, enabling better decision-making.

Type of Data

It is common among countries, different types of data are increasingly accumulated within healthcare facilities. A group of data of the same type forms a network. This includes voice, video, image and text data. Other actors of each of the networks include the contributors (patients) of the data, extractors (medical practitioners) of the data, managers of the data, enablers of the data (IT specialists), and administrative staff, those that make use of the data.

The interest and involvement of the actors with patients' care, come from different angles, such as (1) scheduling of medical appointments with patients, (2) consultations with medical personnel, (3) medical tests and treatment, (4) the use of various tools and medical apparatus, and (5) IT infrastructure and systems used to store, manage and retrieve the types of data.

Analytics Tools (Level 'C')

The four most common data analytics tools are predictive, prescriptive, descriptive and diagnostic (Shao et al., 2014). In healthcare, Raghupathi and Raghupathi (2014) state that predictive analytics anticipate risks by analysing historical health data and patterns. According to Rumsfeld, Joynt and Maddox (2016), prescriptive analytics support medical decisions on individual cases by assessing the risks and benefits of the available solutions. Mathew and Pillai (2015) state that descriptive analytics summarise the past and present data used to inform healthcare decisions. Bottomline, diagnostic analytics help find out why certain things are happening.

Each of these tools can add value to healthcare activities but from different perspectives. Therefore, there should be criteria for selecting the appropriateness of the tools. The choice of tools is determined by the healthcare facility's need from the existing big data. By establishing why, they intend to use the big data, the organisation can narrow down what tool is best suitable for their goals. Thus, there will be risks and challenges during analysis if an inappropriate or less appropriate tool is selected. Potentially, this results in incorrect diagnoses, medications and/or counselling.

Validation of the Framework

Even though some empirically validated artefacts exist, none can be used as a sole basis for research because of their nature of generalisability from one facility or country to another. This makes it an early exploratory study in the context of both developed and developing countries. As a result, it can be difficult to validate the Framework because of the uniqueness of 'healthcare big data analytics' within context and relevance. Thus, the influencing factors are useful.

The outcome of this chapter was validated to ensure that the influencing factors (actors) are still applicable in healthcare contexts in different countries as they were a decade ago. This was against the existing model using the influencing factors, including integration, structure, skill, availability, data set, data integrity and translation. The IS frameworks can be validated in different ways, such as through case descriptions, or mapping the components against requirements (Mueller, Viering, Legner & Riempp, 2010). Belle et al. (2015) argue that validation of Framework can be objective or subjective. The influencing factors were used in validating the outcome of the chapter by employing subjective reasoning.

The integration of patients' data sets, including their risk profile, can advance healthcare services (Elgendy & Elragal, 2014). Availability of patients' big data is critical primarily to achieve clinical predictive analytics (Bates et al., 2014). This helps to ensure ethical standards and manage privacy concerns. Data sets are most purposeful through predictive and diagnostic analytics tools in developing patient care decisions (Wang & Hajli, 2017). Belle et al. (2015) explain that skillsets are crucially essential in using big data analytics tools to form decision-making and achieve healthcare solutions. Based on the validation, this chapter is considered suitable enough for a better understanding of selecting analytics tools to improve healthcare big data usefulness by health facilities.

Implication of Practice

The factors revealed in this chapter are intended to contribute to healthcare practice towards improving service delivery by health facilities (hospitals or clinics) from the following angles: in the development or review of policies, rules and regulations towards addressing some of the challenges that have been encountered in healthcare for many years.

In practice, the implementation of the Framework requires the formulation of templates for each of the levels, as depicted in Figure 5.1. The templates should consist of critical success factors, which are environment- and context-based. This is to ensure that the implementation of the Framework appropriately guides the selection and use of analytics tools, making healthcare big data more useful, and, improving service delivery. Only then, the Framework can help bridge existing gaps, through:

1   enlightening practitioners on the factors that influence big data analytics in the healthcare environment,
2   being a step-by-step guide on factors considered prior to selecting a data analytics tool and
3   improving the quality of services using big data analytics.

In addition, prior to implementing the Framework, big data users (healthcare practitioners) must be educated on the basics of big data and analytics. Therefore, the Framework can further guide them on a step-by-step basis to put that knowledge into practice.

Summary

This chapter helps to address some of the challenges encountered in the healthcare environment from an IS research viewpoint. A solution is proposed through a framework to better understand the factors to consider before selecting and using big data analytics tools. This is primarily to increase the usefulness of big data for healthcare services, particularly in developing countries. This chapter highlights that successful selection and implementation of big data analytics tools require knowledge of the components within the Framework. Through the Framework and the influencing factors, the chapter adds to academia in IS and Health sciences' understanding of the use and roles of big data by health facilities. In addition, the chapter can be of importance and benefit to academics mainly because of its empirical nature.

This chapter addresses an area of big data analytics and healthcare in health facilities that has not previously been explored. Therefore, the Framework can be beneficially explored further to create artefacts for validation and credibility for future studies in big data analytics and healthcare big data in many countries. Based on the analysis, findings and interpretation, further research on this chapter is recommended. Since the Framework has not yet been applied, future studies could focus on applying this Framework to a healthcare-based case study. Additionally, the use of different theories is encouraged.

References

Abarda, A., Bentaleb, Y., & Mharzi, H. (2017). A divided latent class analysis for big data. *Procedia Computer Science, 110,* 428–433. https://doi.org/10.1016/j.procs.2017.06.111.

Abouzahra, M. (2011). Causes of failure in healthcare IT projects. In: *3rd international conference on advanced management science* (Vol. 19), 4–6 January. Singapore: IACSIT Press.

Alaboudi, A., Atkins, A., Sharp, B., Balkhair, A., Alzahrani, M., & Sunbul, T. (2016). Barriers and challenges in adopting Saudi telemedicine network: The perceptions of decision makers of healthcare facilities in Saudi Arabia. *Journal of Infection and Public Health, 9*(6), 725–733. https://doi.org/10.1016/j.jiph.2016.09.001

Archenaa, J., & Mary Anita, E. A. (2015). A survey of big data analytics in healthcare and government. *Procedia Computer Science, 50*(1), 408–413. https://doi.org/10.1016/j.procs.2015.04.021.

Bates, D. W., Saria, S., Ohno-Machado, L., Shah, A., & Escobar, G. (2014). Big data in health care: Using analytics to identify and manage high-risk and high-cost patients. *Health Affairs, 33*(7), 1123–1131. https://doi.org/10.1377/hlthaff.2014.0041.

Belle, A., Thiagarajan, R., Soroushmehr, S. M. R., Navidi, F., Beard, D. A., & Najarian, K. (2015). Big data analytics in healthcare. *BioMed Research International, 2015.* https://doi.org/10.1155/2015/370194.

Bottles, K., Begoli, E., & Worley, B. (2014). Understanding the pros and cons of big data analytics. *Physician Executive, 40*(4), 6–12.

Busagala, L. S., & Kawono, G. C. (2013). Perceptions and adoption of information and communication technology for healthcare services in Tanzania. *International Journal of Computing & ICT Research, 7*(1), 12–21.

Callon, M. (1986). Some elements of a sociology of translation: Domestication of the scallops and the fishermen of St Brieuc Bay. In: Law, J. (ed) *Power, action & belief: A new sociology of knowledge?* (pp. 196–229). London: Routledge.

Chang, B., Tsai, H., Tsai, C., Kuo, C., & Chen, C. (2016). Integration and optimisation of multiple big data processing platforms. *Engineering Computations, 33*(6), 1680–1704. https://doi.org/10.1108/EC-08-2015-0247.

Dwiartama, A., & Rosin, C. (2014). Exploring agency beyond humans: The compatibility of Actor-Network Theory (ANT) and resilience thinking. *Ecology and Society, 19*(3), 1–11.

Elgendy, N., & Elragal, A. (2014). Big data analytics: A literature review paper. In: Perner, P. (ed.), *Advances in data mining. Applications and theoretical aspects.* ICDM 2014. Lecture Notes in Computer Science, Vol. 8557. Cham: Springer. https://doi.org/10.1007/978-3-319-08976-8_16.

Eswari, T., Sampath, P., & Lavanya, S. (2015). Predictive methodology for diabetic data analysis in big data. *Procedia Computer Science, 50,* 203–208. https://doi.org/10.1016/j.procs.2015.04.069.

Gandomi, A., & Haider, M. (2015). Beyond the hype: Big data concepts, methods, and analytics. *International Journal of Information Management, 35*(2), 137–144. https://doi.org/10.1016/j.ijinfomgt.2014.10.007.

Ganjir, V., Sarkar, B. K., & Kumar, R. R. (2016). Big data analytics for healthcare. *International Journal of Research in Engineering, Technology and Science, 6,* 1–6.

Hermon, R., & Williams, P. A. (2014). Big data in healthcare: What is it used for? In: *Proceedings of the 3rd Australian eHealth informatics and security conference,* 1–3 December, Perth, Western Australia.

Horowitz, L.S. (2012). Translation alignment: Actor-network theory, resistance, and the power dynamics of alliance in New *Caledonia. Antipode,* 44(3), 806–827.

Jagadish, H. V., Gehrke, J., Labrinidis, A., Papakonstantinou, Y., Patel, J. M., Ramakrishnan, R., & Shahabi, C. (2014). Big data and its technical challenges. *Communications of the ACM, 57*(7), 86–94. https://doi.org/10.1145/2611567.

Kankanhalli, A., Hahn, J., Tan, S., & Gao, G. (2016). Big data and analytics in healthcare: Introduction to the special section. *Information Systems Frontiers, 18*(2), 233–235. https://doi.org/10.1007/s10796-016-9641-2.

Kavitha, R., Kannan, E. & Kotteswaran, S. (2016). Implementation of cloud based Electronic Health Record (EHR) for Indian healthcare needs, *Indian Journal of Science and Technology 9*(3), 1–5. https://doi.org/10.17485/ijst/2016/ v9i3/86391.

Kitchin, R. (2014). Big Data, new epistemologies and paradigm shifts. *Big Data & Society, 1*(1), 1–12. https://doi.org/10.1177/2053951714528481.

Kumar, H., & Singh, N. (2017). Review paper on Big Data in healthcare informatics. *International Research Journal of Engineering and Technology, 4*(2), 197–201.

Kwon, O., Lee, N., & Shin, B. (2014). Data quality management, data usage experience and acquisition intention of big data analytics. *International Journal of Information Management, 34*(3), 387–394. https://doi.org/10.1016/j.ijinfomgt.2014.02.002.

Labrinidis, A., & Jagadish, H. V. (2012). Challenges and opportunities with big data. *Proceedings of the VLDB Endowment, 5*(12), 2032–2033. https://doi.org/10.14778/2367502.2367572

Law, J. (1992). Notes on the theory of the actor-network: Ordering, strategy, and heterogeneity. *Systems Practice, 5*(4), 379–393. https://doi.org/10.1007/BF01059830.

Lee, C. H., & Yoon, H. J. (2017). Medical big data: Promise and challenges. *Kidney Research and Clinical Practice, 36*(1), 3–11. https://doi.org/10.23876/j.krcp.2017.36.1.3.

Li, D., Yao, Y., & Shao, Z. F. (2014). Big Data in the Smart City. *Geomatics and Information Science of Wuhan University, 39*(6), 630–640. https://doi.org/10.13203/j.whugis20140135

Liu, W., & Park, E. K. (2014). Big data as an e-health service. In: *2014 international conference on computing, networking and communications (ICNC)* (pp. 982–988), 3–6 February, Honolulu, HI, USA. IEEE. https://doi.org/10.1109/ICCNC.2014.6785471.

Luna, D. R., Mayan, J. C., García, M. J., Almerares, A. A., & House, h, M. (2014). Challenges and potential solutions for big data implementations in developing countries. *Yearbook of Medical Informatics, 23*(01), 36–41. https://doi.org/10.15265/IY-2014-0012.

Malaka, I., & Brown, I. (2015). Challenges to the organisational adoption of big data analytics: A case study in the South African telecommunications industry. In: *Proceedings of the annual research conference on South African institute of computer scientists and information technologists* (p. 27), 28–30 September, Stellenbosch, South Africa. ACM. https://doi.org/10.1145/2815782.2815793.

Marjani, M., Nasaruddin, F., Gani, A., Karim, A., Hashem, I. A. T., Siddiqa, A., & Yaqoob, I. (2017). Big IoT data analytics: Architecture, opportunities, and open research challenges. *IEEE Access, 5,* 5247–5261. https://doi.10.1109/ACCESS.2017.2689040.

Mathew, P.S. & Pillai, A.S. (2015). Big data solutions in healthcare: Problems and perspectives, *In Proceedings of the International Conference on Innovations in Information, Embedded and Communication Systems (ICIIECS)* (pp. 1–6). IEEE, Coimbatore, March 19–20, 2015.

Micheni, E. M. (2015). Diffusion of big data and analytics in developing countries. *The International Journal of Engineering and Science, 4*(8), 44–50.

Mishra, S., Kalra, A., & Choudhary, K. (2013). Influence of information and communication technology in health sectors. *International Journal of Soft Computing and Engineering, 3*(5), 66–68.

Mueller, B., Viering, G., Legner, C., & Riempp, G. (2010). Understanding the economic potential of service-oriented architecture. *Journal of Management Information Systems, 26*(4), 145–180. https://doi.org/10.2753/MIS0742-1222260406.

Nambiar, R., Bhardwaj, R., Sethi, A., & Vargheese, R. (2013). A look at challenges and opportunities of big data analytics in healthcare. In: *International conference on big data* (pp. 17–22), 6–9 October 2013, Silicon Valley, CA, USA. IEEE. https://doi.org/10.1109/BigData.2013.6691753.

Nativi, S., Mazzetti, P., Santoro, M., Papeschi, F., Craglia, M., & Ochiai, O. (2015). Big data challenges in building the global earth observation system of systems. *Environmental Modelling & Software, 68,* 1–26. https://doi.org/10.1016/j.envsoft.2015.01.017.

Peek, N., Holmes, J. H., & Sun, J. (2014). Technical challenges for big data in biomedicine and health: Data sources, infrastructure, and analytics. *Yearbook Medical Information, 9*(1), 42–47. https://doi.org/10.15265/IY-2014-0018.

Prasad, P. (2017). Crafting qualitative research: *Beyond positivist traditions*. New York: Routledge. https://doi.org/10.4324/9781315715070.

Purkayastha, S., & Braa, J. (2013). Big data analytics for developing countries – Using the cloud for operational BI IN health. *The Electronic Journal of Information Systems in Developing Countries, 59*(1), 1–17. https://doi.org/10.1002/j.1681-4835.2013.tb00420.x.

Raghupathi, W., & Raghupathi, V. (2014). Big data analytics in healthcare: Promise and potential. *Health Information Science and Systems, 2*(1), 1–10. https://doi.org/10.1186/2047-2501-2-3.

Rumsfeld, J. S., Joynt, K. E., & Maddox, T. M. (2016). Big data analytics to improve cardiovascular care: Promise and challenges. *Nature Reviews Cardiology, 13*(6), 350–359. https://doi.org/10.1038/nrcardio.2016.42.

Sarkar, B. K. (2017). Big data for secure healthcare system: A conceptual design. *Complex & Intelligent Systems, 3*(2), 133–151. https://doi.org/10.1007/s40747-017-0040-1.

Schüll, A., & Maslan, N. (2018). On the adoption of big data analytics: Interdependencies of contextual factors. In: *International conference on enterprise information systems* (1) (pp. 425–431), 21–24 March, Funchal, Madeira, Portugal.

Scotland, J. (2012). Exploring the philosophical underpinnings of research: Relating ontology and epistemology to the methodology and methods of the scientific, interpretive, and critical research paradigms. *English Language Teaching, 5*(9), 1–8.

Shahbaz, M., Gao, C., Zhai, L., Shahzad, F., & Hu, Y. (2019). Investigating the adoption of big data analytics in healthcare: The moderating role of resistance to change. *Journal of Big Data, 6*(1), 1–20. https://doi.org/10.1186/s40537-019-0170-y.

Shao, G., Shin, S. J., & Jain, S. (2014). Data analytics using simulation for smart manufacturing. In *Proceedings of the Winter Simulation Conference 2014* (pp. 2192–2203). IEEE.

Shu, H. (2016). Big data analytics: Six techniques. *Geo-Spatial Information Science, 19*(2), 119–128. https://doi.org/10.1080/10095020.2016.1182307.

Song, T. M., & Ryu, S. (2015). Big data analysis framework for healthcare and social sectors in Korea. *Healthcare Informatics Research, 21*(1), 3–9. https://doi.org/10.4258/hir.2015.21.1.3.

Wang, Y., & Hajli, N. (2017). Exploring the path to big data analytics success in healthcare. *Journal of Business Research, 70*, 287–299. https://doi.org/10.1016/j.jbusres.2016.08.002.

Walsham, G. (2015). *Interpreting information systems in organisations.* London: Cambridge Press.

Watson, H. J. (2014). Tutorial: Big data analytics: Concepts, technologies, and applications. *Communications of the Association for Information Systems, 34*(1), 1247–1268. https://doi.org/10.17705/1CAIS.03462.

Yanow, D., & Schwart-Shea, P. (2015). *Interpretation and method: Empirical research methods and the interpretive turn.* New York: Routledge.

Yu, T. K., Lin, M. L., & Liao, Y. K. (2017). Understanding factors influencing information communication technology adoption behavior: The moderators of information literacy and digital skills. *Computers in Human Behaviour, 71*, 196–208. https://doi.org/10.1016/j.chb.2017.02.005

Zaman, I., Pazouki, K., Norman, R., Younessi, S., & Coleman, S. (2017). Challenges and opportunities of big data analytics for upcoming regulations and future transformation of the shipping industry. *Procedia Engineering, 194*, 537–544. https://doi.org/10.1016/j.proeng.2017.08.182

6 The Interpretivist and Analytics Approaches for Healthcare Big Data Analytics

Introduction

In the areas of health, big data analytics is one of the most challenging undertakings in recent years. In practice, healthcare practitioners struggle with putting the data into digitised forms such as electronic health records (EHR), making the data sets more useful for actionable insights and applying the data sets in an integrated manner to solve complicated health operations. Although not without challenges, big data analytics brings a fresh perspective to easing complex and unwieldy healthcare data sets.

In an ever-growing-driven society, big data and analytics are fuelling the digital revolution (Maniak, Jayne, Iqbal and Doctor, 2015). Fervently, big data is produced regularly using information technology (IT) solutions such as cloud computing, social media and the Internet of Things (Zakir, Seymour & Berg, 2015). Big data analytics is useful in revealing patterns that exist within data sets from which knowledge is gained, the knowledge economy is enriched and services are improved through better decision-making (Iqbal et al., 2020). It is on the basics of it premise that big data analytics is defined as the methods used to study and process high volume and varied types of data sets (Gandomi & Haider, 2015). Iqbal et al. (2020) assert that big data analytics uses techniques to uncover hidden patterns and identify relationships within big data. Similarly, Acharjya and Ahmed (2016) state that big data analytics processes data of high volume, variety, veracity and velocity using different computational techniques.

Despite its enticing and interesting premise, big data analytics come with challenges. Acharjya and Ahmed (2016) explain that most of the data analytics methods, such as data mining and statistical analysis, cannot manage large volumes of data sets successfully because of synchronisation challenges between analytics tools and database systems. These challenges are synonymous and associated with sensitivity in that some information can be restricted. From a different angle, Katal, Wazid and Goudars (2013) postulate that one of the challenges of analytics tools is the designing of systems that can manage big data efficiently and can filter out vital data from the large volumes of data. Other crucial challenges can be attributed to the mono-approach in using analytics tools for analysing healthcare big data, to leverage solutions for service delivery by health facilities.

Along the same line of argument, Kaisler, Armour, Espinosa and Money (2013) state that another problem with analytics tools is how to describe the essential characteristics of big data from a qualitative perspective. This is attributable to Sharma's (2015) concern about the capabilities of the existing analytics techniques to enable and support organisational aims and objectives. According to LaValle et al. (2011), the current single approach lacks a detailed examination of huge data sets, which big data deserves, to increase purposefulness and usefulness. Therefore, there is a need to explore alternatives, to combine big data analytics with a methodological approach. Such an approach is to increase the value of big data in advanced manner, by understanding why and how data sets transform from one point to another (Gandomi & Haider, 2015).

The interpretivist approach allows for alternative options that leads to alternative interpretations, meaning that there is no correct or incorrect route to reality or knowledge (Antwi & Hamza, 2015). Walsham (1995) argues that there are no 'correct' or 'incorrect' theories if viewed from the interpretivist perspective. Correctness is subject to understanding and associated significant. In cognisance, the interpretivist approach helps to gain knowledge of reality through social constructions such as language, shared meanings, tools and documents (Walsham, 2006). This means that the approach can be used complementarily with analytics methods to unpack and gain a deeper understanding of data sets. According to Myers (2009), within the interpretivist premise, access to reality is socially constructed through means such as consciousness and shared meanings. Arguably, this means that an entity can have value only if meaning is associated with it. According to Marshall, Cardon, Poddar and Fontenot (2013), through social construction, realities are revealed to be enquiry and interaction.

Various stakeholders, such as software developers, managers, users and suppliers, use analytics methods to analyse big data in organisations (Skok & Legge, 2001). Due to the variety of stakeholders and interrelationships between them, examining big data analytics becomes a complex situation in a social context such as an organisation (Watson, 2014). Giddens (1984) refers to social context as a society of people governed by policy and culture. Abdel-Fattah (2015) states that an interpretivist research approach is suitable for comprehending the influences at play and capturing the complexity and contextual richness in such a social context. Lukka (2014) states that the interpretivist research approach offers a deep insight into social reality. Thus, the interpretivist approach is usually employed to gain a better understanding of a phenomenon by examining it in its natural context.

Thus, the interpretivist approach, from the perspective of subjectivism, is required to enact and bridge that gap created from the mono-approach in using the analytics methods. From the interpretivist perspective, the actor-network theory (ANT) is employed to complement analytics methods and propose a multilevel approach to big data analysis. ANT is a sociotechnical theory that is primarily concerned with actors (human and non-human), networks, and the relationships and interactions between actors within heterogeneous networks (Callon, 1986; Iyamu, 2021). The theory can be used to define data sets and human actors; examine how the actors' networks are formed and stabilised; how data sets are categorised into networks and how to gain a better understanding of the data sets and actors' relationship and interaction.

From the discussion above, the objectives of this chapter are formulated as follows, to (1) identify some of the gaps created from the mono-approach in using the analytics method for big data analysis; and (2) propose a model through which the interpretivist approach can be combined with analytics methods for big data analysis and to leverage organisational (health facility) objectives. Based on these objectives, the chapter is divided into six main sections. First, the introduction provides an overview of the chapter. In the second section, a review of literature, to identify the existing gaps is presented. The third section covers how to employ techniques for analysis of big data in the context of healthcare. Next, the relevant factors discovered, and a model that depicts a complementary approach are presented and discussed, respectively. Thereafter, implications of use are explained in the section that follows. Finally, the chapter is summarised.

Literature Review

Based on the objectives of the chapter as stated above, a review of works in the areas of big data analytics and interpretivist approach was conducted. Through the review, historical insight into the possibility of combining the two concepts, big data analytics and interpretivist approach for big data analysis, is gained. According to Iyamu and Roode (2010, p. 2), the combined use of two approaches is not necessarily to compare but to highlight the importance and usefulness of the approaches in a complementary fashion.

Big data analytics encompasses various techniques such as descriptive, predictive and prescriptive analytics for analysing large volumes and a variety of data sets, both structured and unstructured (Sun, Sun & Strang, 2018). Descriptive analytics deals with describing past events, while predictive analytics focuses on future activities and how to influence them, and prescriptive analytics refers to decision-making mechanisms and tools (Rehman, Chang, Batool & Wah, 2016). According to Wang, Kung and Byrd (2018), big data analytics can provide fresh insights and improve processes for many environments. This is due to the ability of big data analytics to improve the quality and accuracy of decisions, boost organisational growth through effective decision-making and offer a holistic view for meeting future organisational needs (Sun, Song, Jara & Bie, 2016).

Big data analytics lead to valuable knowledge for many organisations. LaValle et al. (2011) classify the capability of big data analytics into three categories, namely, aspirational (future or intended use of data sets), experienced (practical use of data sets) and transformed (manipulation of data sets). The classifications make attribution to an organisation's operations and risk management (Sivarajah, Kamal, Irani & Weerakkody, 2017). Many organisations aspire to seek the meaning of lived experiences and a deeper understanding from data sets through the interpretation of the text (Jha & Bose, 2016). Chen, Preston and Swink (2015) assert that insights resulting from big data analytics can transform organisational models and strategies. Akter et al. (2016) state that big data analytics can deliver competitive advantages and returns on investments for organisations.

Data sets are generated from various sources, and for this reason, data heterogeneity poses a challenge for big data analytics (Sun, Song, Jara & Bie, 2016). For several reasons, some organisations struggle to gain from the benefits, such as transformation, which big data analytics potentially presents (Wang, Kung & Byrd, 2018). From the explanation in Katal, Wazid and Goudar (2013), there are four main analytical challenges with big data, which are (1) the inability to deal effectively with data that comes in large volumes and is varied in nature; (2) the availability of data storage systems that can efficiently store big data; (3) making decisions as to which data is necessary for analysis and (4) to gain the most value out of the data that has been analysed previously. Currently, the challenges encountered with big data analytics can be addressed using the interpretivist approach, as this allows for various alternative approaches and from different perspectives.

Big data analytics require interpretation to gain deeper insight, regardless of the methods or viewpoints (descriptive, predictive or prescriptive). Chapter 7 demonstrates how big data analytics methods can be combined with ANT from an interpretivist perspective. Najafabadi et al. (2015) argue that the difficulties are caused by the increase in data sources and data types that are associated with big data analytics, thus presenting inherent practical challenges. Also, some unique challenges are faced by big data analytics, such as (1) effectively dealing with streaming data that is moving at a rapid rate; (2) the distributed nature of the data sources; (3) the expansion capabilities available for analysis algorithms and (4) the high dimensionality of data – large number of features and attributes in a data set (Najafabadi et al., 2015; Rumsfeld, Joynt & Maddox, 2016).

Critically, the interpretivist approach can be useful to analytics tools in the analysis of big data in that the approach guides enquiry on why things are the way they are. Also, the interpretivist approach helps to probe and associate meaning with existing facts or materials, including big data. The intentions of the interpretivist approach are grounded in theory building and conceptual thinking, which can be of use in examining big data from its numerous sources, varieties and velocity (Khan, 2014). Ultimately, applying the interpretivist approach for investigation depends on the investigator (researcher) and the amount and types of available data viewed from the scientific and social worlds. It is assumed that the validity of research conducted from an interpretivist approach by gathering in-depth and rich qualitative data focuses on reality and context, according to Wohlin and Aurum (2015).

The interpretivist approach can be employed in either the qualitative or the quantitative enquiry. Some of the strengths of the interpretive approach are as follows:

i   the ability to provide valuable information and generate additional and new knowledge;
ii it enables flexibility in creating meanings that are introduced by unanticipated data and
iii it assists in providing a means in which meaning about a phenomenon can be ascribed, described and discovered through the analysis and understanding of big data, from its complex volume, velocity and variety.

Some of the challenges of analytics methods include the analysis of integrated (variety of) data and the transformation of big data (Sivarajah, Kamal, Irani & Weerakkody, 2017). According to Mikalef, Pappas, Krogstie and Giannakos (2018), analytics methods lack the required capability to transform big data into actionable insight for organisations. The interpretivist approach can be employed from this angle to close this gap because the interpretivist approach allows and enables the analysis of multiple stages of innovation and can be linked to different theories (Jha & Bose, 2016).

Analysis of Healthcare Big Data

The historical challenges identified in the above section spurn the objectives of this chapter, which is to provide a solution that can enhance healthcare big data usefulness. It is on this basis that a model is developed and discussed. After processing (analysis), it is intended to make healthcare big data more meaningful to the social world with a specific focus on reality and cultures. This broadens an understanding to a wider populace among the actors of healthcare and its related activities. Thus, the objectives of the chapter are to (1) identify some of the gaps that are created by using analytics tools as a single approach for big data analysis; and (2) propose a method through which the interpretivist approach can be employed with data analytics methods to leverage organisational aims and objectives. Based on the two objectives, the following questions are formulated: (1) what are some of the uncovered gaps in the single use of analytics method for analysis? (2) how can the interpretivist approach be combined with analytics methods for the analysis of big data purposes?

From an enhancement perspective, big data analytics enable organisations (healthcare facilities) to analyse an immense volume, variety and velocity of data (Wang, Chen, Hong & Kang, 2018). The analysis from extant studies reveals that the challenges remain in using analytics methods (Choi, Chan & Yue, 2017). Mikalef, Pappas, Krogstie and Giannakos (2018) argue that big data analysis is often challenged because of its complexity and multifaceted tasks, which sometimes happen to enhance organisational objectives. The challenges are caused by the mono-approach of using the analytics tools in big data analysis, which could have been done at more than one level.

In achieving the objectives of the chapter, the questions what are some of the uncovered gaps created by using analytics methods as a single approach in the analysis of healthcare big data? And how can the interpretivist approach be combined with analytics methods for big data analysis? are examined. Some gaps are identified in applying big data analytics in the healthcare environment. This is irrespective of the analytics methods applied in the analysis of big data. The main factors that create gaps in the application of big data analytics are algorithm adaption and use, facilitating contradiction, filtration of big data and integration.

Algorithm Adaption and Use

Algorithms (newly developed or existing ones) are often required to analyse big data sets (Chen & Lin, 2014). The need for algorithms is primarily because of the high dimension of the data sets, which has substantial amounts of attributes from various sources associated with the big data (Zhou, Pan, Wang & Vasilakos, 2017). This means that there is a need for solutions that allow defining and formulating the necessary criteria for data representation that will provide valuable meanings (Acharjya & Ahmed, 2016; Manekar, 2017). Despite the application of algorithms, challenges remain in the analysis of big data. Najafabadi et al. (2015) attribute the challenges to the increasing number of data types and data sources constantly associated with big data, affecting sustainability and reliability in the results obtained.

Hermeneutic Circle Technique

These challenges can be eased if the data sets are decomposed into smaller units by applying the interpretivist approach. A way to achieve this is by applying the principle of the hermeneutic circle technique. Klein and Myers (1999) state that the hermeneutic circle advocates that an understanding of complex data sets emanates from the meaning of smaller parts of a data set and their associations. In using the hermeneutic circle, the interpretation process is twofold (Klein & Myers, 1999). The first step begins from a preliminary understanding of the smaller units to the entire data set, and the second step involves an overall understanding of the entire data set back to an enriched appreciation of the individual smaller units. Essentially, it is an iterative process considering the symbiotic meaning of the smaller units and the entire data set of which it forms a part.

Facilitate Contradiction

Regularly, there are incompleteness and inconsistency in big data, which often result in discrepancies and contradictions. This necessitates the use of technologies to facilitate the process of crosschecking contradictory cases introduced by the incompleteness and inconsistency in big data (Jagadish et al., 2014). The contradictions are also attributed to the diverse sources and wavering reliability in big data analytics. To achieve an organisation's objectives in the use of big data, contradictions need to be facilitated. Even though analytics tools have been applied in the analysis of big data, the contradictions persist.

The contradictory challenge can be attributed to a lack of subjective reasoning from an interpretivist perspective, which does not allow data sets to be unpacked into specific viewpoints. By taking a subjective view and position, data sets can be analysed from the awareness of goals and objectives (Friedman & Wyatt, 2006). The interpretation of data and requirements based on subjective reasoning impacts the transformation of events, such as from diagnosis to treatment. Such interpretation helps to better decompose data sets, gain comprehensiveness, improve understanding and make provisions for the most appropriate solutions.

Filtration of Big Data

Big data will continue to be big data in that the data sets will not stop increasing in volume, variety and velocity. The increasing nature of big data does not make it easy for the analytics tools to achieve organisational objectives. The increase in big data sometimes results in complexity, which cannot be economically feasible for an organisation. According to Mohamed and Al-Jaroodi (2014), there is a need for real-time solutions that can filter and summarise the big data in leveraging business goals and objectives.

Data sets can be filtered using descriptive, predictive and prescriptive tools in the analysis of big data. This can only happen by applying the interpretivist approach, allowing data to be viewed from real-world perspectives. Thanh and Thanh (2015) state that using the interpretivist approach, an insightful understanding can be gained from the perspectives of the collected data. This is because the interpretivist approach enables the portrayal of a complex and ever-changing reality often found in big data analytics and leads to a more inclusive understanding of the data (Chen, Shek & Bu, 2011).

Integration

Data sources in big data analytics are highly distributed, which brings about challenges such as integration, access and distribution (Wang, Chen, Hong & Kang, 2018). Due to this observation by the previous authors, the need to create techniques to properly prepare distributed data for integration and management of big data towards organisational objectives becomes a necessity. According to Saldžiūnas and Skyrius (2017), the results from big data analytics are largely influenced by the complementarity between the logical model of a database system and the analysis effort. The authors further argue that a missing middle is integrating database systems and analytical tools in performance and processing. The analytics tools are major differentiators between high-performing and low-performing organisations because they allow pro-activeness and promote competitiveness and sustainability (Wamba et al., 2017). This poses a need for the autonomous use of analytical tools from a logical database model, which must be interpretivist in nature.

The interpretivist approach has been employed many times in the past, where there were integration challenges concerning data sets. For example, the acceptance of multiple perspectives with differing aspects of big data was used to form and underpin a comprehensive cognisance of data sets through an integration approach (Thanh & Thanh, 2015). The interpretivist approach can be employed to disintegrate or integrate attributes in big data based on the subjective view of the experts. Khanal (2013) states that using either sequential (where data is collected and analysed per data type) or concurrent (where data of different types is collected per stage) methodological strategies, integration challenges with data can be addressed. In addition, the use of data conversion and combination strategies in the interpretivist approach was employed by Henderson (2005), to address data integration challenges within the context in an environment.

Big Data Analytics and the Interpretivist Approach

Analytical methods (or tools) for big data analysis are the technologies and algorithms used in the analysis of big data for pattern recognition among data elements, the identification of risk areas to achieve organisational goals and objectives and to facilitate decision-making (Bates et al., 2014; Guleria & Sood, 2017). In addition, Akter and Wamba (2016) argue that analytics tools are used in the extraction and interpretation of information from big data analysis.

Big data analytics encompasses various analytical techniques. The most common ones, descriptive, predictive and prescriptive analytics, as shown in Figure 6.1, focus on distinct deliverables towards leveraging health facility goals and objectives. Employing and managing the tools to enhance a health facility require a better understanding of the challenges faced.

Different types of analytics tools under the categorise of descriptive, prescriptive or predictive (Wang, Zhang, et al., 2018). The analytics tools use algorithmic methods to describe and summarise knowledge patterns (Waller & Fawcett, 2013). In addition, Hazen, Boone, Ezell and Jones-Farmer (2014) state that big data analytics tools are used to probe data and discern patterns for informed business decision-making. The use of analytics tools is also a process of intelligence mining from data sets.

Big data analytics tools, such as descriptive, prescriptive and predictive, are often viewed from both business (healthcare included) and technology perspectives because of the alignment between business and IT units, which remain a critical aspect of an organisation. This allows the encompassing of the analytics tools into technical and non-technical domains in assessing

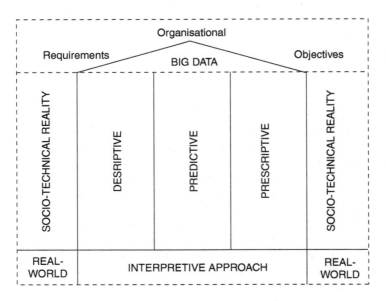

Figure 6.1 Complementary use of big data analytics and *interpretivist* approach

their usefulness within context and relevance. Watson (2014) distinguishes between the three analytical methods to understand their impacts on architecture and technology.

The interpretivist approach enables the use of the hermeneutics technique to decompose data sets into smaller units. The decomposition facilitates a better understanding of the smaller units and the associations among the data sets. The interpretivist approach from the subjectivism stance enhances data analysis from various perspectives, which were derived from the organisational objectives that the data needs to address (Friedman & Wyatt, 2006). This approach is intended to ensure that contradictions are avoided in the process of big data analysis. Due to the complex and volatile nature of big data analytics, achieving healthcare objectives is not as easy as claimed. Based on this foreseen challenge, Chen, Shek and Bu (2011) state that the interpretivist approach can provide an in-depth understanding of complex data sets through forming and underpinning multiple interpretations of a specific healthcare context. In Chapter 7, a model in which ANT is combined with big data analytics to analyse big data is presented.

Implications of Practice

The combination of the interpretivist approach with the big data analytics for big data analysis to leverage healthcare objectives has three main implications of practice: cyber security, healthcare transformation and scientific translation. The implications are tabulated in Table 6.1.

Table 6.1 Implications of practice

Implication	Big data analytics	Interpretivist approach
Cyber security	Healthcare big data analytics can be used to prevent and mitigate against security threats in the cyber space by identifying, accessing and detecting anomalies in systems and networks. This includes gathering and analysing patients' big data generated from computer systems to gain in-depth understanding and discover patterns that can assist in better detecting and responding to cyber threats to patients' personal information.	Detecting patterns towards protecting cyberspace is usually an objective, which does not always cover angles of threat possibilities. The approach needs to include a process that allows patterns of events to be followed and traced. Thus, the analysis cannot always be objective. It does require subjectivism to gain deeper insights into situations and circumstances on why certain things happen or did not happen about responses to patients' health condition.
Healthcare transformation	The analytics methods can enable health facilities to drive towards operational efficiency and strategic innovation, enhance healthcare capabilities and increase competitiveness.	Allows and enables the researchers in the areas of health and IT to gain a richer understanding of the processing of patients' big data by bridging the gap between health-related data and decision-making. Through this means, theoretical and practical understanding can be reached, which helps to generate innovative ideas for the transformation of healthcare initiatives and processes.
Scientific translation	In practice, the analytics methods can be used for translation and transformation of data for healthcare enhancement. This includes the transfer of patient's data sets into information and knowledge to create intelligent processes.	The translation and transformation of patients' data sets into information and knowledge cannot be done one way or through a strictly defined pattern. This is to ensure richness and more purposefulness. It requires interpretation of patients' big data from a subjective point of view.

Table 6.1 summarises the implications of the complementary use of analytics tools and the interpretivist approach. As shown in the table above, it is of fundamental importance for health facility's aims and objectives to combine analytics tools with the interpretivist approach in big data analysis. In practice, the combination of analytics tools with the interpretivist approach can

help cover a wide spectrum of health facility logic from both quantitative and qualitative viewpoints. This is irrespective of the size and nature of the health facility's focus.

Summary

This chapter makes it possible to understand how the interpretivist approach can be combined with analytics tools for the purpose of analysing big data, to assist in leveraging health facilities' objectives. Therefore, the chapter is intended to benefit academics, organisations and professionals that focus on big data and analytics. For academics, this chapter provokes discourse on the complementary use of big data analytics and interpretivist approach, which does not exist at the time of writing this chapter and book. The discourse can be viewed from both social and scientific perspectives. The chapter contributes to the academic domain by adding to the existing literature in the areas of big data analytics, interpretivist approach and field of information systems. From the healthcare perspective, the benefits come from gaining a better understanding of the gaps in applying big data analytics, as revealed in the implication of practice section of the chapter. In addition, the chapter proposes how analytics tools can be combined with the interpretivist approach for healthcare purposes.

However, there is more work to be done in this area of big data analytics and the interpretivist approach. This includes putting into practice the solution proposed in this chapter. A case study can be conducted to assess the theory of combining both analytics tools with the interpretivist approach for big data analysis.

References

Abdel-Fattah, M. A. (2015). Grounded theory and action research as pillars for interpretivist information systems research: A comparative study. *Egyptian Informatics Journal*, *16*(3), 309–327. https://doi.org/10.1016/j.eij.2015.07.002.

Acharjya, D. P., & Ahmed, K. (2016). A survey on big data analytics: Challenges, open research issues and tools. *International Journal Advanced Computer Science and Applications*, *7*(2), 511–518.

Akter, S., & Wamba, S. F. (2016). Big data analytics in E-commerce: A systematic review and agenda for future research. *Electronic Markets*, *26*(2), 73–194. https://doi.org/10.1007/s12525-016-0219-0.

Akter, S., Wamba, S. F., Gunasekaran, A., Dubey, R., & Childe, S. J. (2016). How to improve firm performance using big data analytics capability and business strategy alignment? *International Journal of Production Economics*, *182*, 113–131. https://doi.org/10.1016/j.ijpe.2016.08.018.

Antwi, S. K., & Hamza, K. (2015). Qualitative and quantitative research paradigms in business research: A philosophical reflection. *European Journal of Business and Management*, *7*(3), 217–225.

Bates, D. W., Saria, S., Ohno-Machado, L., Shah, A., & Escobar, G. (2014). Big data in health care: Using analytics to identify and manage high-risk and high-cost patients. *Health Affairs, 33*(7), 1123–1131. https://doi.org/10.1377/hlthaff.2014.0041.

Callon, M. (1986). Some elements of a sociology of translation: Domestication of the scallops and the fishermen of St Brieuc Bay. In: Law, J. (ed.), *Power, action and belief: A new sociology of knowledge?* (pp. 196–233). London: Routledge and Kegan Paul.

Chen, X. W., & Lin, X. (2014). Big data deep learning: Challenges and perspectives. *IEEE Accesss, 2*, 514–525. https://doi.org/10.1109/ACCESS.2014.2325029.

Chen, D. Q., Preston, D. S., & Swink, M. (2015). How the use of big data analytics affects value creation in supply chain management. *Journal of Management Information Systems, 32*(4), 4–39. https://doi.org/10.1080/07421222.2015.1138364.

Chen, Y. Y., Shek, D. T., & Bu, F. F. (2011). Applications of interpretivist and constructionist research methods in adolescent research: Philosophy, principles and examples. *International Journal of Adolescent Medicine and Health, 23*(2), 129–139. https://doi.org/10.1515/ijamh.2011.022.

Choi, T. M., Chan, H. K., & Yue, X. (2017). Recent development in big data analytics for business operations and risk management. *IEEE Transactions on Cybernetics, 47*(1), 81–92. https://doi.org/10.1109/TCYB.2015.2507599.

Friedman, C. P., & Wyatt, J. C. (2006). Subjectivist approaches to evaluation. In: Hannah, K. J. & Ball, M. J. (eds), *Evaluation methods in biomedical informatics. Health informatics* (pp. 248–266). New York: Springer. https://doi.org/10.1007/0-387-30677-3_9.

Gandomi, A., & Haider, M. (2015). Beyond the hype: Big data concepts, methods, and analytics. *International Journal of Information Management, 35*(2), 137–144. https://doi.org/10.1016/j.ijinfomgt.2014.10.007.

Giddens, A. (1984). *The constitution of society: Outline of the theory of structuration.* Cambridge: John Polity Press.

Guleria, P., & Sood, M. (2017). Big data analytics: Predicting academic course preference using hadoop inspired mapreduce. In: *4th international conference on image information processing (ICIIP)*, 21–23 December, Shimla, India. IEEE. https://doi.org/10.1109/ICIIP.2017.8313734.

Hazen, B. T., Boone, C. A., Ezell, J. D., & Jones-Farmer, L. A. (2014). Data quality for data science, predictive analytics, and big data in supply chain management: An introduction to the problem and suggestions for research and applications. *International Journal of Production Economics, 154*, 72–80. https://doi.org/10.1016/j.ijpe.2014.04.018.

Henderson, A. (2005). The value of integrating interpretivist research approaches in the exposition of healthcare context. *Journal of Advanced Nursing, 52*(5), 554–560. https://doi.org/10.1111/j.1365-2648.2005.03622.x.

Iqbal, R., Doctor, F., More, B., Mahmud, S., & Yousuf, U. (2020). Big data analytics and computational intelligence for cyber–physical systems: Recent trends and state of the art applications. *Future Generation Computer Systems, 105*, 766–778. https://doi.org/10.1016/j.future.2017.10.021.

Iyamu, T., & Roode, D. (2010). The use of structuration and actor-network theory for analysis: A case study of a financial institution in South Africa. *International Journal of Actor-Network Theory and Technological Innovation, 2*(1), 1–26. https://doi.org/10.4018/978-1-4666-1559-5.ch001.

Jagadish, H. V., Gehrke, J., Labrinidis, A., Papakonstantinou, Y., Patel, J. M., Ramakrishnan, R., & Shahabi, C. (2014). Big data and its technical challenges. *Communications of the ACM, 57*(7), 86–94. https://doi.org/10.1145/2611567.

Jha, A. K., & Bose, I. (2016). Innovation research in information systems: A commentary on contemporary trends and issues. *Information & Management, 53*(3), 297–306. https://doi.org/10.1016/j.im.2015.10.007.

Kaisler, S., Armour, F., Espinosa, J. A., & Money, W. (2013). Big data: Issues and challenges moving forward. In: *46th Hawaii international conference on System sciences (HICSS)* (pp. 995–1004), 7–10 January, Wailea, HI, USA. IEEE. https://doi.org/10.1109/HICSS.2013.645.

Katal, A., Wazid, M., & Goudar, R. H. (2013). Big data: Issues, challenges, tools and good practices. In: *6th international conference on contemporary computing (IC3)* (pp. 404–409), 8–10 August, Noida, India. IEEE. https://doi.org/10.1109/IC3.2013.6612229

Khan, S. N. (2014). Qualitative research method: Grounded theory. *International Journal of Business and Management, 9*(11), 224–234. https://doi:10.5539/ijbm.v9n11p224.

Khanal, R. C. (2013). Concerns and challenges of data integration from objective post-positivist approach and a subjective non-positivist interpretivist approach and their validity/credibility issues. *Journal of the Institute of Engineering, 9*(1), 115–129.

Klein, H. K., & Myers, M. D. (1999). A set of principles for conducting and evaluating interpretivist field studies in information systems. *Management Information Systems Quarterly, 23*(1), 67–93. https://doi.org/10.2307/249410.

Lavalle, S., Lesser, E., Shockley, R., Hopkins, M. S., & Kruschwitz, N. (2011). Big data, analytics and the path from insights to value. *Massachusetts Institute of Technology Sloan Management Review, 52*(2), 21–32.

Lukka, K. (2014). Exploring the possibilities for causal explanation in interpretivist research. *Accounting, Organisations and Society, 39*(7), 559–566. https://doi.org/10.1016/j.aos.2014.06.002.

Manekar, S. A. (2017). Opportunity and challenges for migrating big data analytics in cloud. In: *IOP conference series: Materials science and engineering, 225*(1), 012148.

Maniak, T., Jayne, C., Iqbal, R., & Doctor, F. (2015). Automated intelligent system for sound signalling device quality assurance. *Information Sciences, 294*, 600–611. https://doi.org/10.1016/j.ins.2014.09.042.

Marshall, B., Cardon, P., Poddar, A., & Fontenot, R. (2013). Does sample size matter in qualitative research?: A review of qualitative interviews in IS research. *Journal of Computer Information Systems, 54*(1), 11–22. https://doi.org/10.1080/08874417.2013.11645667.

Mikalef, P., Pappas, I. O., Krogstie, J., & Giannakos, M. (2018). Big data analytics capabilities: A systematic literature review and research agenda. *Information Systems and e-Business Management, 16*(3), 547–578. https://doi.org/10.1007/s10257-017-0362-y.

Mohamed, N., & Al-Jaroodi, J. (2014). Real-time big data analytics: Applications and challenges. In: *Proceedings of international conference on high performance computing & simulation (HPCS)* (pp. 305–310), 21–25 July 2014, Bologna, Italy. IEEE. https://doi.org/10.1109/HPCSim.2014.6903700.

Myers, M. D. (2009). *Qualitative research in business & management*. Los Angeles, CA: Sage.

Najafabadi, M. M., Villanustre, F., Khoshgoftaar, T. M., Seliya, N., Wald, R., & Muharemagic, E. (2015). Deep learning applications and challenges in big data analytics. *Journal of Big Data, 2*(1), 1–13. https://doi.org/10.1186/s40537-014-0007-7.

Rehman, M. H., Chang, V., Batool, A., & Wah, T. Y. (2016). Big data reduction framework for value creation in sustainable enterprises. *International Journal of Information Management, 36*(6), 917–928. https://doi.org/10.1016/j.ijinfomgt.2016.05.013.

Rumsfeld, J. S., Joynt, K. E., & Maddox, T. M. (2016). Big data analytics to improve cardiovascular care: Promise and challenges. *Nature Reviews Cardiology, 13*(6), 350–364. https://doi.org/10.1038/nrcardio.2016.42.

Saldžiūnas, K., & Skyrius, R. (2017). The challenge of big data analytics in the mobile communications sector. *Ekonomika, 96*(2), 110–121.

Sharma, S. (2015). An extended classification and comparison of nosql big data models. *arXiv*, preprint arXiv:1509.08035.

Sivarajah, U., Kamal, M. M., Irani, Z., & Weerakkody, V. (2017). Critical analysis of Big Data challenges and analytical methods. *Journal of Business Research, 70*, 263–286. https://doi.org/10.1016/j.jbusres.2016.08.001.

Skok, W., & Legge, M. (2001, April). Evaluating enterprise resource planning (ERP) systems using an interpretive approach. In: *Proceedings of the 2001 ACM SIGCPR conference on computer personnel research* (pp. 189–197). https://doi.org/10.1145/371209.371234.

Sun, Y., Song, H., Jara, A. J., & Bie, R. (2016). Internet of things and big data analytics for smart and connected communities. *IEEE Access, 4*, 766–773. https://doi.org/10.1109/ACCESS.2016.2529723.

Sun, Z., Sun, L., & Strang, K. (2018). Big data analytics services for enhancing business intelligence. *Journal of Computer Information Systems, 58*(2), 162–169. https://doi.org/10.1080/08874417.2016.1220239.

Thanh, N. C., & Thanh, T. T. (2015). The interconnection between interpretivist paradigm and qualitative methods in education. *American Journal of Educational Science, 1*(2), 24–27.

Waller, M. A., & Fawcett, S. E. (2013). Data science, predictive analytics, and big data: A revolution that will transform supply chain design and management. *Journal of Business Logistics, 34*(2), 77–84. https://doi.org/10.1111/jbl.12010.

Walsham, G. (1995). The emergence of interpretivism in IS research. *Information Systems Research, 6*(4), 376–394. https://doi.org/10.1287/isre.6.4.376.

Walsham, G. (2006). Doing interpretive research. *European Journal of Information Systems, 15*(3), 320–330. https://doi.org/10.1057/palgrave.ejis.3000589.

Wamba, S. F., Gunasekaran, A., Akter, S., Ren, S. J. F., Dubey, R., & Childe, S. J. (2017). Big data analytics and firm performance: Effects of dynamic capabilities. *Journal of Business Research, 70*, 356–365. https://doi.org/10.1016/j.jbusres.2016.08.009.

Wang, Y., Chen, Q., Hong, T., & Kang, C. (2018). Review of smart meter data analytics: Applications, methodologies, and challenges. *IEEE Transactions on Smart Grid, 6*, 65474–65487. https://doi.org/10.1109/TSG.2018.2818167.

Wang, Y., Kung, L., & Byrd, T. A. (2018). Big data analytics: Understanding its capabilities and potential benefits for healthcare organisations. *Technological Forecasting and Social Change, 126*, 3–13. https://doi.org/10.1016/j.techfore.2015.12.019.

Wang, J., Zhang, W., Shi, Y., Duan, S., & Liu, J. (2018). Industrial big data analytics: Challenges, methodologies, and applications. *arXiv*, preprint arXiv: 1807.01016.

Watson, H. J. (2014). Tutorial: Big data analytics: Concepts, technologies, and applications. *Communication of the Association for Information Systems, 34*(65), 1247–1268. https://doi.org/10.17705/1CAIS.03462.

Wohlin, C., & Aurum, A. (2015). Towards a decision-making structure for selecting a research design in empirical software engineering. *Empirical Software Engineering, 20*(6), 1427–1455. https://doi.org/10.1007/s10664-014-9319-7.

Zakir, J., Seymour, T., & Berg, K. (2015). Big data analytics. *Issues in Information Systems, 16*(2), 81–90.

Zhou, L., Pan, S., Wang, J., & Vasilakos, A. V. (2017). Machine learning on big data: Opportunities and challenges. *Neurocomputing, 237,* 350–361. https://doi.org/10.1016/j.neucom.2017.01.026

7 A Multi-Level Approach for Analysis of Healthcare Big Data

Introduction

Health-related big data is increasingly too complex for a single analysis method if the healthcare service level is to improve. Thus, a multi-level approach that offers analysis at micro and macro levels is required. The multi-level approach helps to reduce the complexity in patients' big data by splitting and putting the data sets into context perspectives and appropriately, from the points of generating the data to its management and use. Thus, the approach offers ratification of data fragmentation and lack of uniform digitisation of patients' big data, which usually impede efficiency and result in poor service delivery because some health practitioners struggle with differentiation and appropriation when it comes to data manipulations and activities associated with computing. Understandably, many health practitioners are not trained, at least, at basic, in the areas of computerisation of data.

Big data are characterised by large volume, velocity and variety (Kitchin, 2013). Although previous chapter provides a good explanation of the characteristics, I am compelled to do so again for the interest of this chapter's focus. Ghazal et al. (2013) explain the characteristics of big data in a bit more detailed fashion as follows: (i) volume, a huge amount of data, which is not easy to handle and process; (ii) velocity, entails the speed of data that flows in and out of an environment, which makes it difficult to manipulate; and (iii) variety, ranges and types of data from various sources that are not always easy to assimilate. Along the same line of understanding, Zikopoulos and Eaton (2011) describe big data as representing a new era in exploring and utilising improved services for organisational purposes. Based on its diverse and versatile nature, big data can be applied to many areas, including complex and real-time situations (Najafabadi et al., 2015).

Organisations use big data for various services and different reasons, including efficiency, sustainability and competitiveness. Irrespective of size, variety and complexity, big data can be harnessed within context and relevance towards achieving organisational goals and objectives in any area, including healthcare and social media. Kambatla, Kollias, Kumar and Grama (2014) argued that big data could be simply interpreted as a set of data that is

DOI: 10.4324/9781003251064-7

more than what an organisation can easily manage effectively and efficiently. Hence, analytics is required to extract value and make it easy to use for organisations' activities, including richer insight for sustainability and service delivery. Also, harnessing big data through analytics can deliver increased value because it intends to reveal and present a more complete story and reality about specifics of an organisation (Foster, 2014).

The most significant breakthrough from the emergence and evolving nature of big data analytics (BDA) is the technological tools (methods), which include descriptive, prescriptive and predictive analytics approaches. However, the benefits and excitements of big data have for many years been suppressed by its challenges. According to Sharma (2015, p. 3), 'scientists are optimistic about the Big Data, but express equally low confidence in the data access capabilities of the existing techniques'. The low confidence carries significant weight because organisations and investors rely on experts' viewpoints. This raises the need, and provides enough justification, to explore alternatives that combine BDA tools with a methodological approach at both micro and macro levels of analysis. The actor-network theory (ANT) is a useful method of analysis due to its focus on network heterogeneity, actors' activities and translation of various events within moments.

The current approach of big data analysis, using analytics tools, does not allow the translation of data sets from a subjective perspective, as, also explained in previous chapter, to increase the value of big data by understanding why and how data manifest themselves in the way they do (Gandomi & Haider, 2015). This negatively impacts the accuracy, redundancy and usefulness of data sets, which affects the value of operations and competitive effectiveness in many organisations (Ghazal et al., 2013). Also, the current single approach lacks detailed examination of huge data sets, which big data deserves, to ensure purposefulness and usefulness (LaValle et al., 2011). Thus, only through a holistic demystification of big data values can it be enhanced in harness and achievement, to improve service delivery. In the context of this chapter, demystification entails a multi-level analysis of big data at the micro and macro levels.

Fundamentally, the multi-level analysis consists of 5 main deeds: (a) defining data, (b) defining human actors activities, (3) examining how actor-networks are formed and stabilised, (4) how data sets are categorised into actor-networks and (5) how to better understand data and actors' relationships and reproductive actions. Such analysis is intended to focus on both current and futuristic states of data sets within an environment. As a result, some of the important questions in approaching any BDA assignment or project include (i) what are the requirements? (Gandomi & Haider, 2015), (ii) what are the deliverables? (Russom, 2011), (iii) who are the users and stakeholders? (LaValle et al., 2011) and (iv) where are the stakeholders? (LaValle et al., 2011). These questions encompass heterogeneous actor-networks, including data, processes, technologies and humans seeking to improve an approach towards finding new things. Sharma (2015) emphasises that the current state of research art in big data is still far behind its maturity, and the scope of demystification seeks continuous active research engagement to derive innovative approaches and findings.

This chapter focuses on exploring BDA tools, examining methodological techniques (ANT) for analysis, and proposing a multi-level approach, which can be used to improve the quality and richness of data sets through analytics. Thus, the question is, how can BDA be conducted at two levels, using a combination of an analytics tool and theoretical framework? Thus, BDA tools and ANT are examined in a complementary fashion. This is considered a novel or fresh perspective because there is apparent no study or book where ANT was complementarily used with BDA tools.

For clarity and better understanding, this chapter is divided into six main sequential sections. The first section introduces the chapter, where its objective is clearly stated. A literature review is conducted on BDA and ANT as presented in the second section. In the third section, BDA is discussed in detail. The fourth section presents and provides a comprehensive explanation on how the multi-level approach can be employed for big data analysis. In the fifth section, the implication of practice in using the multi-level approach for big data analysis is prudently covered. A summary of the chapter is provided in the last section.

Review of Related Works

The literature review is divided into two parts, namely BDA and ANT. This explores the gap and sets the path to gaining an understanding of how BDA and ANT can be complementary to analyse data sets within an organisation.

Big Data Analytics in Organisations

Big data is seen as a collection of data that has grown tremendously beyond the ability of commonly used software tools to capture, manage and process (Wu, Zhu, Wu & Ding, 2014). This is an emphasis, not a repetition, since it is the chapter and book's focus: three main perspectives characterise growth: volume, variety and velocity. Data velocity is much more than a bandwidth issue; it is used for measuring the speed of data creation, streaming and aggregation (Kaisler, Armour, Espinosa & Money, 2013). The vast use of big data makes it essential always to imbibe an approach that allows the interrogation of why things happen in the ways that they do, rather than solely of what happened. However, BDA has so far been static and lean more towards a quantitative, positivist paradigm. This means that there is little or no innovation in the areas of BDA.

Analytics of big data is commonly conducted from three main perspectives using: descriptive, predictive and prescriptive methods (Zakir, Seymour & Berg, 2015). The methods are briefly discussed as follows:

i Descriptive analytics – focuses on the current and available data. According to Evans and Lindner (2012, p. 2), 'descriptive analytics can be used to examine historical data for similar products, such as the number of units sold, the price at each point of sale, starting and ending inventories, and special promotions'.

ii Prescriptive analytics – reveals what actions should be taken, which usually results in creating rules and recommendations going forward. The descriptive analytics for data analysis is mainly to gain insights into both the past and current performances of an organisation, towards making informed decisions. Even though prescriptive analytics is a valuable approach in many ways, it is rarely employed by organisations (Hazen, Boone, Ezell & Jones-Farmer, 2014).

iii Predictive analytics – uses big data to identify past patterns and predict the future within specific needs and activities. Shmueli and Koppius (2011) argued that the predictive analytics tool does not only assist in creating useful models, but the approach also plays a significant role in building theory. Many organisations continue to explore the potentials of the predictive analytics approach for their health facilities (hospitals and clinics), but from different perspectives (Zakir, Seymour & Berg, 2015). Some organisations use the approach in sales, marketing, lead source, frequency of communications, types of communications and social media. Hazen, Boone, Ezell and Jones-Farmer (2014) argued that predictive analytics describes the data set to be leveraged for future purposes. At the same time, organisations such as the health facilities employ the approach for a more complex forecast. The predictive analytics approach concerns characterising a system that was not operating optimally (Waller & Fawcett, 2013).

Irrespective of the BDA option selected, there are challenges, which often emanate from evidence relating to the efficacy and effectiveness of the data sets and the services they are supposed to enable and support (Wang, Kung & Byrd, 2018). According to Katal, Wazid and Goudar (2013), one of the main challenges for information systems and technologies (IS/IT) specialists and health practitioners is filtering the most important and relevant elements of big data for service delivery purposes. McAfee et al. (2012) highlight that the technical challenges of using big data are very real, but the managerial challenges are even greater. Hence, a single approach will continuously be short or problematic in finding the solutions to the challenges. Otherwise, BDA remain a major challenge for organisations, healthcare facilities included(Kaisler, Armour, Espinosa & Money, 2013).

The underlying consequences of BDA and the diversity of application characteristics pose significant challenges for society and the economy (Kambatla, Kollias, Kumar & Grama, 2014). However, Gandomi and Haider (2015) suggest that massive volumes of semi-structured data can be mined to improve service delivery and competitiveness using BDA tools. Thus, individual or combined tools from descriptive analytics, prescriptive analytics and predictive analytics, are employed to guide various types of decision-making (Sun, Sun & Strang, 2018). This effort does not seem to solve the challenges of holistic and in-depth extraction of useful elements from big data, currently encountered (Zakir, Seymour & Berg, 2015). This includes understanding groups' creation, relationships between data sets and interactions among data within heterogeneous networks. Within this context and basics, a multi-level approach is proposed, which complements the use of BDA with ANT as a methodological approach.

Actor-Network Theory

The rationale for employing ANT includes its focus on the formulation of networks, relations among actors and heterogeneity of networks. No other theory seems to focus on a combination of these entities. ANT is a socio-technical theory that focuses on shifting negotiation, accounts of how activities involving human and non-human actors are translated from one moment or stage to another, and their relationship within heterogeneous networks (Iyamu, 2021). In ANT, the actor is both human and non-human, that is, 'anything that modifies a situation by making a difference' (Bryson, Crosby & Bryson, 2009, p. 71). Data sets and analytics tools are also actors, used and reused within environments (networks). According to Pollack, Costello and Sankaran (2013), ANT primarily focuses on tracing networks of associations that occur between actors, including building an understanding of interaction. Couldry (2008) argues that ANT is a highly influential account within the sociology of science that seeks to explain social order through the networks of connections among human and non-human actors, including technologies and objects.

ANT is increasingly used for data analysis, particularly because of its detailed descriptive and narrative emphasis and ontological association. Some of the studies where ANT has been applied in recent years vary, across all sectors. Examples are Foster (2014), Horowitz (2012), and Dery, Hall, Wailes and Wiblen (2013). Pollack, Costello and Sankaran (2013) explained that ANT encompasses many levels of analysis from both narrative and descriptive angles. From an ANT standpoint, there is no shortage of non-human actors that can influence data from size, velocity and variety perspectives. In ANT, it is possible and desirable to view humans and non-humans in the same analytical terms (Law, 1986, p. 258). One of the main tenets of ANT is translation (Iyamu, 2021), as shown in Figure 7.1.

Translation involves associating heterogeneous networks within which actors are identified, interests are aligned, tasks are assigned and action plans are established (Callon, 1986). Translation consists of four moments, which are intertwined and connected, namely problematisation, interessement, enrolment and mobilisation (Callon, 1986). Problematisation is a stage where a problem is defined based on requirements (Horowitz, 2012). In ANT, a problem is not necessarily something broken or negative but an innovative improvement to a situation. Based on the problematised issue, actors consciously or unconsciously show their interest in an activity. During the moment of Interessement, stakeholders' interests are established, drawing

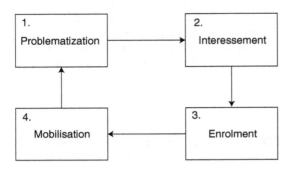

Figure 7.1 Four moments of translation (Callon, 1986)

from their understanding of the problematised issue (Alcouffe, Berland & Levant, 2008). When it comes to Enrolment, alliance actor-networks are formed, stakeholders form groupings of common interests. Mobilisation is a stage where a set of methods are used to ensure that actions are in accordance with the requirements of the actor-networks (Lee & Oh, 2006). Thus, translation helps to create groupings and relationships through which data can be demystified and transformed for organisational purposes.

Transformation happens through moments of translation based on earlier associations of actors within heterogeneous networks (Iyamu, 2021). In ANT, it is only when associations have been formed or accepted that some actors are perceived as organising and others as organised (Wissink, 2013). This type of association helps to organise both semi-structured and structured data sets into a more useful purpose.

Understanding Big Data Analytics

Based on the chapter's objective, which is to construct and propose a multi-level approach that can be used to analyse big data, the interpretivist approach was employed. According to Walsham (2006, p. 320), 'Our theories concerning reality are ways of making sense of the world, and shared meanings are a form of inter-subjectivity rather than objectivity'. Interpretivism is a rich mechanism; hence, ANT is continuously associated with it in the field of IS to examine, gain insights and discover new ideas or innovations. There is currently no formula or single approach of complementary formation in applying BDA with a sociotechnical theory. The complementarity of both ANT and BDA tools is used to construct reality from a social world perspective, concerning a new approach, to advance data analytics for analysis purposes. It can be complementarily used with ANT from a methodological perspective to analyse big data.

BDA helps an organisation harness its data for more purposefulness and to improve ease of use towards proactively identifying new opportunities.

However, challenges manifest from a lack of an in-depth extraction of elements from big data. According to Gandomi and Haider (2015), some organisations focus on predictive analytics and structured data and ignore the largest component of big data, the unstructured part. To extract useful and most relevance information and gain more knowledge from huge data sets, scalable analytics is required (Talia, 2013). At this point, ANT is approached from an interpretivist perspective. This is to advance the use of BDA from both operational and strategic perspectives, including the unstructured aspect of big data. The interpretivist approach begins from the position that our knowledge of reality is a social construction of human actions (Walsham, 2006), which is highly required in a sense making situation of this nature.

Through subjective understanding and interpretive analysis, it was gathered from studies such as Mgudlwa and Iyamu (2021); Sun, Sun and Strang (2018); Gandomi and Haider (2015) and LaValle et al. (2011) that an understanding of BDA and getting substantial value for organisational purposes is more than the mere use of software tools. It first requires understanding the main factors, which can deterministically affect the outcome. This includes three main factors: (i) complementarity of analytics tools with method (Waller & Fawcett, 2013); (ii) levels of big data analysis and (iii) heterogeneity of organisational data sets (Breckels et al., 2016).

Complementarity of Analytics Tools with a Method

The ability and opportunism to be effective, efficient and remain agile helps an organisation, to continuously improve in pursuit of service delivery. This can also help identify insights for immediate decision-making. However, from an analytics perspective, the quest to improve services is not always as easy as envisaged (Sun, Sun & Strang, 2018). This difficulty can be problematic for both the enabler (IT) and the enabled (health systems' users and healthcare managers). According to Katal, Wazid and Goudar (2013), some of the challenges that exist which IT specialists do sometimes struggle with include designing systems that would be used to manage large volumes of data from various sources and maintain high levels of velocity for health facilities' efficient and effective use.

The use of ANT for analysis is not new. The theory has been used for over three decades, primarily to interrogate social structure, scientific and technological networks (Horowitz, 2012). One of the motivating factors is that the theory is scalable and flexible in that it can be combined with other approaches or techniques for analysis purposes. Thus, ANT is considered appropriate for understanding, formulating and stabilising groupings, referred to as networks of data sets, in analysing big data at the strategic level in an environment.

There is no single technology or approach that encompasses BDA. The challenge which data analytics encounters is an opportunity for complementarity. Technologies and approaches can be combined to enhance the quality of analytics. Thus, the complementarity of analytics tools with a method enhances and improves the quality of analysis for operational and strategic efficiency in using big data for healthcare service delivery. The combined use of analytics tools and methodological approach must be conducted at two different levels, namely operational and strategic, towards achieving organisational goals and objectives.

Levels of Analytics

There is a fundamental technical challenge in making use of big data. Those (such as IT specialists) who know or understand what big data means and entails do not understand how to extract a detailed and most relevant elements, to create more value and benefits, for healthcare purposes. This is intended to fortify and enhance the ability to work faster, stay agile and identify insights for immediate decision-making. This could be attributed to the complexity of big data and the know-how instrument for conducting the analysis tasks. According to Najafabadi et al. (2015), in the past, strategies and solutions for data storage and retrieval were challenged by increasing massive volumes of data from different sources.

As revealed from the literature review, incompatibility of formats, inconsistency of data and large volumes of data are some of the obstacles that can affect or influence BDA for services within the healthcare environments (Wang, Kung & Byrd, 2018). Underlying this challenge, analysis is crucial at different levels to make it easier and possible in enabling data volume, ensuring continued accuracy and supporting (near) real-time processing. Another necessity for advocating for multi levels of analysis is because many stakeholders engage with their big data from different angles that include interrelationship and interconnectivity. Some stakeholders are at the operational level, and others are at the strategic level, a divide that boosts the usefulness of big data in an organisation.

The first level, in the context of this chapter and book, is christened with term 'in-tive', the last four letter of descriptive, predictive and prescriptive analytics tools. The output from this level is for operational use. This is a level at which more stakeholders are engaged in many organisations, healthcare facilities included. The second level creates networks and establishes the connections and relationships that exist among the data sets, from one process or activity to another. Thereafter, it finds components and elements that were unclear beforehand, which must be guided by organisational requirements to exhume values. Analysis at both levels is influenced by varied data sets in their heterogeneous state, which requires an exploratory approach to gain more benefits.

Heterogeneous Data Set

As health facilities grow, units are created for expanded functions and responsibilities. As such, organisational data is scattered across the units. Some of the data sets are therefore duplicated over a period. As a result, the data is sometimes interoperated for service delivery, which is often a challenging task to undertake. This, therefore, requires heterogeneity in its analytics. This is to be holistic and uncover hidden entities across the data sets.

The heterogeneity of data sets increases the size of big data. This often poses major challenges in the attempt to understand the available data and how it can be analysed. According to Breckels et al. (2016), meaningful integration of heterogeneous data is a major challenge. Thus, a detailed approach split into levels is needed, to accommodate the heterogeneity of data sets from various sources (Pincus & Musen, 2003).

Multi-Level Approach for Big Data Analysis

The multi-level approach, which combines operational (macro) and strategic (micro) is purposely to bring about advancement, innovation, and a fresh perspective in the analysis of big data, from epistemological and ontological standpoints. The micro level defines and establishes network formation and interaction, while the macro level focuses on the current BDA approach. Wright and Boswell (2002) emphasise the importance of integrating both micro and macro levels of analyses. In Evans and Lindner's (2012) assessment, the tools used in descriptive analytics, predictive analytics and prescriptive analytics are different. However, some software applications can combine the three approaches, which enacts an epistemological stance. According to Bleakley (2012), ANT is not primarily interested in epistemologies but in ontologies, including how meanings are generated within networks and how the different networks are formulated and significantly shape activities. Fenwick (2010) argues that networks of prescription and networks of negotiation co-exist from an ontological perspective to form the same standards of activities.

A multi-level approach for big data analysis, which is developed, is presented in this chapter as Figure 7.2. The approach consists of operational and strategic levels of analysis aimed at demystifying data sets using healthcare requirements. The divide between operational and strategic levels of analysis, using both analytics tools and a method, is critically significant for BDA from the depth and detailed perspectives, in achieving healthcare requirements.

The multi-level approach combines micro and macro, a process for transforming big data into a more meaningful and useful artefacts, in an organisation. The approach is intended to increase the benefits of big data analysis in an organisation. Significantly, the approach unpacks complex and huge data sets into perspectives and relevance at the micro level, which is strategic. At the operational level, that is, the macro level, the approach reduces complex data sets into actionable artefacts for more effective and accurate decision-making. The micro- and macro-transformative processes are primarily for more demystification of big data at both strategic and operational levels to enhance health facilities (hospitals and clinics) capability and advance service delivery.

As shown in Figure 7.2, the multi-level approach primarily aims to gain new insights from big data for decision-making at operational and strategic

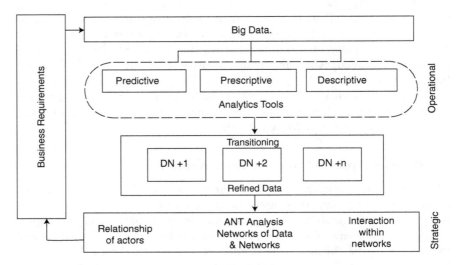

Figure 7.2 Multi-level analysis of big data

levels in an organisation (health facility) intended to provide more details about activities concerning data sets in improving service delivery. The main components of the multi-level approach are requirements, big data, operational level, and strategic level, discussed as follows:

Healthcare Requirements

In some quarters, BDA is considered as a new and emerging field. From this angle, it is argued to require integration of the state-of-the-art computational and statistical techniques, to enable and allow service quality and value extraction from a volume of diverse data sets. The data sets are gathered from different sources by using various techniques. Initially, the data sets are considered raw and make little or no sense, which the healthcare requirements help demystify for purposeful use.

Big Data

As a unique way of re-echoing its meaning, I describe BDA as the science of examining raw data to conclude accumulated information over a period. Evidently, BDA is used in many industries including healthcare facilities, to make better decisions through descriptive analytics, prescriptive analytics or predictive analytics approaches. Wang, Kung and Byrd (2018) explained that the predictive analytics approach could assess models for futuristic tenacities gain. Also, BDA is a form of science that can verify or disprove existing models or theories. BDA is distinguished from data mining based on the scope, purpose and focus of the analysis, which makes it more complex and more difficult if applied in a mono approach.

Using descriptive analytics, prescriptive analytics or predictive analytics, traces actions and responses that are fundamental in BDA usefulness. ANT complements at the point where it allows and enables traces of associations, re-associations and reassembly of actors and their reproductive actions within networks (environment). According to Bryson, Crosby and Bryson (2009), associations can be traced through ANT by allowing actors to reassemble in a social network.

Operational Level

At the operational level, different moments and their translations influence technical and non-technical situations of big data. Using different analytics tools, the situations can be categorised into volume, variety and velocity of big data in any environment. Predictive is an analysis of likely scenarios of what might happen. The deliverables are usually a predictive forecast. According to Shmueli and Koppius (2011), predictive analytics can focus on predictors (human actors) and methods (non-human) that reproduce refined data and transparent models. Waller and Fawcett (2013) explained that the predictive analytics approach attempts to quickly and inexpensively approximate relationships between variables, subjects or objects. For a prescriptive analytics technology to be transformative, it must be able to process hybrid data. Descriptive analytics is the approach that focuses on uncovering patterns that offer insight into an organisation. A simple example of descriptive analytics would be assessing credible risks and categorising patients (customers) by their health condition (or product preferences) and incident cycle.

Strategic Level

In complement with analytics tools, ANT as a method is appropriate at the strategic level of big data analysis mainly because of its specific focuses. ANT has specific focuses on (i) shifting negotiations; (ii) associations or connections with non-human elements or aspects of the situation and (iii) accounts for associations are produced, become stabilised and legitimised, or change, through strengthening or weakening of networks, respectively. As a method, Latour (2005) argues that ANT strength can be drawn from groupings as defined, such as how actions manifest; and an understanding of facts vs 'matters of concern'.

ANT as a lens is appropriate in viewing things from many ways, by identifying groups, intended and intended actions and their consequences. Gao (2005) argues that ANT examines actors' various motivations and reproductive actions within requirements and is, therefore, different from other socio-technical theories.

In summary, the micro level facilitates the strategic outcomes from an analysis angle, while the macro level guides data splits for operational constructs and demystifications. At the micro level, the first level of analysis clarifies the ontologies of big data and its entities within specific environments. The macro level is epistemologies, the second level of analysis to understand big data subjects, objects, devices, contexts and cultural factors. At this level, the application of moments of translation from the perspective of ANT is proposed, as shown in Figure 7.1.

Understanding the Impact of Multi-Level Approach

In an understanding of the impact of the multi-level approach, the role of ANT is reiterated. Data sets from BDA can be less stable without categorising their networks. Data as actors can be classified through moments of translations from the perspective of ANT. Iyamu and Roode (2012) explained that the idea of problematisation is mainly to foster relationships, allocate and reallocate facilities among actors. The facilities are dictated by specific requirements within which BDA is conducted. Through interessement, an actor takes a set of actions to impose and stabilise the identity of other actors in the same network. Dery, Hall, Wailes and Wiblen (2013) suggest that interessement helps to create the conditions for the third moment of actor-network formation, enrolment, which involves the definition of actors' roles and responsibilities in the network. According to Unnithan, Nguyen, Fraunholz and Tatnall (2013), enrolment facilitates a situation where actors accept the roles that have been defined for them in their various networks. In summary, Fenwick (2011) states that the problem is divided into spaces and actions according to issues of relationship, roles and differences become connected and mobilised into networks.

Based on the multi-level approach for big data analysis, three factors stand out, actor-networks, actors and relationships, and BDA, as shown in Figure 7.3. The factors are discussed from the perspective of the multi-level approach.

Actor-Networks

Figure 7.3 presents the heterogeneous networks within which big data can be demystified towards achieving improved services for competitiveness and sustainability. The multi-level approach of analysis unveils the signification of actors' relationships within networks. This approach reduces big data to small data, making each data set more purposeful, meaningful and useful. Also, each data set becomes easier to associate with other objects and subjects, such as sales, marketing and health conditions.

Actors and Relationship

As shown in Figure 7.3, the impact of multi-level analytics is threefold, which enacts understanding and usefulness of big data in an organisation. First, the

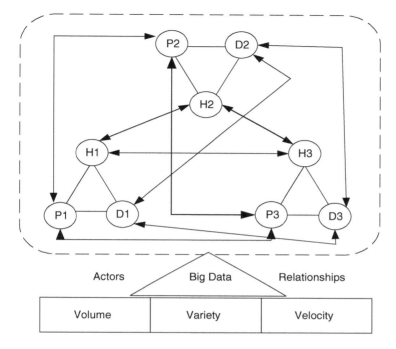

Figure 7.3 Heterogeneity of big data

bigness of the data must be understood, which the analytics tools focus on. Only then can it be effectively and efficiently used to communicate and interact among actors for the good of an organisation, in improving services. Second, the associated factors, which are technical and non-technical, must be clearly defined by using moments of translation to examine how networks are formed and stabilised. This helps to streamline and clarify the relationship among the actors, which guides the ease of big data use for organisation purposes. Finally, the healthcare requirements function as a catalyst to the existence of big data in an organisation. The three components are tightly related and connected in the context of the multi-level approach for big data analysis purposes. Therefore, the three components cannot be viewed or treated in isolation if analysis of big data is to be conducted, to advance usefulness and promote ease of use in an environment.

Big Data Analytics

The intention is often to apply BDA, to explore huge data sets using sophisticated software to identify undiscovered patterns and establish hidden relationships. Data analytics focuses on inference, the process of deriving a conclusion based solely on what is already known by the analyst or researcher.

This enables the process of examining and understanding data sets to uncover and extract trends and patterns, unfamiliar correlations, customer preferences and other useful health-related information. According to Russom (2011), data analytics tools are used to create analytic models or fashion complex queries. The process requires using techniques such as text analytics, machine learning, predictive analytics, data mining, statistical methods and natural language processing for health facilities' activities. Zaslavsky, Perera and Georgakopoulos (2013) argue that the concept of big data is defined based on its main characteristics, which have been stated many times in this book, include volume, variety and velocity. In different ways and levels, volume, variety and velocity expand the capability to enhance services.

By using ANT's moments of translation for analysis, the epistemology of big data can be better understood through a heterogeneity of networks. The process is facilitated where new networks start to operate in a target-oriented (requirements based) approach to implement the solution proposed. This can lead to strengthening and stabilising big data purposeful usage within networks. Fenwick (2010) suggests that the conclusion drawn from the analysis helps to assess and examine the usefulness of big data within an environment (network).

Summary

Big data analysis can be conducted by using the multi-level approach, a complementarity of ANT and analytics tools, as proposed in this chapter. The ANT's moments of translation provide a useful lens to examine and understand BDA. Using the translations process at the strategic level of analysis is reasonable and makes it easier to trace how varieties of data accelerate in their various sizes, according to requirements. By drawing on the four moments of translation from ANT, big data are analysed and fortified for strategic use and purposes.

The multi-level approach adds much value to big data analysis from a more theoretical, practical and methodological approach, benefiting the health sector and academic domains. Practically and methodologically, health facilities will realistically understand the roles and influences of human and data networks while applying analytics tools, including the ability and usefulness of splitting the analysis into operational and strategic levels. To the academic domain, the chapter contributes from both theoretical and methodological perspectives in that it brings rigour into exploring and gaining insightful circumstance about big data without losing both human and non-human factors. In addition, this chapter contributes to existing literature, but from IT, health informatics and data management angles.

However, the chapter lays a foundation for future studies and triggers further multi-level big data analysis discourse. Some areas for further research include security within the networks, particularly in the healthcare and finance sectors. Also, further studies to integrate ANT with BDA tools into one entity will be of interest to both organisations and academics.

References

Alcouffe, S., Berland, N., & Levant, Y. (2008). Actor-networks and the diffusion of management accounting innovations: A comparative study. *Management Accounting Research, 19*(1), 1–17. https://doi.org/10.1016/j.mar.2007.04.001.

Bleakley, A. (2012). The proof is in the pudding: Putting actor-network-theory to work in medical education. *Medical Teacher, 34*(6), 462–467. https://doi.org/10.3109/0142159X.2012.671977.

Breckels, L. M., Holden, S. B., Wojnar, D., Mulvey, C. M., Christoforou, A., Groen, A., Trotter, M. W., Kohlbacher, O., Lilley, K. S., & Gatto, L. (2016). Learning from heterogeneous data sources: An application in spatial proteomics. *PLoS Computational Biology, 12*(5), e1004920. https://doi.org/10.1371/journal.pcbi.1004920.

Bryson, J. M., Crosby, B. C., & Bryson, J. K. (2009). Understanding strategic planning and the formulation and implementation of strategic plans as a way of knowing: The contributions of actor-network theory. *International Public Management Journal, 12*(2), 172–207. https://doi.org/10.1080/10967490902873473.

Callon, M. (1986). Some elements of a sociology of translation: Domestication of the scallops and the fishermen of St Brieuc Bay. In: Law, J. (ed.), *Power, action and belief: A new sociology of knowledge?* (pp. 196–233). London: Routledge and Kegan Paul.

Couldry, N. (2008). Actor network theory and media: Do they connect and on what terms? In: Hepp, A., Krotz, F., Moores, S., & Winter, C. (eds), *Connectivity, networks and flows: Conceptualizing contemporary communications* (pp. 93–110). Cresskill, NJ: Hampton Press, Inc.

Dery, K., Hall, R., Wailes, N., & Wiblen, S. (2013). Lost in translation? An actor-network approach to HRIS implementation. *The Journal of Strategic Information Systems, 22*(3), 225–237. https://doi.org/10.1016/j.jsis.2013.03.002.

Evans, J. R., & Lindner, C. H. (2012). Business analytics: The next frontier for decision sciences. *Decision Line, 43*(2), 4–6.

Fenwick, T. (2011). Reading educational reform with actor network theory: Fluid spaces, otherings, and ambivalences. *Educational Philosophy and Theory, 43*(s1), 114–134. https://doi.org/10.1111/j.1469-5812.2009.00609.x.

Fenwick, T. J. (2010). (un) Doing standards in education with actor-network theory. *Journal of Education Policy, 25*(2), 117–133. https://doi.org/10.1080/02680930903314277.

Foster, L. A. (2014). Critical cultural translation: A socio-legal framework for regulatory orders. *Indiana Journal of Global Legal Studies, 21*(1), 79–105.

Gandomi, A., & Haider, M. (2015). Beyond the hype: Big data concepts, methods, and analytics. *International Journal of Information Management, 35*(2), 137–144. https://doi.org/10.1016/j.ijinfomgt.2014.10.007.

Gao, P. (2005). Using actor-network theory to analyse strategy formulation. *Information Systems Journal, 15*(3), 255–275. https://doi.org/10.1111/j.1365-2575.2005.00197.x.

Ghazal, A., Rabl, T., Hu, M., Raab, F., Poess, M., Crolotte, A., & Jacobsen, H. A. (2013). BigBench: Towards an industry standard benchmark for big data analytics. In: *Proceedings of the 2013 ACM SIGMOD international conference on management of data* (pp. 1197–1208), 22–27 June, New York, NY, USA. ACM. https://doi.org/10.1145/2463676.2463712.

Hazen, B. T., Boone, C. A., Ezell, J. D., & Jones-Farmer, L. A. (2014). Data quality for data science, predictive analytics, and big data in supply chain management: An introduction to the problem and suggestions for research and applications.

International Journal of Production Economics, 154, 72–80. https://doi.org/10.1016/j.ijpe.2014.04.018.

Horowitz, L. S. (2012). Translation alignment: Actor-network theory, resistance, and the power dynamics of alliance in new caledonia. *Antipode, 44*(3), 806–827. https://doi.org/10.1111/j.1467-8330.2011.00926.x.

Iyamu, T. (2021). *Applying theories for information systems research.* London: Routledge. https://doi.org/10.4324/9781003184119.

Iyamu, T., & Roode, D. (2012). The use of structuration theory and actor network theory for analysis: Case study of a financial institution in South Africa. In *Social influences on information and communication technology innovations* (pp. 1–19). IGI Global. https://doi.org/10.4018/978-1-4666-1559-5.ch001.

Kaisler, S., Armour, F., Espinosa, J. A., & Money, W. (2013, January). Big data: Issues and challenges moving forward. In: *2013 46th Hawaii international conference on system sciences (HICSS)* (pp. 995–1004), 7–10 January, Wailea, HI, USA. IEEE. https://doi.org/10.1109/HICSS.2013.645.

Kambatla, K., Kollias, G., Kumar, V., & Grama, A. (2014). Trends in big data analytics. *Journal of Parallel and Distributed Computing, 74*(7), 2561–2573. https://doi.org/10.1016/j.jpdc.2014.01.003.

Katal, A., Wazid, M., & Goudar, R. H. (2013, August). Big data: Issues, challenges, tools and good practices. In: *2013 sixth international conference on contemporary computing (IC3)* (pp. 404–409), 8–10 August, Noida, India. IEEE. https://doi.org/10.1109/IC3.2013.6612229.

Kitchin, R. (2013). Big data and human geography: Opportunities, challenges and risks. *Dialogues in Human Geography, 3*(3), 262–267. https://doi.org/10.1177/2043820613513388.

Latour, B. (2005). *Reassembling the social: An introduction to actor-network-theory.* Oxford: Oxford University Press.

LaValle, S., Lesser, E., Shockley, R., Hopkins, M. S., & Kruschwitz, N. (2011). Big data, analytics and the path from insights to value. *Massachusetts Institute of Technology Sloan Management Review, 52*(2), 21–32.

Law, J. (1986). On the methods of long-distance control: Vessels, navigation and the Portuguese route to India. In: Law, J. (ed.), *Power, action, and belief: A new sociology of knowledge* (pp. 234–263). London: Routledge & Kegan Paul.

Lee, H., & Oh, S. (2006). A standards war waged by a developing country: Understanding international standard setting from the actor-network perspective. *The Journal of Strategic Information Systems, 15*(3), 177–195. https://doi.org/10.1016/j.jsis.2005.10.002.

McAfee, A., Brynjolfsson, E., Davenport, T. H., Patil, D. J., & Barton, D. (2012). Big data: The management revolution. *Harvard Business Review, 90*(10), 60–68.

Mgudlwa, S., & Iyamu, T. (2021). A framework for accessing patient big data: ANT view of a South African health facility. *The African Journal of Information Systems, 13*(2), 225–240.

Najafabadi, M. M., Villanustre, F., Khoshgoftaar, T. M., Seliya, N., Wald, R., & Muharemagic, E. (2015). Deep learning applications and challenges in big data analytics. *Journal of Big Data, 2*(1), 1–21. https://doi.org/10.1186/s40537-014-0007-7.

Pincus, Z., & Musen, M. A. (2003). Contextualizing heterogeneous data for integration and inference. In: *AMIA annual symposium proceedings* (Vol. 2003, p. 514). American Medical Informatics Association, 8–12 November, Marriott Wardman Park, Washington, DC, USA.

Pollack, J., Costello, K., & Sankaran, S. (2013). Applying actor–network theory as a sensemaking framework for complex organisational change programs. *International Journal of Project Management, 31*(8), 1118–1128. https://doi.org/10.1016/j.ijproman.2012.12.007.

Russom, P. (2011). Big data analytics. *The Data Warehouse Institute best practices report, Fourth quarter, 19*(4), 1–34.

Sharma, S. (2015). An extended classification and comparison of NoSQL big data models. *arXiv*, preprint arXiv:1509.08035.

Shmueli, G., & Koppius, O. R. (2011). Predictive analytics in information systems research. *Management Information System Quarterly, 35*(3), 553–572. https://doi.org/10.2307/23042796

Sun, Z., Sun, L., & Strang, K. (2018). Big data analytics services for enhancing business intelligence. *Journal of Computer Information Systems, 58*(2), 162–169. https://doi.org/10.1080/08874417.2016.1220239.

Talia, D. (2013). Clouds for scalable big-data analytics. *Computer, 46*(5), 98–101.

Unnithan, C., Nguyen, L., Fraunholz, B., & Tatnall, A. (2013). RFID translation into Australian hospitals: An exploration through Actor-Network Theoretical (ANT) lens. In: *2013 international conference on information society (i-Society)* (pp. 85–90), 24–26 June, Toronto, ON, Canada. IEEE.

Waller, M. A., & Fawcett, S. E. (2013). Data science, predictive analytics, and big data: A revolution that will transform supply chain design and management. *Journal of Business Logistics, 34*(2), 77–84. https://doi.org/10.1111/jbl.12010.

Walsham, G. (2006). Doing interpretive research. *European Journal of Information Systems, 15*(3), 320–330. https://doi.org/10.1057/palgrave.ejis.3000589.

Wang, Y., Kung, L., & Byrd, T. A. (2018). Big data analytics: Understanding its capabilities and potential benefits for healthcare organisations. *Technological Forecasting and Social Change, 126*, 3–13. https://doi.org/10.1016/j.techfore.2015.12.019.

Wissink, B. (2013). Enclave urbanism in Mumbai: An actor-network-theory analysis of urban (dis) connection. *Geoforum, 47*, 1–11. https://doi.org/10.1016/j.geoforum.2013.02.009.

Wright, P. M., & Boswell, W. R. (2002). Desegregating HRM: A review and synthesis of micro and macro human resource management research. *Journal of Management, 28*(3), 247–276. https://doi.org/10.1016/S0149-2063(02)00128-9.

Wu, X., Zhu, X., Wu, G. Q., & Ding, W. (2014). Data mining with big data. *IEEE Transactions on Knowledge and Data Engineering, 26*(1), 97–107.

Zakir, J., Seymour, T., & Berg, K. (2015). Big data analytics. *Issue in Information Systems, 16*(2), 81–90.

Zaslavsky, A., Perera, C., & Georgakopoulos, D. (2013). Sensing as a service and big data. *arXiv*, preprint arXiv:1301.0159.

Zikopoulos, P., & Eaton, C. (2011). *Understanding big data: Analytics for enterprise class Hadoop and streaming data*. Emeryville: McGraw-Hill Osborne Media.

8 Transforming Big Data for Healthcare Service Delivery

Introduction

Due to the essentiality of healthcare, delivery of quality service is crucial (Cresswell, Worth & Sheikh, 2010). However, there have been many cases of wrong diagnoses and medications by practitioners in many health facilities (hospitals and clinics), in many countries (Lewandowski et al., 2017). Thus, the governments of many countries employ approaches, such as big data analytics (BDA) and information technology (IT) solutions, to improve the quality of healthcare (Sacristán & Dilla, 2015). In Fico et al.'s (2016) assessment, IT advancements enable and support systems, improving health activities, such as diagnosis, medications and treatments, from big data perspectives. The use of big data can improve the quality of healthcare delivering due to its characteristics, which include volume, variety and velocity (Priyanka & Kulennavar, 2014). Some IT solutions enable healthcare big data to create and store data sets at unprecedented size (volume), types (variety) and speed (velocity) (Ganjir, Sarkar & Kumar, 2016). However, the various sources of big data can also create limitations to its access, quality and use, thereby constraining activities towards improving patients' care (Nativi et al., 2015).

The use of big data for specific purposes requires harnessing its capabilities from both technology and human standpoints. Thus, analytics tools are needed, used to analyse diverse big data types at immense velocity and in real-time (Priyanka & Kulennavar, 2014). Despite the impressive premise, BDA can be a disruptive phenomenon from perspectives, such as privacy and standardisation (Bello-Orgaz, Jung & Camacho, 2016). This is attributed to the largeness and complexity of the data sets involved, which analytics tools have so far found difficult to address at socio-technical levels (Ularu, Puican, Apostu & Velicanu, 2012).

One of BDA challenges are the magnitude of data sets and the difficulties associated with validating long-term predictions for diagnoses and medications' purposes (Kambatla, Kollias, Kumar & Grama, 2014). According to Esposito, Ficco, Palmieri and Castiglione (2015), users (practitioners) must know the details of the activity, to provide proper and accurate service using

DOI: 10.4324/9781003251064-8

big data. On the technological front, the challenges include integration with other systems and analysing various healthcare big data to address impending problems (Kankanhalli, Hahn, Tan & Gao, 2016). Thus, scalability is a fundamental challenge for BDA and ontological extraction and semantic inference to support innovative processes (Esposito, Ficco, Palmieri & Castiglione, 2015) in providing patients with desirable care. The analytics tools also pose challenges to both scientists and IT specialists in different ways (Nativi et al., 2015). From the academic front, BDA is a disruptive innovation that reconfigures how research is conducted and has epistemological implications for data revolution (Kitchin, 2014). From both empirical and experimental perspectives, it was revealed that big data presents technical challenges to analytics tools due to its volume, variety and velocity (Priyanka & Kulennavar, 2014).

Patients' big data and other materialistic artefacts (such as medical apparatus) form networks, a state of realism, which the ontological stance focuses on (Scotland, 2012). In the course of health activities, the networks become heterogeneous, which also increases the levels of security, making it more difficult for analytics tools to produce useful and purposeful data from analysis (Archenaa & Anita, 2015). Also, the realistic state is that health big data is independent of patients and health professionals, including researchers (Scotland, 2012). Thus, the decision to examine and understand how healthcare big data can be transformed to increase usefulness and purposefulness is a reality that must be addressed. The interpretive epistemology guided this from a subjectivist perspective, which is based on the phenomena of reality. Epistemology focuses on the nature and forms of knowledge created and gained (Tsang, 2014).

The problem is that patients and some health practitioners do not know how their big data exists and, most importantly, what to expect from the data sets. This is due to the rawness and complexity of big data evolution, which many health practitioners do not know how to analyse the socio-technical aspects, to understand why things happen the way they do within patients' big data. Thus, the objective of this chapter is to develop a framework to guide analysis that can translate and transform big data into a more useful and purposeful resource for health practitioners, thereby improving services to the patients. In achieving the objective, the ontological stance is employed as the means, and epistemology as the end, through the interpretive approach. Thus, the focus is on the interaction between the actors, including health facilities, health practitioners, patients and healthcare big data, to understand how they are interconnected, to improving care and saving lives. From this perspective, actor-network theory (ANT) becomes crucial in examining relationships in which actors participate and influence the shape of the heterogeneous networks (Dwiartama & Rosin, 2014). Characteristically, analytics tools focus on prediction, which ANT rejects about actors and their activities and interests (Wissink, 2013). Therefore, assumptions and preconceived ideas are discarded to focus on the reality at the time, interpretively. This also can be attributed to the fact that heterogeneous components of healthcare big data do not precede their interactions but rather emerge through related activities.

ANT offers a different type of analysis by focusing on the relational effect shaped by the interaction between humans and non-humans in their heterogeneous networks. The framework guides the transformation of healthcare big data from ontological to epistemological positions towards improving patients' care. Using ANT for the analysis and transformation of healthcare big data, the challenges in healthcare BDA in technological, social and policy barriers can be addressed, making this chapter useful to the health profession and academia.

The remainder of the chapter is structured into six main sections. It beings with the introduction section, which provides an overview to the focus of the chapter. A review of literature that was conducted in twofold, healthcare big data and moments of translation of ANT, is presented in the second section. This section is followed by a discussion about ANT's view of healthcare big data. The fourth section presents the framework with a comprehensive discussion. The fifth section covers the implication of practice. The chapter is summarised in the final section.

Literature Review

A review of the core aspects of the chapter, big data in health environment and ANT is presented in this section. Big data is reviewed from the perspective of health, whereas the discussion on ANT focuses on moments of translation.

Healthcare Big Data

Health facilities greatly depend on big data to provide care to patients (Hansen, Miron-Shatz, Lau & Paton, 2014). Big data in the healthcare environment constitutes various data accumulated from various sources and at different speeds (Priyanka & Kulennavar, 2014). More specifically, healthcare big data consists of large and complex patients' data sets, which cannot be handled with the traditional systems (Ganjir, Sarkar & Kumar, 2016). According to Panahiazar, Taslimitehrani, Jadhav and Pathak (2014), big data in healthcare holds a lot of potential benefits in its premedical ability to improve clinical decisions. Other highlighted benefits that can be achieved through big data include early disease detection and overall management of health activities (Giambrone, Hemmings, Sturm & Fleischut, 2015).

However, big data in healthcare hold challenges that are mostly related to its characteristics, volume, variety, velocity and veracity (Acharjya & Ahmed, 2016). One of the challenges is that the size of healthcare data sets affects important aspects, such as storage, processing and the analysis of the big data (Sacristán & Dilla, 2015). Another challenge in utilising big data is its vast amount of data within the legacy systems, which is hard to relate to other data sets from different sources (Archenaa & Anita, 2015).

Conversely, the realisation of these benefits can only be fulfilled by analysing the big data, according to Sacristán and Dilla (2015). Wyber et al. (2015) state that the analysis of big data can help improve healthcare outcomes. Inherently, this brings the need for analytics solutions, which are more integrated and secured (Nepal, Ranjan & Choo, 2015), hence the introduction of BDA. Analytics tools can be used to solve the complexities that reside within healthcare big data (Peek, Holmes & Sun, 2014). But has it really worked and provided the solutions various health facilities need?

Big data and analytics face challenges influenced by different factors, such as volume, complexity, and levels of security. As a result, it is difficult to create efficient and strong analytics methods that are essential to improving health services (Peek, Holmes & Sun, 2014). Thus, some tools, such as MapReduce, Hadoop and STORM, have been designed to store, analyse, visualise and secure data sets, in addressing some of the challenges encountered in the use of big data (Ganjir, Sarkar & Kumar, 2016). Even though the existing solutions seem to hold promise, healthcare big data still encounter challenges of resolving complexity and integration, which Rumsfeld, Joynt and Maddox (2016) and other studies emphasised. From Kankanhalli, Hahn, Tan and Gao's (2016) empirical study, it was revealed that the challenges in the analysis of big data stem from the variety and sources of health activities.

The challenges, as discussed above, have been there for many years (Kitchin, 2014). Thus, an additional but different approach to guide the analysis of healthcare big data to improve patients' care, is proposed in this chapter. This approach entails the use of moments of translation as a lens from the perspective of ANT.

Actor-Network Theory: Moments of Translation

ANT is a socio-technical theory, which focuses on the interaction between humans and non-human actors (Iyamu & Roode, 2012). ANT is also described as a theory embedded within science and technologies (Dwiartama & Rosin, 2014), including big data, medical apparatus and instruments. The core elements of ANT are actor and network, which cannot be independent of each other (Thapa, 2011). In ANT, the actor is both a human and non-human entity (Mol, 2010), which Durepo and Mills (2012) describe as having the ability to act and alter each other's actions. From the perspective of ANT, Dery, Hall, Wailes and Wiblen (2013) define a network as a set of actors tied together based on their allied interest, through which they knowingly or unknowingly create a link. The inseparability between actor and network enables them to establish negotiation through translation, using four moments.

ANT has been used to analyse development, implementation and practice of IT solutions, including big data, for many years (Díaz Andrade & Urquhart, 2010). One of ANT's benefits is its recognition of technology and how it is not distinguished from humans but rather how the two are related and equally as influential to one another (Cordella, 2012). This is a critical and major advancement in the health sector in that it is impossible to separate practitioners, patients and big data from each other in providing and receiving services and care. In clarification, Iyamu and Roode (2012) state that even though human and non-human actors are not distinguished, they do differ in purpose, particularly in their roles. It is of no relevance to separate interaction between the actors, nature (such as health) and society (such as patients) while trying to provide and improve healthcare services (Thapa, 2011).

In ANT, networks are heterogeneous (Dery, Hall, Wailes & Wiblen, 2013), within which activities, such as big data, are assembled, disassembled and reassembled (Baiocchi, Graizbord & Rodríguez-Muñiz, 2013). Translation can be described as a process that aims to flatten out the differences between various aspects of technologies and big data through four moments (Díaz Andrade & Urquhart, 2010). Figure 8.1 shows the four moments of translation: problematisation, interessement, enrolment and mobilisation (Callon, 1986).

Problematisation refers to a focal actor's articulation and formulation of a problem within a network (Callon, 1986). Based on the problematised item, interessement occurs, where other actors show and align their interests with the focal actor's (Dwiartama & Rosin, 2014). The third moment is the enrolment stage, wherein actors accept the roles defined and assigned to them by the focal actor towards achieving or finding the solution to the problematised item (Pollack, Costello & Sankaran, 2013). The mobilisation stage is considered a moment of success within the actor-network, in that more actors are attracted and voluntarily take responsibility (Baiocchi, Graizbord & Rodríguez-Muñiz, 2013).

Thus, ANT is used to guide an analysis to investigate, simplify and understand the factors that influence and contribute to the use of big data, processes and the success of technologies (Wissink, 2013). The theory is also used as a socio-technical framework, which helps to explain how technology is developed, implemented and used in society (Dwiartama & Rosin, 2014).

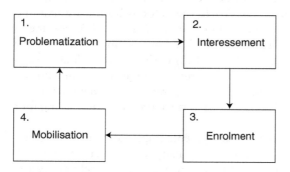

Figure 8.1 Four moments of translation (Callon, 1986)

ANT has been used in various IT developments, including integrating big data with health systems' implementations (Nepal, Ranjan & Choo, 2015). Saedi and Iahad (2013) highlight how ANT can give a clear valuation on the complexity and fluidity of networks while showing a strong impact of technology.

Actor-Network Theory View of Healthcare Big Data

In healthcare, big data is a reality constructed through the interaction between health practitioners and patients, using various communicative schemes. Ontology is thus confirmed and requires the core stakeholders to know how they really work. To make sense of what is known about the current healthcare related activities and processes, there is need to translate big data, to gain deeper insights about experiences and viewpoints to assist in discovering new knowledge and innovation.

The interpretivist approach is employed to gain an alternative understanding of whether the moments of translation of ANT can replace analytics tools in analysing healthcare big data. Thus, the chapter should be viewed from an ontological perspective to which epistemology is the end in advancing quality in the use of health big data, to improve service delivery. Based on the understanding gained, a framework is constructed to foster the transformation of healthcare big data for better quality and usefulness. The transformation is intended to enable sense-making of reality from a social world perspective about healthcare big data. Reality comes from sense-making of the world and shared meanings from subjectivity rather than objectivity (Walsham, 2006).

From an ANT perspective, actors within the healthcare environment include practitioners, patients, facility and big data. Each actor can change at any point in time, depending on their perceived usefulness, purposes and the degree at which they make a difference. Activities of health are led by practitioners, who get their colleagues to accept how big data (or parts of big data) can be accessed or used to provide care to patients, a process which ANT calls 'translation' (Wissink, 2013). In ANT, moments of translation allow many levels of analysis, which provide an approach for evaluations, in-depth categorisation to improve quality and increased purposefulness (Pollack, Costello & Sankaran, 2013).

Ontologically, humans (health practitioners and patients) and big data are both health and social materials among many realities. The materials exist separately but are inherently inseparable and enacted by their inevitable interaction, as shown in Figure 8.2. Big data does not exist without human activities and interactions, which influence decisions towards patients' care. The process begins with and is shaped by a moment of problematisation, identifying items that require attention. This draws on interest (intreressement) from other actors, such as health specialists, diagnostic type and medical apparatus and tools. The interest does not perform actions by itself but requires certain

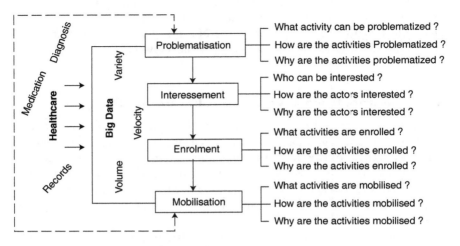

Figure 8.2 ANT for analysis of healthcare big data

actors to provide care and supervise or evaluate the activities. Thereafter, the proceedings are shared with the larger interest groups or the general public through mobilisation by the actors who believe in the care process and potential outcomes. Hence, Muhammad, Teoh and Wickramasinghe (2012) employed ANT to evaluate the Personally Controlled Electronic Health Record (PCEHR) in the Australian context.

Figure 8.2 shows the model constructed and presented in this chapter, primarily to guide the analysis of big data in healthcare environment using ANT. The model illustrates the relationship between healthcare, big data and moments of translation in translation and transformation of big data, to advance healthcare services. Also shown in Figure 8.2 are the primary entities used to elicit information towards the translation and transformation of healthcare big data, including the 'what, why and how' prefixes. The scrutiny and discussion that follow expand more in Figure 8.2, using the four moments of translation from ANT's point of view.

Moments of Translation: Problematisation

It is of interest to both health practitioners and patients to problematise big data that relate to their profession and health condition, respectively. Ontologically, health practitioners and patients account for how they know their individual responsibility. Therefore, aspects of big data that are connected to areas, such as diagnoses, surgical operations and medications, can be problematised to examine and understand the reality of a patient's health condition. Thus, big data reproductively emerge through problematised items within a network consisting of a facility, healthcare practitioners and patients. Actors are more capable of quickly problematising items for possible new opportunities (Montenegro & Bulgacov, 2014). Problematisation of health-related items ignites a new response, which includes referral to specialists for further or detailed examination that generates new knowledge. Epistemologically, the new knowledge can be gained from answers to the questions: What healthcare activities can be problematised? How are the activities of healthcare problematised? and why are the activities problematised?:

What Can Be Problematised?

Problematisation helps to unveil how activities, such as surgical operations, diagnoses and illnesses are conceived from multiple ontological meanings within heterogeneous healthcare facility or networks (Baiocchi, Graizbord & Rodríguez-Muñiz, 2013). Therefore, it is an 'ice breaker' towards knowing, creating an epistemological assumption in delivering a phenomenon in a patient's condition. Also, the types of questions posed during a problematic moment assist in tracing the entities that constitute patients' big data, since they are reproduced through several actions, evolvements of various actors, and transformation towards different directions.

The three main factors often problematised to advancing patients' care in society include practitioners' activity, patients' big data and enabling technology. Thus, the actions of healthcare practitioners are problematised to establish the trajectory of experiments and activities. Big data are problematised to understand their heterogeneous links, which can also be referred to as medical history. The enabling technologies are worth problematising to assess innovations towards support, enablement and management of healthcare activities. However, these factors can also constrain the cause they are supposed to support and enable; hence, it is necessary to explore and understand how they are problematised.

How Are Healthcare Activities Problematised?

ANT warns against preconceived, predictive and presumptive approaches, which means that actors should tell their own stories as they know and experience it (Wissink, 2013). Actors can identify problematic areas and new opportunities, which can be used to reproduce actions in the corresponding complexity and variety of health conditions (Montenegro & Bulgacov, 2014).

Therefore, problematisation is used as an investigative enquiry from three main folds, which are (a) how practitioners are involved in providing care, using related aspects of big data; (b) how big data is accessed and managed to improve healthcare services and (c) how actors make use of IT solutions to interact (practitioners-to-practitioners; practitioners-to-facilities; practitioners-to-patients; facilities-to-facilities; facilities-to-patients and patients-to-patients) and access big data in the course of providing and improving care. Thus, based on evidence from experience or experiments with patients' big data, practitioners problematise care through activities, such as medications, diagnoses, surgical operations and research. Items are not problematised in a vacuum but guided by rationale.

Why Are Healthcare Activities Problematised?

Each diagnosis is unique, so the 'why' informed question becomes an indispensable character in the practitioners' big data attribution of care (Dery, Hall, Wailes & Wiblen, 2013). Within such circumstances, moments of translation offer a different perspective of resilience by focusing on the relational effect shaped by the interaction between humans and non-humans within a healthcare facility (Dwiartama & Rosin, 2014).

Healthcare big data is considered highly sensitive, making accuracy and security crucial components of their activities. This can be established through an understanding of why items are problematised. Thus, patients' stories need to be interrogated and motivated towards accuracy. Also, practitioners' responses need to be examined for quality and appropriateness of IT solution used to provide support and enabling capability. These processes are fundamental to improving the quality of diagnoses and medications, within which health big data are reproduced. Such process-oriented action dictates and enriches the direction and type of care provided and received, which, in turn, defines various types of interests.

Moments of Translation: Interessement

Significantly, actors' interests contribute and determine the types of services provided and received within the healthcare environment. However, from the first aid point of view, it is difficult to ascertain actors' interest in an activity of healthcare without interconnected assessment or interaction. Hence, is it necessary to enquire who can be interested?; how are actors interested in an activity? and why are actors interested in healthcare activities?

Who Can Be Interested in Healthcare Activities?

The problematic assumption that big data, patients and health practitioners are all interested in care is only of ontological subjectivist belief (Dery, Hall, Wailes & Wiblen, 2013). From a problematisation perspective, ANT stresses the pluralist character of coalition among actors, humans and non-humans within heterogeneous networks, to examine the different interests through an epistemological assumption of what can be known (Cordella, 2012).

At the point where interessement occurs, paves ways to examine how actors, such as health practitioners, patients and relations of the patients, contribute to patients' conditions, which are usually reproduced to form health big data. This is examined from the perspective where the interested parties try to convince each other and/or offer alternative solutions about the reality of the patient's medical condition. If the interests are to be analysed valuably, the empirical approach should be employed rather than predictive analytics, descriptive analytics or prescriptive analytics tools. Such investigation is triggered by known and unknown factors, which require an inductive response based on professional skill, experience and knowledge. The classification of what is known, unknown or can be known consciously or unconsciously defines actors' interests in healthcare activities in providing and receiving the services.

How Are Actors Interested in Healthcare Activities?

The actors involved in health activities usually have a common interest to provide care to the patients (Priyanka & Kulennavar, 2014). However, the common interest manifests from different factors, which include well-being, professional ethics and obligations, job security and technical know-how. The factors influence how actors express their interests, which are sometimes subjectively interpreted by other actors in the wider networks (Iyamu & Roode, 2012). This means that actors' interests are either voluntarily or contractually obliged.

Independent operability is another challenge that affects big data, which analytics tools are not fully capable of resolving (Nativi et al., 2015). Big data and actors with common interests cannot be independent of one another. Therefore, it is crucial to know how the interest of the various actors is drawn, expressed and linked. This assists in analysing big data in terms of how they are stored, accessed and used to provide care to individual patients in different health conditions.

Why Are Actors Interested in Healthcare Activities?

The activities of healthcare are shaped by various types of interests (Giambrone, Hemmings, Sturm & Fleischut, 2015). Typically, for some actors, the rationale behind their interests is known to them but unknown to others. Also, whether known or unknown, the interest is habitually conscious but sometime unconscious to actors. Furthermore, the different interests of the various actors towards patients' medical care determine the type of big data that needs to be stored, retrieved, used and managed (Díaz Andrade & Urquhart, 2010). Different types of interests make it necessary to categorise activities through the evaluation process towards accumulating big data.

Evaluation of a patient's health condition through interessement assists in refining data sets, from positions of differentiation, categorisation and perspective to certainty and specific. This is done by understanding how the interests are linked, from surgical operations, diagnoses and medications to providing care and alternative solutions. Analysis of these details is impossible with any current data analytics tools (Acharjya & Ahmed, 2016).

Moments of Translation: Enrolment

Not every actor that is interested in a health-related activity can or does participate (enrol) in the actual provision and receipt of healthcare, making involvement limited. For example, a relation accompany a patient to a health facility but does not undergo a surgical operation or consume medication on behalf of the relative (patient). From a health professional perspective, limited enrolment of actors causes challenges, such as the capacity to collect, store, use and manage big data due to its rapidly increasing size, variety and speed (Bello-Orgaz, Jung & Camacho, 2016). This problem makes it difficult for health practitioners to have 100% reliance on the information extracted from big data, using analytics tools for decision-making (Ularu, Puican, Apostu & Velicanu, 2012). This problem can be addressed by enrolling different actors as they connect or associate with activity, from health, big data and IT perspectives. This includes knowing what must be enrolled, how they should participate and why actors should participate in healthcare activities.

What Healthcare Activities Are Enrolled?

Human and non-human, such as surgical operations, diagnosis, medications and facilities, are enrolled individually or collectively, depending on the patients' health conditions and the facility involved (Panahiazar, Taslimitehrani, Jadhav & Pathak, 2014). From an ANT perspective, enrolment can be used to trace the networks of connections between actors through their participation, as they influence and are influenced by other actors in the process of mediation and the shifting negotiation (Pollack, Costello & Sankaran, 2013).

Enrolment in healthcare activities is influenced by various factors, such as source, type of big data and variety. Enrolment of facilities and other actors is used to trace, track and monitor activities in providing care using health big data. It is, therefore, necessary to establish actors' participation as it influences decision-making on how services are provided. There have been many cases of a low ratio of medical practitioners to patients, which is considered to enact poor service delivery, particularly in developing countries. Fortin et al. (2005) explained that the ratio of general practitioners to patients in the Saguenay region (Québec, Canada) is 9.0 per 10,000.

How Are Actors Enrolled in Healthcare Activities?

Practitioners often have relevant detailed knowledge about the conditions of patients to whom they provide care. This type of knowledge is reproduced within heterogeneous networks to improve the quality of data sets for decision-making. According to Montenegro and Bulgacov (2014), a combined knowledge of actors represents a significant basis for making intelligent choices between feasible options.

Enrolment of actors is done on a case-by-case basis depending on the types of care needed by the patient, determined by areas of specialisation and available health facility. Also, enrolment of actors can be carried out through various means, such as physical presence, electronic records or documentation, and virtual connectivity. This process requires analysis that is empirical, which enable tracing and tracking of activities, to determine the influence and roles of actors.

Why Do Actors Enrol in Healthcare Activities?

There are many realities in each patient's big data. As a result, a broadened narrative to understand factors of influence for enrolment is critical. Also, multiple sources of big data, as in the health environment, is another challenge (Hansen, Miron-Shatz, Lau & Paton, 2014), which requires highly skilled personnel from IT or the health profession or both, to analyse.

Consciously or unconsciously, health practitioners provide care to patients within heterogeneous networks, using available resources, such as big data, medical apparatus and IIT solutions. What is even more important is how the networks are initiated or formed, enabling practitioners and patients to provide and receive healthcare, respectively. Also, enrolment takes place at different times during care, increasing the data sources as activities transform. This is significant to the activities of healthcare in its sensitive status. For example, times of registering specimen, and diagnosis, are critical to their results, which constitute big data, and are reproduced over time, in a patient's subsequent visit to the health facility.

Moments of Translation: Mobilisation

Healthcare big data manifests from sources such as interaction and translation, which Pollack, Costello and Sankaran (2013) describe as actions that are not independent choices but rather the result of a diffused network of influence by actors. Therefore, the reproductive aspects of big data for healthcare purposes are accepted by interested actors through mobilisation within heterogeneous networks. Due to big data reproductive nature, it is significant to examine what exactly was mobilised, why such mobilisation took place and how the activities were mobilised in each patient's health condition.

What Healthcare Activities Are Mobilised?

Both positive and negative or disputed results from health activities about patients' conditions can be mobilised by the focal actor, who is appointed or volunteered to be the spokesperson. The mobilised items are not necessarily agreed upon by all stakeholders or interested parties (Tsang, 2014). Thus, conclusions are reached from the subjective, interpretivist approach of consciousness. It is therefore safe to say that position, based on interpretivism

118 *Transforming Big Data for Service Delivery*

is of relativism that is often mediated by consciousness, without which the outcomes of health activities are meaningless. As a result, many realities can be individually and socially constructed about patients through a network, to produce and reproduce big data. However, ethics and privacy take precedence due to the sensitive nature of the health environment. Hence, there is an obligatory passage point (OPP) on how the activities are mobilised in many instances. OPP is defined as the communication channel between actors (Iyamu, 2021). It makes the focal actor indispensable (Callon, 1986).

How Are Health Activities Mobilised?

The contributions of health big data in providing and improving care can only be recognised through actors' interaction and relationships among health practitioners, facilities and patients, which an actor coordinates in the form of mobilisation. The spokespersons can be practitioners (representative/appointed) from the facilities or patients (or patients' relations/friends), or both. Mobilisation takes place within heterogeneous networks that are consciously or unconsciously formed, which reproduces many realities. Also, ANT's focus on how many realities are experienced and enacted by different actors, without neglecting their inter-relatedness, makes it significantly a useful tool in the fast-paced and complex area of healthcare (Cresswell, Worth & Sheikh, 2010). This type of activity brings about new knowledge, which modifies existing big data.

Why Are Healthcare Activities Mobilised?

Mobilisation allows an investigation to seek why things happen the way they do within context and relevance. Mobilisation of health activities, therefore, assists in testing some of the realities that are associated with them. However, not all outcomes or items from healthcare activities undergo mobilisation. This is ascribed to the sensitive and private nature of the environment (Bello-Orgaz, Jung & Camacho, 2016). As a result, some information is incomplete when objectivism is implored to collect data about certain patients' conditions, such as human immunodeficiency virus (HIV).

Even though each diagnosis is unique, individuals often construct many realities through their interaction with related health facilities and big data. Thus, mobilisation assists in tracing the creation, evolution and dissolution of heterogeneous networks within which healthcare big data is constituted.

Translation of Healthcare Big Data

In the quest to improve the quality of health-related care, the large volume of big data, including their velocity and variety, should be analysed effectively, to provide answers to new challenges (Archenaa & Anita, 2015). Based on

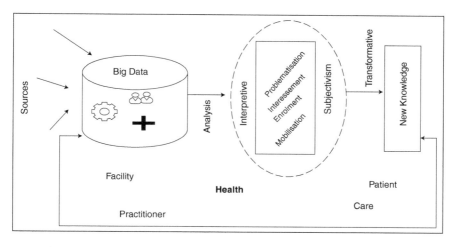

Figure 8.3 Big data transformative in healthcare

the explanation and discussion presented above, there are three main areas through which the use of ANT for analysis of big data can improve the quality of healthcare services. These are (i) a detailed decomposition of healthcare big data for units-based analysis into sources and types of data sets; (ii) criticality of subjective, interpretive analysis; (iii) interactive scheme that envelops human and non-human actors. Based on the findings, a framework as shown in Figure 8.3 is developed.

As shown in Figure 8.3, the relationships between human and non-human actors are instrumental to providing and receiving healthcare services, using big data, as enabled and supported by IT solutions. Based on such ontological assumptions, Callon (1986) suggests that through the study of scientific theories and technologies, 'things' actively influence the social and natural world. Within this context, the framework guides a multi-level analysis, from the source of big data, categorisation of activities into moments for translation and transformation purposes. This iterative process can produce and reproduce newness in patients' big data for quality and increased usefulness.

Decomposition of Healthcare Big Data

Through the decomposition approach, healthcare big data are detailed into specific sources and respective types of data sets (Bello-Orgaz, Jung & Camacho, 2016). The approach enables a strategic transformation of big data from its complex state of high volume, velocity and varieties into more meaningful and purposeful states. Also, the decomposition of big data assists in optimising modularity and maintaining health data sets to minimise their static dependencies and maximise the cohesiveness of the big data. Thus, decomposition fortifies units of analysis to enable translation and transformation of health big data, to advance services and improve quality of care.

The decomposition approach provides a logical and hierarchical structure of the data sets, allowing and leading to the transformation of big data originality within an environment. Also, the approach enables differentiation between functional and strategic data sets, allowing track and trace of sources and linking them to a single view of individual patients. This helps to separate the differences in many realities existing within the heterogeneous networks, enabling the provision of healthcare services.

Criticality of Subjective, Interpretive Analysis

Identifying quality data from big data in carrying out analysis to discover useful and relevant knowledge to improve decision-making is a major challenge (Hartman et al., 2015). This challenge gets worse, especially in situations that are related to real-time or surgical operations. Many analysis tasks, such as patients' diagnoses and progression of disease outbreaks, are time-critical (Kambatla, Kollias, Kumar & Grama, 2014). Troshani and Wickramasinghe (2014) suggest that the inherent complexity of healthcare environments can be addressed using the ANT analysis.

Through the reproductive actions of both practitioners and patients, data sets are generated and constructed into big data, which are ontologically believed to be of need and purpose for human care. Therefore, translation and transformation of big data to advance care cannot be completely objective without subjective interpretations. Thus, it is critical to be subjective in interpreting patients' big data to trace the trajectory of the condition before opinions can be formed. This approach helps to gain better comprehension of the nature of the relationship that exist between what is known and what can be known about patients' big data.

Interactive Scheme

Each entity or set of big data is a result of human action. Therefore, healthcare big data cannot exist independently of human knowledge, in providing care. Hence, the interaction between the actors is critical. ANT is a useful tool for examining power relationships concerning healthcare reforms and big data transformation (Cresswell, Worth & Sheikh, 2010). The theory poses significant benefits in analysing health big data for patients' care because it envelops human and non-human interactions and relationships in an allied interest. This type of interpretive analysis is set to help uncover and discover new knowledge as the actors tell their unique stories.

Managers need to understand and follow the interaction between humans and non-humans during health activities to improve care. Thus, as shown in

Figure 8.3, managers can use ANT to understand how phenomena like diagnoses and medications are conceived across health practices, manifest from practitioners' experiences and the meanings they associate with the activities. Through such practices and meanings, networks are formed, data sets are generated and enquiries are instituted.

Implications for Practice

In practice, the translation and transformation of healthcare big data have implications for healthcare managers and the enablers (IT), from decomposition, interpretive and interactive perspectives. As shown in Table 8.1, the actors' actions can consciously or unconsciously enable, at the same time constrain the activities and processes of healthcare.

As summarised in Table 8.1, the main implications of practice are for healthcare and IT managers in the three, following ways: (i) the ability to understand the collaboration between health conditions and associated activities, to inform and enable decision-making; (ii) acknowledge and understand that the existence of many intermediaries in health activities impacts the results of healthcare services, which are often unpredictable and (iii) understand the concept of ANT in order to manage and guide the unpredictable interaction and interpretation of actions and communication that happens among the technical and non-technical actors.

Table 8.1 Implication of practice

Translation	Healthcare	IT solution
Decomposition	Know-how on managing: varieties of health conditions; various sources of data sets and different types of data sets.	Enabling the categorisation of the data sets using various devices and mechanisms.
Interpretive	• Translation of facilities, processes and semi-structured data sets. • Affects the quality of service, which ultimately affects care	Provide lens to guide interpretation as they manifest from different interests and sources. Presents the transformed data sets as they are influenced by different activities and processes.
Interactive	• The use of many opinions, unpredictable circumstances and actions. • Impacts quality of service, which ultimately affects care.	Enable and support various tools and channels used for interaction between practitioner-to-patient, practitioner-to-practitioner and patient-to-patient.

Summary

The chapter is intended to benefit health practitioners, IT professionals and academia. Through this chapter, health practitioners can gain better understanding of a detailed analysis of healthcare big data, from human and non-human standpoints. The chapter advances academia's continued investigation into healthcare big data usefulness. Therefore, it can interest IT professionals from different perspectives on how big data translates and transforms through analysis, using ANT, which has always been complexed to understand. Thus, the chapter's contributions are from three viewpoints: first, it contributes theoretically through its addition to the existing literature on how ANT can be used to enrich healthcare big data analysis, conceptually. Second, it methodologically advances the use of ANT as a lens to guide data analysis in IS studies. Finally, the chapter's practical contribution is its guide, which health practitioners can use to analyse big data from an interpretivist perspective.

This chapter triggers the need for further studies where data analytics tools can be combined with moments of translation to explore the possibility of layers of analysis of healthcare big data. This is to continue the investigation for improved quality, increased appropriateness and usefulness of big data for better service delivery.

References

Acharjya, D. P., & Ahmed, K. (2016). A survey on big data analytics: Challenges, open research issues and tools. *International Journal of Advanced Computer Science and Applications,* 7(2), 511–518.

Archenaa, J., & Anita, E. M. (2015). A survey of big data analytics in healthcare and government. *Procedia Computer Science,* 50, 408–413. https://doi.org/10.1016/j.procs.2015.04.021.

Baiocchi, G., Graizbord, D., & Rodríguez-Muñiz, M. (2013). Actor-network theory and the ethnographic imagination: An exercise in translation. *Qualitative Sociology,* 36(4), 323–341. https://doi.org/10.1007/s11133-013-9261-9.

Bello-Orgaz, G., Jung, J. J., & Camacho, D. (2016). Social big data: Recent achievements and new challenges. *Information Fusion,* 28, 45–59. https://doi.org/10.1016/j.inffus.2015.08.005.

Callon, M. (1986). Some elements of a sociology of translation: domestication of the scallops and the fishermen of St Brieuc Bay. In: Law, J. (ed.), *Power, action & belief: A new sociology of knowledge?* (pp. 196–229). London: Routledge & Kegan Paul.

Cordella, A. (2012). Information infrastructure: An actor-network perspective. In: *Social influences on information and communication technology innovations* (pp. 20–39). IGI Global. https://doi.org/10.4018/978-1-4666-1559-5.ch002.

Cresswell, K. M., Worth, A., & Sheikh, A. (2010). Actor-network theory and its role in understanding the implementation of information technology developments in healthcare. *BMC Medical Informatics and Decision Making,* 10(1), 67–79. https://doi.org/10.1186/1472-6947-10-67.

Dery, K., Hall, R., Wailes, N., & Wiblen, S. (2013). Lost in translation? An actor-network approach to HRIS implementation. *The Journal of Strategic Information Systems,* 22(3), 225–237. https://doi.org/10.1016/j.jsis.2013.03.002.

Díaz Andrade, A., & Urquhart, C. (2010). The affordances of actor network theory in ICT for development research. *Information Technology & People, 23*(4), 352–374. https://doi.org/10.1108/09593841011087806.

Durepo, G., & Mills, A. J. (2012). Actor-network theory, ANTi-history and critical organizational historiography. *Organization, 19*(6), 703–721.

Dwiartama, A., & Rosin, C. (2014). Exploring agency beyond humans: The compatibility of actor-network theory (ANT) and resilience thinking. *Ecology and Society, 19*(3), 28–38.

Esposito, C., Ficco, M., Palmieri, F., & Castiglione, A. (2015). A knowledge-based platform for Big Data analytics based on publish/subscribe services and stream processing. *Knowledge-Based Systems, 79*, 3–17. https://doi.org/10.1016/j.knosys.2014.05.003.

Fico, G., Fioravanti, A., Arredondo, M. T., Gorman, J., Diazzi, C., Arcuri, G., ... & Pirini, G. (2016). Integration of personalized healthcare pathways in an ICT platform for diabetes managements: A small-scale exploratory study. *IEEE Journal of Biomedical and Health Informatics, 20*(1), 29–38. https://doi.org/10.1109/JBHI.2014.2367863.

Fortin, M., Bravo, G., Hudon, C., Vanasse, A., & Lapointe, L. (2005). Prevalence of multimorbidity among adults seen in family practice. *The Annals of Family Medicine, 3*(3), 223–228. https://doi.org/10.1370/afm.272.

Ganjir, V., Sarkar, B. K., & Kumar, R. (2016). Big data analytics for healthcare. *International Journal of Research in Engineering, Technology and Science, 6*, 1–6.

Giambrone, G. P., Hemmings, H. C., Sturm, M., & Fleischut, P. M. (2015). Information technology innovation: The power and perils of big data. *British Journal of Anaesthesia, 115*(3), 339–342. https://doi.org/10.1093/bja/aev154.

Hansen, M. M., Miron-Shatz, T., Lau, A. Y. S., & Paton, C. (2014). Big data in science and healthcare: A review of recent literature and perspectives. *Yearbook of Medical Informatics, 23*(01), 21–26. https://doi.org/10.15265/IY-2014-0004.

Iyamu, T., & Roode, D. (2012). The use of structuration theory and actor network theory for analysis: A case study of a financial institution in South Africa. *International Journal of Actor-Network Theory Technological Innovation, 2*(1), 1–26. https://doi.org/10.4018/978-1-4666-1559-5.ch001.

Kambatla, K., Kollias, G., Kumar, V., & Grama, A. (2014). Trends in big data analytics. *Journal of Parallel and Distributed Computing, 74*(7), 2561–2573. https://doi.org/10.1016/j.jpdc.2014.01.003.

Kankanhalli, A., Hahn, J., Tan, S., & Gao, G. (2016). Big data and analytics in healthcare: Introduction to the special section. *Information Systems Frontiers, 18*(2), 233–235. https://doi.org/10.1007/s10796-016-9641-2.

Kitchin, R. (2014). Big Data, new epistemologies and paradigm shifts. *Big Data & Society, 1*(1), 1–12. https://doi.org/10.1177/2053951714528481.

Lewandowski, L. B., Watt, M. H., Schanberg, L. E., Thielman, N. M., & Scott, C. (2017). Missed opportunities for timely diagnosis of pediatric lupus in South Africa: A qualitative study. *Pediatric Rheumatology, 15*(1), 14–23. https://doi.org/10.1186/s12969-017-0144-6.

Mol, A. (2010). Actor-network theory: Sensitive terms and enduring tensions. *Kölner Zeitschrift für Soziologie und Sozialpsychologie. Sonderheft, 50*, 253–269.

Montenegro, L. M., & Bulgacov, S. (2014). Reflections on actor-network theory, governance networks, and strategic outcomes. *BAR-Brazilian Administration Review, 11*(1), 107–124.

Muhammad, I., Teoh, S. Y., & Wickramasinghe, N. (2012). Why using actor network theory (ANT) can help to understand the personally controlled electronic health record (PCEHR) in Australia. *International Journal of Actor-Network Theory and Technological Innovation (IJANTTI)*, *4*(2), 44–60. https://doi.org/10.4018/jantti.2012040105.

Nativi, S., Mazzetti, P., Santoro, M., Papeschi, F., Craglia, M., & Ochiai, O. (2015). Big data challenges in building the global earth observation system of systems. *Environmental Modelling & Software*, *68*, 1–26. https://doi.org/10.1016/j.envsoft.2015.01.017.

Nepal, S., Ranjan, R., & Choo, K. K. R. (2015). Trustworthy processing of healthcare big data in hybrid clouds. *IEEE Cloud Computing*, *2*(2), 78–84. https://doi.org/10.1109/MCC.2015.36.

Panahiazar, M., Taslimitehrani, V., Jadhav, A., & Pathak, J. (2014). Empowering personalised medicine with big data and semantic web technology: Promises, challenges, and use cases. In: *Proceedings of international conference on Big Data* (pp. 790–795), 27–30 October, Washington, DC, USA. IEEE. https://doi.org/10.1109/BigData.2014.7004307

Peek, N., Holmes, J. H., & Sun, J. (2014). Technical challenges for big data in biomedicine and health: Data sources, infrastructure, and analytics. *Yearbook of Medical Informatics*, *9*(1), 42–47. https://doi.org/10.15265/IY-2014-0018.

Pollack, J., Costello, K., & Sankaran, S. (2013). Applying actor–network theory as a sensemaking framework for complex organisational change programs. *International Journal of Project Management*, *31*(8), 1118–1128. https://doi.org/10.1016/j.ijproman.2012.12.007.

Priyanka, K., & Kulennavar, N. (2014). A survey on big data analytics in health care. *International Journal of Computer Science and Information Technologies*, *5*(4), 5865–5868.

Rumsfeld, J. S., Joynt, K. E., & Maddox, T. M. (2016). Big data analytics to improve cardiovascular care: Promise and challenges. *Nature Reviews Cardiology*, *13*(6), 350–359.

Sacristán, J. A., & Dilla, T. (2015). No big data without small data: Learning health care systems begin and end with the individual patient. *Journal of Evaluation in Clinical Practice*, *21*(6), 1014–1017. https://doi.org/10.1111/jep.12350.

Saedi, A., & Iahad, N. A. (2013). An integrated theoretical framework for cloud computing adoption by small and medium-sized enterprises. In: *Proceedings of Pacific Asian conference on information systems (PACIS)* (p. 48), 18–22 June, Jeju Island, Korea.

Scotland, J. (2012). Exploring the philosophical underpinnings of research: Relating ontology and epistemology to the methodology and methods of the scientific, interpretive, and critical research paradigms. *English Language Teaching*, *5*(9), 9–16.

Thapa, D. (2011). The role of ICT actors and networks in development: The case study of a wireless project in Nepal. *The Electronic Journal of Information Systems in Developing Countries*, *49*(1), 1–16. https://doi.org/10.1002/j.1681-4835.2011.tb00345.x.

Troshani, I., & Wickramasinghe, N. (2014). Tackling complexity in e-health with actor-network theory. In *2014 47th Hawaii international conference on system sciences (HICSS)* (pp. 2994–3003), 6–9 January, Waikoloa, HI, USA. IEEE. https://doi.org/10.1109/HICSS.2014.372.

Tsang, E. W. (2014). Case studies and generalisation in information systems research: A critical realist perspective. *The Journal of Strategic Information Systems*, *23*(2), 174–186. https://doi.org/10.1016/j.jsis.2013.09.002.

Ularu, E. G., Puican, F. C., Apostu, A., & Velicanu, M. (2012). Perspectives on big data and big data analytics. *Database Systems Journal*, *3*(4), 3–14.

Walsham, G. (2006). Doing interpretive research. *European Journal of Information Systems*, *15*(3), 320–330. https://doi.org/10.1057/palgrave.ejis.3000589.

Wissink, B. (2013). Enclave urbanism in Mumbai: An actor-network-theory analysis of urban (dis) connection. *Geoforum*, *47*, 1–11. https://doi.org/10.1016/j.geoforum.2013.02.009.

Wyber, R., Vaillancourt, S., Perry, W., Mannava, P., Folaranmi, T., & Celi, L. A. (2015). Big data in global health: Improving health in low- and middle-income countries. *Bulletin of the World Health Organization*, *93*(3), 203–208. https://doi.org/10.2471/BLT.14.139022.

9 The Integration of Social Media with Healthcare Big Data for Services

Introduction

Social media (e.g., Twitter and Facebook) is increasingly a communication tool for patients and healthcare providers to receive and advance services (Lin & Kishore, 2021). From one angle, social media facilitates professional networking, quick clinical education and patients' health promotion. From another perspective, the use of social media affects the relationship between healthcare professionals and patients in that information can be misinterpreted and accountability shifted, particularly when there is compromised activity. Other challenges are lack of reliability; lack of confidentiality and privacy; and inaccurate health advice, which can lead to daunting consequences. Some of the challenges get worse because of the sensitive nature of the healthcare environment due to personalisation and privacy of information.

Social media integration with their professional lives enables some health workers to connect with current best practices and colleagues of common interest in their field. It improves response time, as there are no geographical restrictions or boundaries, allowing users to share text, photos and videos, which is critically essential in the healthcare environment. The integration of social medial with healthcare requires minimum effort to facilitate conversations between health practitioners. In terms of creating awareness, social media can influence behavioural health change. Also, some social media users feel empowered with knowledge and support because of improved response time.

As established in previous chapters, 5, 6, 7 and 8, the term big data is used to describe massive data sets, which are large, and have a more varied and complex structure with the difficulties of storing, analysing and visualising for further processes of results (Sagiroglu & Sinanc, 2013). Thus, the characteristics of big data include size, velocity and variety, which are significant to organisations and businesses for various reasons (Russom, 2011). These characteristics differentiate big data from small data (Katal, Wazid & Goudar, 2013).

In recent years, individuals and organisations' interest in big data has grown rapidly due to its benefits. The interest is across sectors, professions and fields of studies, such as healthcare (Kitchin, 2014; Wang, Kung, Ting & Byrd,

DOI: 10.4324/9781003251064-9

2015). Even though there are benefits to big data, there are numerous challenges as well. For example, the larger the size of data, the more complex it becomes to process. As a result of these attributes and factors, Syed, Gillela and Venugopal (2013) suggest that the size of big data makes it complicated to process using on-hand database management tools or the traditional data processing applications, as it often exceeds the capacity of conventional database systems. This is one of the challenges that has been experienced with social media over the years (Schroeder, 2014).

Social media produces a huge data size, with over a billion users worldwide, due to its rapidly increasing audience and subscribers (Carr & Hayes, 2015). The size and velocity of social media big data are based on data generated in minutes and daily from various social network platforms, such as Twitter and Facebook, which have no limitations to users (Young, 2014). To this end, there are claims by authors, such as Romero, Galuba, Asur and Huberman (2011), that the growth of social media has provided millions of users with the opportunity to create and share content on a larger scale than it has ever had before.

Big data is most relevant and useful to organisations, such as healthcare service providers, with the use of big data and social media for health purposes is growing in popularity in recent years (Mayer-Schönberger & Cukier, 2013). Thus, McCormack, Friedrich, Fahrenwald and Specker (2014) propose the analysis of big data for futuristic purposes and environmental trends. However, the use of social media and big data to improve healthcare delivery is challenged and hindered by factors, which include integration (Hashem et al., 2015), security and privacy (Househ, Borycki & Kushniruk, 2014) and complexity of technology (Koster, Stewart & Kolker, 2016). This could explain why healthcare research has not yet been covered extensively (De Choudhury, Gamon, Counts & Horvitz, 2013). This factor shapes the main motivations of this chapter, which integration of social media with big data, to advance the services that are provided to patients.

Thus, the question posed in this chapter is, how can social media be integrated with healthcare big data to improve service delivery? In answering the question, the factors that influence social media and big data from a healthcare perspective are examined using the following questions to navigate through available information: (i) What factors shape the value obtained from social media and big data? (ii) What factors influence the use of big data for healthcare service delivery?

This chapter provides a guide that integrate social media with big data, for service delivery by health facilities (hospitals and clinics). The chapter contributes to healthcare workers' awareness of how social media can be used to improve their services to the needy. Also, the chapter provides clarity on how information technology (IT) solutions' enabled social media and big data manifest to influence health practitioners' actions and services.

The remainder of this chapter is organised into five main sections. It begins with a section that introduces the chapter. A review of literature covering big data and social media from a healthcare perspective is presented in the second section. Thereafter, a holistic coverage of the factors that influence social media and big data for healthcare purposes is discussed. In the fourth section, a model including a discussion about integration of social media with big data, to improve healthcare service delivery is presented. Finally, the chapter is summarised.

Big Data and Social Media in Healthcare

In many countries, the use of big data is a challenge, and as such, it is often prioritised along with healthcare and other services (Kaisler, Armour, Espinosa & Money, 2013). This brings different challenges to stakeholders, those involved and concerned with the concept of big data, irrespective of the level and field of work. This is one of the motivating factors behind why research about big data is bound to become more widespread and require more awareness from data scientists and policymakers (Schroeder, 2014) in many areas, including social media and the health sector.

Some health practitioners fear that social media exposes them ethical risk through their networks or compromise patients' privacy via the hacking of their posts. To mitigate against this, social media should be formally integrated with health processes and activities whereby a strategy for security, integrity and confidentiality is implemented, and compliance is enforced. Many healthcare practitioners use social media to communicate and track health-related activities of interest, including correcting misinformation (Bautista, Zhang & Gwizdka, 2021). Many patients use social media to seek information about a disease and support groups to share experiences and information of common interest (Gupta, Khan & Kumar, 2022).

Social media provides a connecting link to the public domain for patients and health professionals to interact about health-related issues (Gupta, Khan & Kumar, 2022). This makes it difficult for either the patients or health workers not to stop using social media. In addition to health-related activities, the platforms connect many health workers' personal lives with their profession. Thus, it is inevitable to address the risks posed using social media (Ennis-O-Connor & Mannion, 2020). The integration of social media with healthcare requires authentication as a first step (Bautista, Zhang & Gwizdka, 2021).

Social media is a product of, as well as facilitated by, IT solutions. Within the context of IT applications, Sagiroglu and Sinanc (2013) suggest that information about big data has been very useful to companies or organisations, particularly for gaining richer and deeper insights. This suggestion has been particularly true in health and medicine, through which big data and social media activities can be remotely monitored and controlled, to manage behaviours that can lead to risk and disease outbreaks (Young, 2014). Critically, this is important in that social media is a platform that provides mechanisms for users to connect, communicate and interact with each other and generate big data (Correa, Hinsley and De Zuniga, 2010). Thus, social media platforms are an integral part of big data due to their high volume of user-engagements which produce over 500 million tweets per day on Twitter alone (Young, 2014).

Primarily, subscribers use social media for interaction and information sharing. It is on this basis, Carr and Hayes (2015) described social media as internet-based channels that allow users to interact. Big data presents many benefits to organisation, health facility included. However, new challenges are being presented by its existence, and these challenges are concerned with how information is stored, shared and managed (Kwon, Lee & Shin, 2014). Some of the challenges affect both the end-users and the IT solutions that host social media. Within this context, Yin et al. (2012) suggest that social media brings about difficulties in sifting relevant information, which is sometimes due to its massive volumes.

Another major challenge with big data is dissemination, which could be attributed to both hardware and software, due to the huge size and high speed of the data sets (Kaisler, Armour, Espinosa & Money, 2013). In addition, Marx (2013) suggests that big data challenges also come from the need to engineer tools for stability and longevity, in that many software tools cannot handle the challenge and crash often. For such reasons, big data implementations need to be analysed and executed as accurately as possible (Sagiroglu & Sinanc, 2013) in areas such as the health sector.

Big data generated by social media hold numerous benefits for organisations and the healthcare sector, in particular. However, the use of social media in the healthcare environment poses some challenges, including the threat to privacy and the need to continuously monitor and manage where and when possible (Katal, Wazid & Goudar, 2013). The emergent threats to users' online privacy come from other users' social media, making them particularly bad, as the victims are often not involved in the process of uploading the content. The users cannot take any pre-emptive cautions, as the amount of data uploaded varies so much that it cannot be detected manually (Smith, Szongott, Henne & Von Voigt, 2012).

Like many other sectors, the healthcare industry experiences many challenges, ranging from healthcare quality to strategic and operational efficiency. Rehman, Naz and Razzak (2021) argue that analytics is needed to enhance data quality in addressing challenges. However, big data analytics (BDA) on its own is not enough because the challenges extend to accessing of data, regulatory compliance, information security, interoperability, manageability and reusability, owing to the versatile nature of social media. Abkenar, Kashani, Mahdipour and Jameii (2021) empirically add that some of the challenges manifest from complications in identifying and tracking social media users, which ultimately makes assessing some types of information difficult. Also, the challenges increase the heterogeneity of patients' (social media users) data, which become difficult to put into perspective in data locality, velocity and availability.

Factors Influencing Social Media and Big Data for Healthcare Purposes

This chapter aims to help understand the complexities of integrating social media with healthcare big data to improve service delivery. Based on the aim, it is critical to gain insight into how interactions on social media platforms are influenced. The influence is synonymous with the meanings that human beings associate with various contexts and their relations with each other.

The aim is intended to enhance the quality and richness of data in terms of the consistency of the meaning associated with the concepts and the challenges encountered. In doing so, the aim is divided into two objectives, to be more horizontal in finding and gaining deeper perspective, for richer answers: (1) to comprehend the roles and effects of social media in delivering healthcare services; and (2) to examine how big data from social media can be used for healthcare services. Another rationale for splitting the objective is to have a good spread of corroborative and contrasting events.

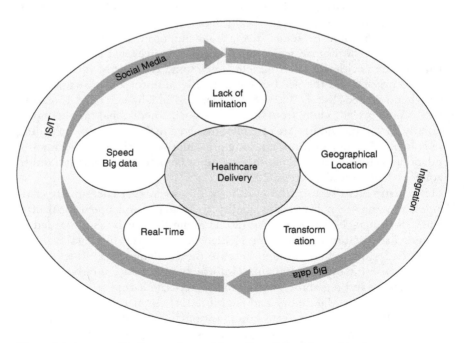

Figure 9.1 Factors of influence for social media and healthcare big data

This helps to examine and gain a better comprehension of social reality in the healthcare environment, from integration with social media perspective. This includes exploring the factors and trends that manifest to determine circumstance in the process of integrating IT solutions with other healthcare services components. Two questions are formulated, towards achieving the objectives as stated above: (i) What are the roles and effects of social media in delivering healthcare services? And (ii) how can big data from social media be used to carry out healthcare services? These questions are to determine how both social media and healthcare services can be integrated. Factors extracted from both questions are combined, as shown in Figure 9.1. The relationship between the factors and how they are interconnected to influence improved healthcare services using social media big data are illustrated in Figure 9.1.

What are the roles and effects of Social Media in delivering healthcare services?

Using social media, big data are gathered, which has provides benefits and challenges when used for healthcare services. Primarily, through the big data generated, both healthcare service providers and receivers are connected. Even though challenges exist, there is a growing trend in using social media technology by patients to seek and search for health information (Househ, Borycki & Kushniruk, 2014). Thus, Vance, Howe and Dellavalle (2009) highlighted the social media platforms, such as Facebook, MySpace and Twitter, are rapidly increasing as sources of big data for healthcare services.

The benefits and challenges of using social media to gather big data for healthcare come from both technical and non-technical perspectives. From the angles of benefits and challenges, De Choudhury, Gamon, Counts and Horvitz (2013) examined the potential of social media as a tool in detecting and predicting affective disorders in individuals. Thus, within the context of healthcare, some of the factors that influence social media and big data include (i) lack of limitation to accumulation of big data; (ii) ease of connectivity among subscribers; (iii) lack of geographical boundaries and (iv) real-time access to big data. These factors are discussed as follows:

a   Lack of limitation – There is no limit to the amount of data accumulated and shared between social media users. However, the infrastructures used to store the big data are sometimes challenged, from either the users or host's, or both perspectives. There is a constant flow of big data accumulated at an unprecedented rate, which sometime presents new challenges. These challenges are due to the rapid volume and variety of big data collected, which ultimately change their velocity at different rates, influencing decision-making (Feldman, Martin & Skotnes, 2012, p. 10).

Depending on the capacity of the hardware, both users and host providers do sometimes run out of storage space (Hashem et al., 2015). The amount of data generated from activities facilitated by the internet and mobile technologies is unprecedented (Vayena, Salathé, Madoff & Brownstein, 2015). However, this challenge seems easier to manage by both users and those hosting the infrastructures (Wang, Kung, Ting & Byrd, 2015; Hassan Zadeh, Zolbanin, Sharda & Delen, 2019).

b   Ease of connectivity – Social media platforms have made it easier for people-to-people, people-to-business and business-to-business to connect. The connectivity has increased visibility, which manifests to add value for some of the users. From a technical perspective, connectivity through social media is effortless in that the infrastructures are scalable and reused (Christodoulakis et al., 2016). Various technologies and devices, such as database technologies and patient monitoring and sensor technologies, are used to generate health big data by hospitals and medical organisations at an unusual speed.

One of the premises of social media in healthcare is in its support and enablement of patient-to-patient, patient-to-facility and facility-to-facility engagement (Gupta, Khan & Kumar, 2022). Social media convergence enables personalisation in terms of messaging and model of information and service delivery. Personalisation is a challenge that will always exist within healthcare big data. Thus, Kayyali, Knott and Van Kuiken (2013) argued that privacy concerns would continue to be problematic in using big data for healthcare services.

c   Real-time – Another important benefit of social media is allowing real-time big data capturing and accessing. In some medical situations, access to real-time big data that covers areas, such as trauma monitoring for blood pressure and bedside heart monitors, is essential to life or death (Zhao et al., 2021). Real-time access to health activities is critical, particularly in monitoring to give immediate alerts of changes in patient status and correlate with patient records (Boer et al., 2021).

Also, real-time requires compatibility with various devices, allowing usage, accessibility and management of social media and big data at any time and from any geographical location. Kayyali, Knott and Van Kuiken (2013) explained that irrespective of the challenges, integrating social media with big data by IT allows medical personnel and health facilities to deliver evidence-based care that is more coordinated and personalised. This has the potential to improve performance in areas such as prevention and care coordination.

In situations where patients' data may be collected through automated systems and in real-time, there is a high possibility of constraints (Naslund, Bondre, Torous & Aschbrenner, 2020). Thus, software applications and other devices used to store, access and manage health data should be integrated with mechanisms, such as privacy protection, access control and secure transmission modules (Lin & Kishore, 2021).

d   Speed of social media and big data – Enabled by IT solutions, the use of social media enhances speedy patients' consultation with physicians, administering of patients' chronic medications and ease of monitoring of patients' progress. For example, by integrating big data with legacy IT systems, health practitioners can automatically monitor drug safety by tracking warning signals triggered by alarm systems (Wang, Kung, Ting & Byrd, 2015). Thus, Kayyali, Knott and Van Kuiken (2013) argue that IT solution for integration of systems, such as HealthConnect with big data, improves cardiovascular disease outcomes and promotes the use of electronic health records for data exchange across medical facilities.

The use of social media for health services enables rapid transmission through a wide community, user interaction and dissemination of health information (Zhao et al., 2021). This contributes to the increasing interest in the integration of social media with healthcare big data. For example, through social media, De Choudhury, Gamon, Counts and Horvitz (2013) employ big data to learn about people's social and psychological behaviour to predict their vulnerabilities to depression.

How can big data from social media be used to carry out healthcare services?

Evidently, the communications and interactions between patients and medical practitioners through technological devices are mostly wireless, which results in various security threats and challenges to personal information (Al Ameen, Liu & Kwak, 2012; Chen & Wang, 2021). Primarily, the factors, which can influence big data within the healthcare environment, include (i) lack of geographical boundaries; (ii) transformation and (iii) security and privacy, discussed in detail below:

a   Lack of geographical boundaries – IT solutions are used to facilitate activities towards improving the efficiency and quality of healthcare services (Ukoha & Stranieri, 2021). Users are not restricted to their geographical locations in the application of social media. One of the reasons is the integration of technologies, such as cloud computing, to perform massive-scale, complex and sensitive tasks, including big data (Hashem et al., 2015). This makes the use and dissemination of big data to be more purposeful.

Also, the lack of geographical boundaries increases communication between distant medical practitioners and patients. This eradicates duplication and replication of infrastructures. Technological devices can collect, access and manage big data remotely and from different locations (Al Ameen, Liu & Kwak, 2012). However, the host databases should be situated in a secure location.

b   Transformation – Rapidly increasing patients' heterogeneous big data helps to provide a valuable resource for use in improving healthcare delivery services, including medical decision-making (Christodoulakis et al., 2016). There has been optimism in using big data to transform healthcare in recent years, but some structural issues continue to be obstacles (Kayyali, Knott & Van Kuiken, 2013). However, the transformation is difficult due to identity manipulation and misinformation about patients' records, privacy and security concerns (Ali, Balta & Papadopoulos, 2022).

Healthcare transformation can gain from integrating IT solutions with big data (Wang, Kung, Ting & Byrd, 2015). Innovation such as digitisation is instrumental to accelerating the transformation of healthcare services (Koster, Stewart & Kolker, 2016). Integrating social media and big data helps eliminate the need to maintain expensive computing hardware, dedicated storage space and software applications (Hashem et al., 2015). Thus, integrating IT solutions' capabilities is key to healthcare transformation (Wang, Kung, Ting & Byrd, 2015).

c   Security and privacy – This poses challenges to both the users and technology host providers. The users must be wary about the privacy of their personal information continuously. The IT solutions provider manages the volume of the big data, organises its variety and responds to the rapid speed (velocity) at which they receive, process and disseminate the big data. Feldman, Martin and Skotnes (2012) argue that patients' big data privacy has increasingly become a matter of attention and concern as social media expose personal data to potential misuse.

Even though Kayyali, Knott and Van Kuiken (2013) highlighted some benefits of healthcare big data, such as enabling faster identification of high-risk patients, more effective interventions and closer monitoring, there are security challenges. The challenges emanate from evidence relating to how the efficacy and effectiveness of big data from social media are currently limited due to security and privacy concerns (Househ, Borycki & Kushniruk, 2014). The main challenges are security and privacy.

Integration of Social Media with Health Big Data

As presented above, the factors that influence social media and big data for healthcare service delivery are interpreted. From the interpretation, four factors are found to be critical in achieving the objectives of the chapter. As shown in Figure 9.2, the four factors must be tightly connected to achieve improved healthcare service delivery through social media and big data by integrating IT solutions. The factors are (i) analytics of big data; (ii) the roles and influence of big data from social media; (iii) integration of big data with social media, using IT solutions and (iv) healthcare and privacy within the context of big data that comes from social media.

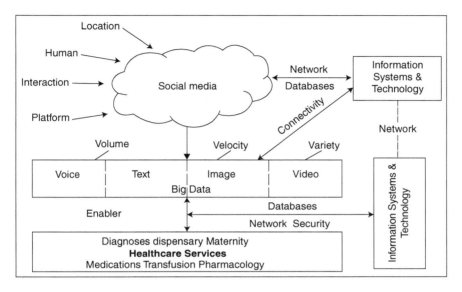

Figure 9.2 IT integration of social media with healthcare big data

Big Data and Analytics

The continuous increase in speed and variety of big data makes it necessary for analysis to be constantly conducted before the data sets are used. Regular analysis of healthcare big data of each patient is important due to the numerous activities that they carry out on the patients, using various apparatus and diagnostics tools (Christodoulakis et al., 2016). Thus, different analytics tools have been introduced and applied over the years. However, some analytics tools have been noticed to be problematic for reasons such as lack of capability for real-time, lack of sensitivity and slow response time. This has contributed to making big data and data analytics tools slow or disruptive to innovations, primarily because they are difficult to integrate, in Kitchin's (2014) assessment.

Also, continuous and rapid change in the size and variety of big data is a challenge that affects how the data sets are stored, processed and transmitted, ultimately influencing the analysis. The constant increases in big data volume, variety and speed make it even more complex and difficult for organisations to achieve their objectives (Sagiroglu & Sinanc, 2013). The complexities and challenges impact big data at various levels of security and privacy; hence, there is a need to conduct regular analysis. Therefore, integrating the tools and artefacts involved in the collection, storage and analytics is critical. This is primarily to reduce the complexity and enhance the capacity to enable and support healthcare for improved services to society.

Thus, there is a need for analytics tools, which can be integrated with the enabling and associated artefacts, such as operating systems, databases and healthcare applications. The integration helps flexibility and compatibility between social media BDA tools, and other IT supporting and enabling solutions within healthcare services. As the data increases in size and complexity, the integration maintains and enhances the connectivity and relationship between BDA tools and social media platforms to improve healthcare services.

Social Media and IT solutions

The increasing volume and expected speed of data sets are caused and influenced by various factors, including database and network capacity. This indicates that social media and healthcare big data can be queried or requested in real-time. However, for epidemiological and biomedical data, there is often a delay between when people contract a virus or disease and the release of the data (Young, 2014). This could be associated with the different systems and technologies used to host, connect and transmit big data.

The use of social media continues to expand the reach of internet networks and other IT associated components vastly. The IT unit provides systems (solutions) for accessing and interacting with social media networks, comprising hosting, processing and transmission devices. One of the challenges is that some of these devices are not or cannot be integrated. Hence, some social media platforms, such as YouTube, Facebook and Twitter, are too often treated as stand-alone elements rather than part of an integrated system for health-related processes and activities (Bautista, Zhang & Gwizdka, 2021). The integration of these systems and devices is significant as to how they respond and the result they reproduce.

Over the years, an increasing number of patients and healthcare service providers have embraced social media for health-related activities and processes. Even though subscribers and medical practitioners use social media for the same health-related activities, the motive or rationale can often be different. However, little is known yet about the motives behind patients' and health professionals' use of social media for health-related reasons (Antheunis, Tates & Nieboer, 2013). This necessitates tighter security and privacy of social media big data for health-related activities by both patients and health professionals.

Healthcare and Privacy

Health-related issues are at all times considered to be private due to their nature of sensitivity and care. This is primarily to protect both the service providers and those requiring the services. As a result, many healthcare service providers have policies on code of conduct, which are intended to guide the privacy of their activities. However, the challenges persist because research on healthcare information systems (HISs) pays little attention to privacy protection (Shi, M., Jiang, Hu & Shang, 2020). A common understanding is that the privacy of patients' big data is a foremost security concern in healthcare and must be enforced by using strong technology, such as cryptography, irrespective of the source of data. Hsu, Lee and Su (2013) proposed a framework to protect patients' electronic healthcare records (EHRs) in search of solutions.

Consequently, big data sets that generate diagnoses, medications and other health-related activities for care must be secured and adhere to the privacy policies. This is supported and enabled by the software and hardware that hosts and facilitates the use of social media with healthcare big data. Therefore, big data generated from social media activities requires a security-integrated approach to enable and support IT artefacts, including network, internet and databases. This is primarily to address security and privacy concerns, to which Al Ameen, Liu and Kwak (2012) suggest that there should be more focus on wireless sensor networks and applications. This approach will assist in controlling and managing flows and accessibility of the big data sets in their increasing volume, speed and variety.

IT solutions and Integration

The flow of materials, products and services at both short-term and long-term operations are facilitated, enabled and supported by IT solutions, such as software, hardware and network. These flows are engineered through the linkage between the solutions of IT, which include cloud and databases. None of the artefacts could execute operations in isolation. Thus, integration with IT constitutes interrelations and connectivity among its solutions

The IT solutions that are associated with the various entities, such as cloud, network and data, must be integrated to use big data from social media for healthcare services. On the one hand, healthcare big data is hosted by necessary interconnected and interrelated software and hardware. On the other hand, social media is enabled and powered by network connectivity. There is a relationship between big data and networks in every social media and healthcare operation, reproducing big data.

Summary

This chapter is intended to benefit both healthcare and academic domains from theoretical, methodological and practical perspectives. Theoretically, this chapter reveals the factors that can influence social media big data for improved healthcare, which both organisations and academics will find useful. In addition, the use of social media big data as a form of research has become a trend, which ultimately draws the attention of both businesses and the healthcare sectors. Another theoretically important contribution is that this chapter adds to the existing literature from three dimensional angles, big data, healthcare and social media. Methodologically, integrating the three areas highlighted by the chapter contributes to both organisations and academics through its approach towards real revealed circumstances. This includes how social media generated big data can improve health-related services, including remote monitoring and surveillance of risk behaviours and disease outbreaks. A practical contribution of the chapter is in its insights, which managers and academia can consider, to better understand the influencing factors towards managing, storing and retrieving social media big data, and using IT solutions to transform them for improved healthcare services to the society.

Having identified the primary areas of concern and benefits in the intersection between social media, healthcare and big data, it is essential to consider ethical issues. The privacy of patients' big data must be prioritised and guided by ethical considerations of the communities. This is one of the areas for future studies as research in healthcare, and social media big data continue to evolve, particularly in developing countries.

References

Abkenar, S. B., Kashani, M. H., Mahdipour, E., & Jameii, S. M. (2021). Big data analytics meets social media: A systematic review of techniques, open issues, and future directions. *Telematics and Informatics, 57*, 101517. https://doi.org/10.1016/j.tele.2020.101517

Al Ameen, M., Liu, J., & Kwak, K. (2012). Security and privacy issues in wireless sensor networks for healthcare applications. *Journal of Medical Systems, 36*(1), 93–101. https://doi.org/10.1007/s10916-010-9449-4

Antheunis, M. L., Tates, K., & Nieboer, T. E. (2013). Patients' and health professionals' use of social media in health care: Motives, barriers and expectations. *Patient Education and Counseling, 92*(3), 426–431. https://doi.org/10.1016/j.pec.2013.06.020

Bautista, J. R., Zhang, Y., & Gwizdka, J. (2021). Healthcare professionals' acts of correcting health misinformation on social media. *International Journal of Medical Informatics, 148*, 104375. https://doi.org/10.1016/j.ijmedinf.2021.104375

Carr, C. T., & Hayes, R. A. (2015). Social media: Defining, developing, and divining. *Atlantic Journal of Communication, 23*(1), 46–65. https://doi.org/10.1080/15456870.2015.972282

Chen, J., & Wang, Y. (2021). Social media use for health purposes: systematic review. *Journal of medical Internet research, 23*(5), e17917. https://doi.org/10.2196/17917

Christodoulakis, A., Karanikas, H., Billiris, A., Thireos, E., & Pelekis, N. (2016). "Big data" in health care. *Archives of Hellenic Medicine/Arheia Ellenikes Iatrikes, 33*(4), 489–497.

Correa, T., Hinsley, A. W., & De Zuniga, H. G. (2010). Who interacts on the web?: The intersection of users' personality and social media use. *Computers in Human Behaviour, 26*(2), 247–253. https://doi.org/10.1016/j.chb.2009.09.003

De Choudhury, M., Gamon, M., Counts, S., & Horvitz, E. (2013). Predicting depression via social media. In: *Proceedings of the international AAAI conference on web* and social media (ICWSM) (p. 2). https://ojs.aaai.org/index.php/ICWSM/article/view/14432

Ennis-O-Connor, M., & Mannion, R. (2020, May). Social media networks and leadership ethics in healthcare. In: *Healthcare management forum* (Vol. 33, No. 3, pp. 145–148). Los Angeles, CA: Sage. https://doi.org/10.1177/0840470419893773

Feldman, B., Martin, E. M., & Skotnes, T. (2012). Big data in healthcare hype and hope. *Dr. Bonnie, 360.*

Gupta, P., Khan, A., & Kumar, A. (2022). Social media use by patients in health care: A scoping review. *International Journal of Healthcare Management*, 15(2), 121–131. https://doi.org/10.1080/20479700.2020.1860563

Hashem, I. A. T., Yaqoob, I., Anuar, N. B., Mokhtar, S., Gani, A., & Khan, S. U. (2015). The rise of "big data" on cloud computing: Review and open research issues. *Information Systems*, 47, 98–115. https://doi.org/10.1016/j.is.2014.07.006

Hassan Zadeh, A., Zolbanin, H. M., Sharda, R., & Delen, D. (2019). Social media for nowcasting flu activity: Spatio-temporal big data analysis. *Information Systems Frontiers*, 21(4), 743-760.

Househ, M., Borycki, E., & Kushniruk, A. (2014). Empowering patients through social media: The benefits and challenges. *Health Informatics Journal*, 20(1), 50–58. https://doi.org/10.1177/1460458213476969

Hsu, C. L., Lee, M. R., & Su, C. H. (2013). The role of privacy protection in healthcare information systems adoption. *Journal of Medical Systems*, 37(5), 1–12. https://doi.org/10.1007/s10916-013-9966-z

Kaisler, S., Armour, F., Espinosa, J. A., & Money, W. (2013). Big data: Issues and challenges moving forward. In: *46th Hawaii international conference on system sciences (HICSS)* (pp. 995–1004). IEEE. https://doi.org/10.1109/HICSS.2013.645.

Katal, A., Wazid, M., & Goudar, R. H. (2013). Big data: Issues, challenges, tools and good practices. In: *2013 sixth international conference on contemporary computing (IC3)* (pp. 404–409). IEEE. https://doi.org/10.1109/IC3.2013.6612229

Kayyali, B., Knott, D., & Van Kuiken, S. (2013). The big-data revolution in US health care: Accelerating value and innovation. *Mc Kinsey & Company*, 2(8), 1–13.

Kitchin, R. (2014). Big Data, new epistemologies and paradigm shifts. *Big Data & Society*, 1(1). https://doi.org/10.1177/2053951714528481

Koster, J., Stewart, E., & Kolker, E. (2016). Health care transformation: A strategy rooted in data and analytics. *Academic Medicine*, 91(2), 165–167. https://doi.org/10.1097/ACM.0000000000001047

Kwon, O., Lee, N., & Shin, B. (2014). Data quality management, data usage experience and acquisition intention of big data analytics. *International Journal of Information Management*, 34(3), 387–394. https://doi.org/10.1016/j.ijinfomgt.2014.02.002

Lin, X., & Kishore, R. (2021). Social media-enabled healthcare: A conceptual model of social media affordances, online social support, and health behaviors and outcomes. *Technological Forecasting and Social Change*, 166, 120574. https://doi.org/10.1016/j.techfore.2021.120574

Marx, V. (2013). The big challenges of big data. *Nature*, 498(7453), 255–260. https://doi.org/10.1038/498255a

Mayer-Schönberger, V., & Cukier, K. (2013). *Big data: A revolution that will transform how we live, work, and think*. London: Hachette.

McCormack, L. A., Friedrich, C., Fahrenwald, N., & Specker, B. (2014). Feasibility and acceptability of alternate methods of postnatal data collection. *Maternal and Child Health Journal*, 18(4), 852–857. https://doi.org/10.1007/s10995-013-1310-1

Naslund, J. A., Bondre, A., Torous, J., & Aschbrenner, K. A. (2020). Social media and mental health: benefits, risks, and opportunities for research and practice. *Journal of technology in behavioral science*, *5*(3), 245-257.

Rehman, A., Naz, S., & Razzak, I. (2021). Leveraging big data analytics in healthcare enhancement: Trends, challenges and opportunities. *Multimedia Systems*, 1–33. https://doi.org/10.1007/s00530-020-00736-8

Romero, D. M., Galuba, W., Asur, S., & Huberman, B. A. (2011). Influence and passivity in social media. In: *Proceedings of the 20th international conference companion on world wide web* (pp. 113–114). ACM. https://doi.org/10.1007/978-3-642-23808-6_2

Russom, P. (2011). Big data analytics. *TDWI best practices report, Fourth Quarter, 19*(4), 1–34.

Sagiroglu, S., & Sinanc, D. (2013, May). Big data: A review. In: *2013 international conference on collaboration technologies and systems (CTS)* (pp. 42–47). IEEE. https://doi.org/10.1109/CTS.2013.6567202

Schroeder, R. (2014). Big Data and the brave new world of social media research. *Big Data & Society*, *1*(2), 1-11. https://doi.org/10.1177/2053951714563194

Shi, M., Jiang, R., Hu, X., & Shang, J. (2020). A privacy protection method for health care big data management based on risk access control. *Health care management science*, *23*(3), 427-442.

Smith, M., Szongott, C., Henne, B., & Von Voigt, G. (2012). Big data privacy issues in public social media. In: *2012 6th IEEE international conference on digital ecosystems technologies (DEST)* (pp. 1–6). IEEE. https://doi.org/10.1109/DEST.2012.6227909

Syed, A., Gillela, K., & Venugopal, C. (2013). The future revolution on big data. *International Journal of Advanced Research in Computer and Communication Engineering*, *2*(6), 2446–2451.

Ukoha, C., & Stranieri, A. (2021). On the value of social media in health care. *Journal of Technology in Behavioral Science*, *6*(2), 419-426.

Vance, K., Howe, W., & Dellavalle, R. P. (2009). Social internet sites as a source of public health information. *Dermatologic Clinics*, *27*(2), 133–136. https://doi.org/10.1016/j.det.2008.11.010

Vayena, E., Salathé, M., Madoff, L. C., & Brownstein, J. S. (2015). Ethical challenges of big data in public health. *PLoS Computational Biology*, *11*(2), 1–7. https://doi.org/10.1371/journal.pcbi.1003904

Wang, Y., Kung, L., Ting, C., & Byrd, T. A. (2015). Beyond a technical perspective: Understanding big data capabilities in health care. In: *48th Hawaii international conference on system sciences (HICSS)* (pp. 3044–3053). IEEE. https://doi.org/10.1109/HICSS.2015.368

Yin, J., Lampert, A., Cameron, M., Robinson, B., & Power, R. (2012). Using social media to enhance emergency situation awareness. *IEEE Intelligent Systems*, *27*(6), 52–59.

Young, S. D. (2014). Behavioural insights on big data: Using social media for predicting biomedical outcomes. *Trends in Microbiology*, *22*(11), 601–602. https://doi.org/10.1016/j.tim.2014.08.004

Zhao, J., Han, H., Zhong, B., Xie, W., Chen, Y., & Zhi, M. (2021). Health information on social media helps mitigate Crohn's disease symptoms and improves patients' clinical course. *Computers in Human Behavior*, *115*, 106588. https://doi.org/10.1016/j.chb.2020.106588

10 Actor-Network Theory View of Healthcare Big Data

Introduction

Medical practitioners and support personnel uphold the responsibility of storing large amounts and various types of patients' data sets such as medical histories, diagnoses and other materials related to health conditions. Thus, tools or methods are needed to harness and gain from the benefits of the healthcare data set (Chawla & Davis, 2013; Miah, Camilleri & Vu, 2022). A patient's data set embodies the characteristics of big data in that they are in volume, variety (structured and unstructured), velocity, veracity and validity. One of the benefits of big data in healthcare is that it helps to categorise and put in perspective as patients' data set comes in large amounts, from different sources, and has real-time and continuous nature (Sahay, 2016). The benefits include enabling different types of diagnoses, in their volumes, and from various sources, for forecasting and health management of the population (He, Nazir & Hussain, 2021). Applying advanced analysis techniques means that such information could be extracted, and medication could be personalised while also gaining insight into genetic and environmental causes of diseases (Chandarana & Vijayalakshmi, 2014).

One of the primary challenges in using healthcare big data is in its analysis, which perhaps comes from the heterogeneous nature of patients' data sets (Jagadish et al., 2014). Labrinidis and Jagadish (2012) state that heterogeneity, scale, timeliness, complexity and privacy problems hinder progress in creating value from data sets. According to Kuo et al. (2014), healthcare big data is so large, complex and vastly distributed that it becomes very difficult to access or use without appropriate categorisation. Analysis is critical to monitoring and evaluating patients' current and historical health conditions. Also, analysis is frequently needed to predict epidemics that may affect a region (Bates et al., 2014; Roy et al., 2021).

Big data helps to have a full scale, from text to video and images of patient's health data. Big data analysis enables the transformation of healthcare by providing insight into healthcare facilities, which helps with decision-making (Van Biesen et al., 2021). This challenge has long been identified, leading Chawla and Davis (2013) to state that taking the next

DOI: 10.4324/9781003251064-10

big steps in personalised healthcare will require computing and analytics (or analysis) framework to aggregate and integrate big data, to gain deeper insight into patients' data set connectedness, which is not only derived from medical records. Additionally, the challenges with access and use of patients' big data could be caused by numerous groupings, such as administration, nurses, doctors and specialisation areas, including surgery, pathology, gynaecology and dentistry. The different areas require specific attention and type of analysis.

The analysis of the healthcare data set is critical to improving accuracy and consistency for service delivery purposes. Big data analysis helps harness data sets for more purposefulness and improved ease of use towards proactive identification of new opportunities, which spurs the use of actor-network theory (ANT) for analysis from an interpretive perspective. The theory focuses on human and non-human (such as software, computer and process) actors (Callon, 1986; Iyamu, 2021). The theory is concerned with investigating complexity in the relationship and interaction between actors in networks (Heeks & Stanforth, 2015), which can help analyse the groupings nature of the healthcare setting and its associated big data.

Sequentially, this chapter is organised into six main sections. It began with introduction and by problematising the challenges of using big data for healthcare services, in sections one and two, respectively. This is followed by a review of literature, which focuses on the core aspects of the chapter, healthcare big data and ANT. The fourth section presents ANT's view of healthcare data, based on which a framework is developed. The framework is presented and discussed in the fifth section. The summary of the chapter is presented in the final section.

The Chapter Problematised

The functions of healthcare and how care is carried out in many facilities (hospitals and clinics) across the world is increasingly challenging. As a result, patients continue to be incorrectly diagnosed, and some are given incorrect medications. Some of these challenges remain persistent. For instance, in a hospital in 2008, an elderly woman was incorrectly diagnosed and had to be transferred to two different hospitals, in her frail state, to save her life. Additionally, some of the health facilities are challenged when it comes to analyse and management of patients' data sets, which sometimes affect service delivery. There is another case of a patients who was a wrong medication for over 10 tens. Gradually, the situation worsened and caused neurological damage. Had the health condition and medication been adequately monitored through analysis, it could have perhaps been prevented. Primarily, the problem is caused by a lack of appropriate categorisation of patients' big data, making its analysis difficult. As a result, outcomes from the analyses are sometimes skewed, which affect healthcare services delivery.

The question posed in this chapter is: How can big data be used to improve healthcare services? Answers to this question are intended advance the services provided by health facilities in many countries.

Healthcare Big Data and Actor-Network Theory

Healthcare Big Data

There are challenges of disparities of data within healthcare systems in many countries, caused by dysfunction and malaise (Mphatswe et al., 2012; Velpula & Pamula, 2022). According to Leon, Schneider and Daviaud (2012), data challenges in health systems include the complexity of ensuring interoperability and integration of big data with information systems and securing the privacy of information. Big data in healthcare holds potential benefits, in improving clinical decision-making (Panahiazar et al., 2014). Some highlighted benefits in previous studies include early disease detection and overall management of healthcare (Ganjir, Sarkar & Kumar, 2016; Giambrone, Hemmings, Sturm & Fleischut, 2015). However, Sacristán and Dilla (2015) state that these benefits can only be realised by analysing the existing data. Wyber et al. (2015) argue that the analysis of big data can help in improving outcomes in healthcare. Additionally, Tresp et al. (2016) state that the use of information technology (IT) solutions could also improve healthcare.

However, inaccuracies and lack of efficiency within data sets hinder its progression and the realisation of its benefits (He, Nazir & Hussain, 2021). This inherently brings the need for more integrated and secure analytics solutions (Nepal, Ranjan & Choo, 2015; Velpula & Pamula, 2022). Most importantly, the analysis of the data must be computed, as manual analysis might devalue the information sought (Shah, Rabhi & Ray, 2015; Sreedevi, Harshitha, Sugumaran & Shankar, 2022). Hilbert (2016) regards the term big data as a shorter term for big data analysis as it goes as far as the analysis which contributes to better decision-making. Healthcare improvement relies heavily on uncovering the hidden facts within big data, states Ojha and Mathur (2016).

One of the challenges of big data analysis is the magnitude of data sets and the difficulties associated with validating long-term predictions for diagnoses and medication purposes (Kambatla, Kollias, Kumar & Grama, 2014). According to Esposito et al. (2015), users (practitioners) require knowledge of the details of the activity, to provide service using big data properly and accurately. On the technological (IT solutions) front, the challenges include integrating and analysing various healthcare big data to address impending problems (Kankanhalli, Hahn, Tan & Gao, 2016).

Patients' big data and other materialistic artefacts (such as medical apparatus) form networks, a state of realism, which the ontological stance focuses on (Scotland, 2012). During health activities, the networks become heterogeneous, which also increases the levels of security, making it more difficult for analysis, in producing useful and purposeful data (Archenaa & Anita, 2015).

Additionally, the realistic state is that healthcare big data cannot be independent of patients and health professionals (Scotland, 2012). Thus, this chapter aims to examine how healthcare big data can be transformed to increase usefulness and purposefulness.

Actor-Network Theory

ANT is a socio-technical theory embedded within science and technologies (Dery, Hall, Wailes & Wiblen, 2013). The core elements of ANT are the actor, network and translation (Callon, 1986). Irrespective of the context, both actor and network cannot be independent of each other (Teles & Joia, 2011). The actor can make a difference with its network (Walsham, 1997), a health practitioner providing a service (medical treatment) that makes a patient recover from his or her illness. A network is a group of actors (e.g., patient, health practitioner, biodata, and medication) with allied interests (healthcare or well-being). Bleakley (2012) describes ANT as a method that uncovers the initiation of networks and ensures their solidity and growth while also monitoring where they fail due to reliance on third parties. ANT assumes that actors within a network are the cause behind social effects (Latour, 2005).

In ANT, translation is explained as a four-stage transitional process that consists of problematisation, interessement, enrolment and mobilisation, through which events are carried within a network of actors (Callon, 1986). *Problematisation* – to initiate problems as well as to propose solutions (Latour, 2005). Interessement – a process where the focal actor stabilises the identity of other actors and creates links between them (Stanforth, 2006). Enrolment – the approaches through which the focal actor attempts to define and interconnect different roles that allow other actors to relate and execute tasks within the network (Heeks & Stanforth, 2015). Mobilisation – the last stage in the moments of translation when the focal actors ensure that all representatives or spokespersons act according to what are now their aligned interests (Walsham, 1997).

The theory focuses on networks, relationships, interactions in heterogeneous networks, and shifting negotiation (Callon, 1986). On this basis, ANT has been used in the development of various IT solutions (Heeks & Stanforth, 2015). Walsham (1997) argues from an IT perspective that ANT is concerned with human and non-human actors within networks which, in the case of IT, include people, software, computer-network and standards. The theory, ANT, offers a different type of analysis focusing on the relational effect shaped by the interaction between humans and non-humans in their heterogeneous networks. To be more specific, ANT has been used to advance healthcare service initiatives, to explain the complexity of relations within it (Afarikumah & Kwankam, 2013; Lee, Harindranath, Oh & Kim, 2015). This includes Cho, Mathiassen and Nilsson (2008), who applied ANT to examine the healthcare information systems implementation of a radiology network system. Robert et al. (2010) employ ANT to explore how new technologies were adopted for healthcare practices. Bleakley (2012) used ANT to examine how it can be applied in medical education

Actor-Network Theory View

Thus, the theory focuses on examining the relations between health activities and big data, including the roles of medical practitioners, administrators and patients in analysing data towards delivering service. In this respect, ANT helps understand social complexities when employed to examine interaction and relationships between actors within networks (Arnaboldi & Spiller, 2011). Thus, ANT is applied to (i) examine how patients' incidents are transformed from problem (problematisation) to accepted solution (mobilisation) stages and (ii) understand how different networks are usually formed, including the types of data that are generated to influence healthcare services. This is of importance to healthcare studies as it allows a sense of comfort around a sensitive area.

Actors

Health facilities (hospitals and clinics) consist of both human and non-human actors. The actors include employees who are classed into two categories, namely the medical and administrative units. When writing this chapter, the classification was done to distinguish between roles and responsibilities and link them to actions carried out in the course of service delivery to the community. In the context of this chapter, general practitioners (GP) and nurses are referred to as medical staff (health practitioners), while the administrative staff consists of the facility manager and clerical assistants.

The actors mentioned above make use of IT solutions to carry out their responsibilities. The IT solutions included data. Other types of non-human actors included medical apparatus. The data sets consist of medical files, which contain patients' biodata, results from diagnoses, medications and prescriptions. The IT solutions included the computers that are used by both medical and administrative staff. In the health facilities scans are conducted, tasks carried using medical apparatus such as ultrasound machines. Patients' information, including physicians' notes, is captured on hard-copy files in some health facilities.

In health facilities, big data, different types of data were accumulated through medical and administrative activities and processes. This includes voice, text and image. The voice data were gathered and accessed through telephonic communication between medical personnel and administrative employees. Text data set forms part of patients' data set from patients' diagnoses, treatments, prescriptions and medications. Also, images and videos from scans and x-rays are accessed for services based on diagnoses. In some health facilities in many countries, blood samples are sent to the lab; they return the results in paper and electronic (email) forms.

Also, some employees use IT solutions to support the health facility's functions, such as storing and managing patients' information. Usually, the clerical assistants use personal computers to obtain patients' file numbers and extract information such as names, surnames and addresses. Even though the actors are both human and non-human, they depend on each other to accumulate and use big data for healthcare services. This means that the actors inevitably have relationships in providing services. The relationships are formed based on activities or circumstances that bring the actors together into groups, which ANT refers to as networks.

Actor-Networks

Employees in health facilities are usually divided into two main units, the medical and the administrative. The medical unit consists of doctors and nurses. The administrative unit comprises of clerks and the managers. Also, there are groups (networks) of patients. The main groups of patients are sometimes unconsciously formed. They are the chronic and day-to-day groups of patients. Chronic patients are those who required treatments for long-term illnesses. These groups of patients visit the health facility regularly for medical check-ups, collection of medications or medical tests purposes. The day-to-day patients are those that visit health facility once-off, to get specific treatment or information.

Within networks, the actors carry out activities, are involved in events and employed processes by using big data for healthcare services. At one stage or the other during the activities, events, processes, and negotiations take place between the actors, directly or indirectly, consciously or unconsciously. ANT refers to this as moments of translation, stages where interactions shape and reshape decisions. This enables medical practitioners to make better decisions in providing services.

Moments of Translation: Problematisation

Since health facilities focus on patients' medical conditions, problematisation happens through two ways: (1) solicits for care; and (2) document healthcare processes, activities and events, which happen through patients' visits to the facility; and use of telephonic or electronic mail (email) communication between a patient and health practitioners. As the patients' conditions are problematised, a facility accumulates a substantial amount of big data daily. The big data consist of patients' information, including biodata, diagnoses, prescriptions and medications.

This stage was critical in big data accumulation, access and use for healthcare service delivery. This makes problematisation critical in providing healthcare services because healthcare-related decisions are informed and guided by the patients' original information and health records. Once the initial communication has been established through a visit to the facility or telephonically or by email, the process of accumulating big data proceeds through observation and consultation commences.

Observation and consultation were important parts of problematising patients' health conditions before services are rendered. They play a pivotal role in the overall provision of healthcare services. This compels the patient to be open and honest about their health conditions. However, the facility encounters challenges at this stage. Patients are not always forthcoming about the trueness of their health conditions, which shapes the data set and ultimately influences and affects response and care.

How information is collected from the patients also contributes to the problematisation of healthcare. In some small facilities, staff had limited options not to collect personal information in the presence of other patients. Some individuals find this invasive, which leads them to not fully disclose their health conditions. Thus, some patients are a bit uncomfortable with how the medical personnel request personal information from them.

Also, some patients find many healthcare practitioners intimidating, impatient and harsh, leading to some having trouble expressing themselves about their conditions. Thus, some of the patients consider the healthcare to be insensitive towards their health conditions. This type of approach is also associated with unethical behaviour. In addition, some health practitioners in many health facilities are not accommodating, based on their impatience with patients who struggle with articulating or expressing themselves about their health challenges. This is influenced by how and the types of information some of the patients share or disclose.

Language and socio-cultural differences are usually standing issues in many facilities. As a result, some staff found it difficult to communicate with patients, thus resulting in (perceived) intimidation, impatience and harshness. It is understandable that patients who visit a health facility come from various cultural and linguistic backgrounds. This affects the interaction between some of the patients and medical personnel in providing and receiving care. Thus, language interpreters are often used, which takes away the privacy of the patient. This is a prevalent challenge in multilingual environments.

The medical personnel utilise the information collected at this stage to take the treatment process further. Diagnoses, treatments and follow-ups are conducted based on the information gathered and stored. This makes full disclosure of important during problematisation. Although roles have been established at this stage, various factors come into play to determine individuals' interest in the care process.

Moments of Translation: Interessement

For each medical case within a health facility, various actors had an interest. These actors include the patients, their relations, medical personnel and medical aid schemes that cover individuals visiting a health facility. Patients expressed their interest through initiating and discussing their health conditions via telephone or walk-in. Some patients are accompanied by their relations for various reasons (interests), such as to act as an interpreter, guardian (financier) or spokesperson (for those severely ill). The medical aid schemes are more interested in how and what led to the cost.

Patients are particularly interested in the health services offered by the healthcare facility. The services include patients' health assessment, specialist referrals for cases that the facility cannot handle, prescribing and dispensing medications. Patients' relations, including friends, also had interests in the facility's health services. This is often triggered by their concerns for the patients' well-being. These individuals' interest is expressed by ensuring that patients receive help from the health facility. In most emergency cases, a patient is not alone; other people accompany them.

Different factors sway the interests of the various stakeholders about a patient and within a facility. Medical schemes stand to gain financially from the treatment of patients. Patients seek healthcare services from the health facility to improve the state of their health. The medical personnel are also obligated to take an interest in patient care, uphold their professional ethics and secure their jobs. However, the interest of these stakeholders does not guarantee participation in the process of actual care. Different factors drive participation and ensure that individuals fulfil their different roles.

Moments of Translation: Enrolment

Stakeholders participate in various ways such as gathering patients' big data, accessing the big data, using the big data and managing the data set to provide services. The stakeholders' participation is determined by different factors, including professionalism, ethics, care and financial interests.

Patients participate in their own care by visiting a health facility. This is driven by the goal to improve their health conditions. This starts with registration, wherein patients provide their personal details and capture them on the health facility's database. Thereafter, a consultation takes place during which individuals are required to describe their condition for the facility to provide necessary healthcare services, also captured in the database in image or text form. However, participation is not always guaranteed, as some patients often refuse to get treated by a certain practitioner of a race or culture different from theirs.

Medical personnel are wholly involved and participate in providing healthcare for patients because of their caring attitude, professional obligations and ethical code of conduct. As healthcare providers, they have taken an oath that holds them responsible for patients' health. Therefore, their participation is typically to ensure that they give patients the best medical services. That applies to consultation, diagnoses, treatments and the follow-ups granted to patients. Some health facilities has a strategy that aims to ensure participation from its medical personnel. The facility advises patients to provide feedback on the services received. A health facility uses the information provided, to assess the areas they feel are lacking and improve the processes.

Nurses are usually the first line of assistance in every patient's case. Thus, the nurses must perform preliminary tests before the patient sees the medical doctor for consultation and further medical examination. The results obtained from those tests are habitually pivotal to the care process, as this information forms part of the patients' medical record, thus making it important for treatment. The nurses' observation provides doctors with insight into a patient's case before further administering treatment. Therefore, their participation can be monitored by having the observation report aligned with the doctors' findings.

Lastly, administrative personnel ensure that the health facility runs efficiently and effectively, starting from the registration stage until the patient leaves the facility. Each unit of health facility partakes in patient care by ensuring that patients follow a process as they go through their different stages of acquiring healthcare services. The units also act as a liaison between the medical staff and external associations such as the specialists, laboratories and pharmacies that provide services to the facility. Administrative personnel's participation is measured by outcomes and responses from the patients. In many health facilities, the administration unit is overseen by a facility manager. A part of their duty is to ensure that individuals in the unit are present and participative in the activities of the health facility.

Moments of Translation: Mobilisation

Since health facilities provide services to the patients, there often exist spokespersons. Some of the spokespersons are representatives of the facility, while others are usually patients and relatives of the patients. These representatives included the medical personnel and interpreters. The individuals are either appointed or self-appointed. Different factors drive their representation. These individuals are commonly tasked with the responsibility of enforcing participation from the different units within a health facility. The spokespersons are either internal or external to the health facility. Internally, the medical personnel are delegated to speak on behalf of the facility.

Among these spokespersons are nurses and doctors. As the first line of assistance in a health facility, nurses are often delegated as representatives of the patients. They are professionally responsible for communicating a patient's case to the doctor, using the collected information during observation. These individuals provided preliminary analyses of the patient's condition and presented reports to the doctor. However, this is not always the norm, as some patients preferred to consult directly with the doctor.

Also, doctors act as representatives in patients' care processes. This representation is done through referrals and prescription of medications to patients. Patients who could not be further assisted at a health facility are usually referred to a larger facility. Thus, on behalf of the patient, the representative (spokesperson) of the facility communicates with the referred facility to ensure that the other medical practitioners have a clear view of the patient's condition and history. However, this is sometimes challenging, as relatives of some patients raised privacy issues. Consent is required from patients when their medical information is to be shared. This is within the personal information protection laws of different countries. Health facilities are obligated to abide by these laws.

A health facility, in partnership with pharmacies, enables them to prescribe and dispense medications. The facilities can also give their patients the option to collect medications from their preferred pharmacies. In this instance, doctors represent the patient by requesting the prescribed medication to pharmacies with their network.

In some health facilities, patients are allowed to demonstrate and describe their health condition to the medical doctors without third parties, such as nurses or interpreters. In this sense, patients are self-representative. However, this representation is not always effective due to language barriers, hence the need for interpreters. Language as a challenge is a standing issue in the facility as they serve patients of different ethnicities. This makes it harder to obtain information from patients as the medical caregiver or patient struggles to understand what is being said. As a result, the facility may elect interpreters for cases where language is a problem.

As a representative, the interpreter must articulate the patient's problem as best as possible. This is to enable the health practitioner, to conduct accurate diagnoses towards quality health services. However, language and dialect are not easily translatable to the medium of communication, such English or Spanish. This leaves a dent in the information provided, which distorts patients' big data. The medical practitioner needs to have a clear view of a patient's history. This information would allow them to link what is being said by the interpreter to previous occurrences. Furthermore, it would contribute to the solution a medical practitioner provides for the case, which has been a challenge in many countries for many years.

A Framework for Analysis of Healthcare Big Data

Subjective reasoning was employed to understand the factors that stand out and influence healthcare big data in many environments. Garcia and Quek (1997) argue that subjectivism is an essential part of human interaction as it permits a deeper understanding of actors' perspectives, therefore necessary to remain subjective on the human element. Bashir, Syed and Qureshi (2017) suggest that subjective reasoning helps to provide conceivable answers about social phenomena. Based on the subjective understanding as narratively presented above, five factors, namely data set, medical apparatus, data set integrity, data analysis and health organisations, influence big data in many healthcare facilities. As shown in Figure 10.1, these factors are the primary sources, and, at the same time, influence facts and figures in the gathering, storing, accessing, using and managing of healthcare big data in the organisation.

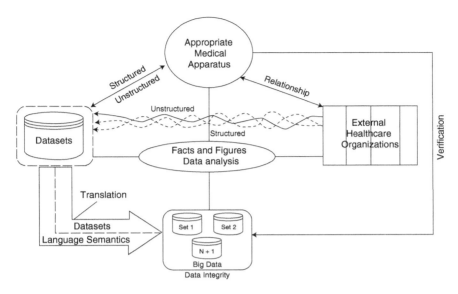

Figure 10.1 Data analysis framework

Data Set

Health facilities accumulate big data, consisting of patients' daily information. This information is obtained during patients' visitations, consultations with medical personnel, diagnoses and medications. A part of this big data comes from within the health facility, and others are gathered from external sources, which can be structured or unstructured data, or both. Also, the data consists of files that store patient information.

Each health facility encounters different challenges while providing healthcare services to patients. Among these challenges are patients refusing to be attended to by medical practitioners of the opposite sex (gender) due to patients' different social and cultural backgrounds, making medical practitioners omit some parts of the treatment process to respect and accommodate individuals' beliefs and traditions. However, these tests are pivotal to the treatment of patients. They assist in providing thorough knowledge of the patients' cases. Furthermore, these tests contribute substantially to a facility's data. Therefore, the exclusion of some parts of healthcare activities negatively affects big data analysis. The medical practitioners are compelled to insert incomplete data in patients' files, further leading to a disjoint in patients' big data due to incompleteness, which can compromise the data set integrity. This brings about the need for translation of the health facility data. Some health facilities ignore the importance of translating the data, making it hard to put certain things into perspectives.

The different cultural backgrounds also affect big data analysis. This puts a health facility in a disadvantage position because of lack of preparedness for analysing big data where patients' cultural backgrounds are involved. Thus, it is essential to customise the analysis (or data analytics tools) to suit the needs of patients, including areas that could have been neglected. This covers broader areas in collecting and analysing data for the benefit of both health practitioners and patients.

Appropriateness of Medical Apparatus

In some instances, many health facilities are classified as small based on the limited health services provided and human capacity. The facility may not be able to conduct certain services due to its limited access to resources, such as a lack of appropriate medical apparatus and personnel. This results in the facility delegating some of its health services to external parties who could perform the tasks. Some of these services included x-rays and other medical tests conducted on patients. This forces patients to visit medical practitioners with whom they are not familiar with, to get that one service or the other.

Delegating health services to external parties affects the facility's big data in different ways, from accuracy to completeness. Even though health facilities interact, there is no guarantee that the information received about a patient and their medication or medical condition is accurate, which could be attributed to limited knowledge, or an understanding of the medical personnel involved. This compromises the facility's data as the x-rays and medical tests may present inaccurate results. Inconsistency within the facility's data is also an issue due to outsourcing some services. In addition, questions about patients' medical condition and history (including the family tree and hereditary diseases) are sometimes omitted intentionally or unconsciously, meaning that the information collected and stored in a patient's medical history may be incomplete; yet the information is used in big data analysis.

Failure to conduct all-inclusive tests impacts the results, as some important issues may be missed and further affects the data set as these results are inconclusive and fail to provide a diagnosis that considers all potential health factors. This causes a disjoint in the patient's big data, resulting in a flawed analysis. Furthermore, combining data from different facilities increases difficulty as it may not coincide. This brings about the issue of verification, as the facility has no means of verifying the data set coming from external sources, which further impacts its integrity. The facility's failure to verify their data means that they must make decisions based on data that is possibly incomplete and inaccurate.

External Healthcare Organisations

Due to many countries' limited resources and infrastructure, some healthcare facilities seek services from different external organisations to support their daily functions. These include external laboratories, specialist facilities within their network and pharmacies that supply medications to the facility. External laboratories are outsourced, to conduct different medical tests that contribute to diagnoses. Once these tests have been conducted, they are sent back to the originator and used to support decision-making regarding a patient's health condition. There are also medical specialists that the facility interacts or consults with. These individuals provide specific expert opinions about a patient's health condition for decision-making, mostly in critical situations. This is done by providing the facility's medical practitioners with deeper insight into individual medical records and challenges. After diagnosis and different medical opinions have been considered, the facility treats patients by prescribing medication. However, some health facilities do not have a pharmacy at its disposal or within its premises, which make collaborate with different medication supplies. The entire processes and channels, as described herewith, contribute various types of data for analysis.

The challenge is that some external laboratories, specialist facilities and pharmacies provide different services, which means that the organisations provide various types of data sets from texts, videos and images in different quantities to the same health facility. The data set is either structured or unstructured. This brings about two challenges, namely data dispersion difficulties and data merging. These entities are constantly divided due to their different functions. Consequently, the data relating to the various units is dispersed when it arrives at the facility, which is a challenge because it affects the continuity of patient information. Furthermore, it becomes even more difficult to merge the facility's data with these external entities.

Language Semantics

Many health facilities take the initiative to employ the service of interpreters during patients' consultations. This measure is intended to curb the language barrier between the medical practitioners and the patients. The interpreters are required to better understand communication between the medical practitioners and the patients who need interpretation. However, despite engaging interpreters, challenges still occur in some instances. The persistence of some of the challenges is often caused by semantics and differences in dialects, such as the case Africa where there are many dialects in a language. The implications of this include miscommunication between the interpreter and the medical practitioners, noting inaccurate information due to an incorrect translation of patients' interactions, which questions the accuracy of data collected during consultations. Furthermore, collecting inaccurate data negatively impacts the analysis, irrespective of the analysis tool that is employed. The results will be flawed as they will be presenting inaccurate conclusions on the patients' cases; hence, many patients have been medical victims over the years.

From another perspective, the engagement of an interpreter by some health facilities during medical consultations between patients and practitioners induces a different type of challenge. One such challenge is privacy. Through policies, many countries insist on the protection of patients' privacy. The involvement of an interpreter means that the patient had to divulge personal information in the presence of a third party. Additionally, there are no non-disclosure agreements lawfully binding the interpreter not to share what was said during the consultation, which puts patients at the risk of having their information shared unfairly or maliciously.

In response to self-protection, some patients do not fully disclose their problems in the presence of a third party. Consequently, this may have serious implications and risks for the patient for not providing complete information about their health condition. Patients are provided with care according to the information they provide, where full diagnoses are not carried out. Even when diagnoses are carried out, it is based on the available information. Furthermore, the information collected during these consultations form part of a facility's big data, which undergoes the analysis. Therefore, patients' failure to disclose their problems holds consequences such as an incomplete data set. In addition to that, the integrity of the data set may be compromised, as the results from the analysis may not reflect patients' real issues.

Data Set Integrity

Healthcare facilities collect a substantial amount of data daily. The data is collected from both internal and external (other organisations) sources. The external organisations included the facilities that provide medical apparatus and the external healthcare organisations that support their daily functions. However, some challenges affect the data accumulated by a facility. These challenges include incomplete data sets, a challenge because they affect the integrity of the data relied upon for patient care.

Moreover, a health facility's data set integrity is sometimes compromised, as revealed in this chapter. This challenge is commonly created during the translation of the communication between the patients and medical practitioners and is enacted due to a lack of verification. Also, a facility can fail to verify data from external sources because they lack the resources to do so. Negatively, this affects the data as the analysis is conducted on inaccurate and incomplete data sets, meaning that some results that influenced some decisions are based on a flawed outcome of the analysis.

Many facilities depend on analysts to translate patients' data to put them into perspectives. However, a health facility encounters challenges in this regard. Currently, there seem to be no proven method for translating data, for healthcare services. From a language perspective, many health facilities cannot guarantee accurate translation from different languages to English and vice versa. From the aspect of data, some health facilities cannot make sense of the copious number of data sets encountered by different units or operations due to the lack of data analysis tools or means of managing the data set. These factors challenge the facility's data set integrity. Furthermore, they compromise patients' health as decisions are made based on the data sets that lack integrity.

Summary

This chapter can benefit many health facilities, professional bodies in many countries and the healthcare sector in general in that the framework (Figure 10.1) helps to reveal and unpack the factors that influence health services from patients' big data viewpoint. Based on these factors, policies and regulations can be formulated and promulgated in practice. In practice, medical practitioners can be better equipped with a guide on using and managing patients' big data towards improved services. Applying the framework would make health practitioners knowledgeable on the issues that hinder big data analysis in providing healthcare services. Health practitioners would also be able to better understand patients' big data by tracing the various sources, types and volumes for operational and strategic activities. Methodologically, although ANT has been used in many IS and Health studies, the challenges of language and culture in providing and receiving healthcare services as revealed in this chapter are not peculiar to any country, which would have been difficult to address without the use of ANT.

References

Afarikumah, E., & Kwankam, S. Y. (2013). Deploying actor-network theory to analyse telemedicine implementation in Ghana. *Science*, *1*(2), 77–84. https://doi.org/10.11648/j.sjph.20130102.15.

Archenaa, J., & Anita, E. M. (2015). A survey of big data analytics in healthcare and government. *Procedia Computer Science*, *50*, 408–413. https://doi.org/10.1016/j.procs.2015.04.021.

Arnaboldi, M., & Spiller, N. (2011). Actor-network theory and stakeholder collaboration: The case of Cultural Districts. *Tourism Management*, *32*(3), 641–654. https://doi.org/10.1016/j.tourman.2010.05.016.

Bashir, S., Syed, S., & Qureshi, J. A. (2017). Philosophical and methodological aspects of a mixed-methods research: A review of the academic literature. *Journal of Independent Studies and Research*, *15*(1), 32–50.

Bates, D. W., Saria, S., Ohno-Machado, L., Shah, A., & Escobar, G. (2014). Big data in health care: Using analytics to identify and manage high-risk and high-cost patients. *Health Affairs*, *33*(7), 1123–1131. https://doi.org/10.1377/hlthaff.2014.0041.

Bleakley, A. (2012). The proof is in the pudding: Putting actor-network-theory to work in medical education. *Medical Teacher*, 34(6), 462–467. https://doi.org/10.3109/0142159X.2012.671977.

Callon, M. (1986). Some elements of a sociology of translation: Domestication of the scallops and the fishermen of St Brieuc Bay. In: Law, J. (ed.), *Power, action and belief: A new sociology of knowledge?* (pp. 196–233). London: Routledge and Kegan Paul.

Chandarana, P., & Vijayalakshmi, M. (2014, April). Big data analytics frameworks. In: *2014 international conference on circuits, systems, communication and information* technology applications *(CSCITA)* (pp. 430–434), April 4–5, Mumbai, India. IEEE. https://doi.org/10.1109/CSCITA.2014.6839299.

Chawla, N. V., & Davis, D. A. (2013). Bringing big data to personalized healthcare: A patient-centred framework. *Journal of General Internal Medicine, 28*(3), 660–665. https://doi.org/10.1007/s11606-013-2455-8.

Cho, S., Mathiassen, L., & Nilsson, A. (2008). Contextual dynamics during health information systems implementation: an event-based actor-network approach. *European Journal of Information Systems, 17*(6), 614–630.

Dery, K., Hall, R., Wailes, N., & Wiblen, S. (2013). Lost in translation? An actor-network approach to HRIS implementation. *The Journal of Strategic Information Systems, 22*(3), 225–237. https://doi.org/10.1016/j.jsis.2013.03.002.

Esposito, K., Maiorino, M. I., Bellastella, G., Chiodini, P., Panagiotakos, D., & Giugliano, D. (2015). A journey into a Mediterranean diet and type 2 diabetes: a systematic review with meta-analyses. *BMJ open, 5*(8), 1–10.

Ganjir, V., Sarkar, B. K., & Kumar, R. R. (2016). Big data analytics for healthcare. *International Journal of Research in Engineering, Technology and Science, 6*, 1–6.

Garcia, L., & Quek, F. (1997). Qualitative research in information systems: Time to be subjective? In: Lee, A. S., Liebenau, J., & DeGross, J. I. (eds), *Information systems and qualitative research. IFIP—The International Federation for Information Processing* (pp. 444–465). Boston, MA: Springer. https://doi.org/10.1007/978-0-387-35309-8_22.

Giambrone, G. P., Hemmings, H. C., Sturm, M., & Fleischut, P. M. (2015). Information technology innovation: The power and perils of big data. *British Journal of Anaesthesia, 115*(3), 339–342. https://doi.org/10.1093/bja/aev154.

He, W., Nazir, S., & Hussain, Z. (2021). Big data insights and comprehensions in industrial healthcare: an overview. *Mobile Information Systems, 2021.* https://doi.org/10.1155/2021/6628739.

Heeks, R., & Stanforth, C. (2015). Technological change in developing countries: Opening the black box of process using actor–network theory. *Development Studies Research, 2*(1), 33–50. https://doi.org/10.1080/21665095.2015.1026610.

Hilbert, M. (2016). Big data for development: A review of promises and challenges. *Development Policy Review, 34*(1), 135–174. https://doi.org/10.1111/dpr.12142.

Jagadish, H. V., Gehrke, J., Labrinidis, A., Papakonstantinou, Y., Patel, J. M., Ramakrishnan, R., & Shahabi, C. (2014). Big data and its technical challenges. *Communications of the ACM, 57*(7), 86–94. https://doi.org/10.1145/2611567.

Kambatla, K., Kollias, G., Kumar, V., & Grama, A. (2014). Trends in big data analytics. *Journal of Parallel and Distributed Computing, 74*(7), 2561–2573. https://doi.org/10.1016/j.jpdc.2014.01.003.

Kankanhalli, A., Hahn, J., Tan, S., & Gao, G. (2016). Big data and analytics in healthcare: Introduction to the special section. *Information Systems Frontiers, 18*(2), 233–235. https://doi.org/10.1007/s10796-016-9641-2.

Kuo, M. H., Sahama, T., Kushniruk, A. W., Borycki, E. M., & Grunwell, D. K. (2014). Health big data analytics: Current perspectives, challenges and potential solutions. *International Journal of Big Data Intelligence, 1*(1–2), 114–126.

Labrinidis, A., & Jagadish, H. V. (2012). Challenges and opportunities with big data. *Proceedings of the VLDB Endowment, 5*(12), 2032–2033. https://doi.org/10.14778/2367502.2367572.

Latour, B. (2005). *Reassembling the social: An introduction to actor-network-theory.* Oxford: Oxford University Press.

Lee, H., Harindranath, G., Oh, S., & Kim, D. J. (2015). Provision of mobile banking services from an actor–network perspective: Implications for convergence and standardisation. *Technological Forecasting and Social Change*, *90*, 551–561. https://doi.org/10.1016/j.techfore.2014.02.007.

Leon, N., Schneider, H., & Daviaud, E. (2012). Applying a framework for assessing the health system challenges to scaling up mHealth in South Africa. *BMC Medical Informatics and Decision Making*, *12*(1), 1–12. https://doi.org/10.1186/1472-6947-12-123.

Miah, S. J., Camilleri, E., & Vu, H. Q. (2022). Big Data in healthcare research: A survey study. *Journal of Computer Information Systems*, *62*(3), 480–492. https://doi.org/10.1080/08874417.2020.1858727

Moore, K. D., Eyestone, K., & Coddington, D. C. (2013). The big deal about big data. *Healthcare Financial Management*, *67*(8), 60–68.

Mphatswe, W., Mate, K. S., Bennett, B., Ngidi, H., Reddy, J., Barker, P. M., & Rollins, N. (2012). Improving public health information: A data quality intervention in KwaZulu-Natal, South Africa. *Bulletin of the World Health Organization*, *90*, 176–182.

Nepal, S., Ranjan, R., & Choo, K. K. R. (2015). Trustworthy processing of healthcare big data in hybrid clouds. *IEEE Cloud Computing*, *2*(2), 78–84. https://doi.org/10.1109/MCC.2015.36.

Ojha, M., & Mathur, K. (2016, March). Proposed application of big data analytics in healthcare at Maharaja Yeshwantrao Hospital. In: *2016 3rd MEC international conference on big data and smart city (ICBDSC)* (pp. 1–7), 15–16 March, Muscat, Oman. IEEE. https://doi.org/10.1109/ICBDSC.2016.7460340.

Panahiazar, M., Taslimitehrani, V., Jadhav, A., & Pathak, J. (2014). Empowering personalized medicine with big data and semantic web technology: Promises, challenges, and use cases. In: *2014 IEEE international conference on big data (Big Data)* (pp. 790–795), 27–30 October, Washington, DC, USA. IEEE. https://doi.org/10.1109/BigData.2014.7004307.

Robert, G., Greenhalgh, T., MacFarlane, F., & Peacock, R. (2010). Adopting and assimilating new non-pharmaceutical technologies into health care: a systematic review. *Journal of health services research & policy*, *15*(4), 243–250.

Roy, V., Shukla, P. K., Gupta, A. K., Goel, V., Shukla, P. K., & Shukla, S. (2021). Taxonomy on EEG artifacts removal methods, issues, and healthcare applications. *Journal of Organizational and End User Computing (JOEUC)*, *33*(1), 19–46. https://doi.org/10.4018/JOEUC.2021010102

Sacristán, J. A., & Dilla, T. (2015). No big data without small data: Learning health care systems begin and end with the individual patient. *Journal of Evaluation in Clinical Practice*, *21*(6), 1014–1017. https://doi.org/10.1111/jep.12350.

Sahay, S. (2016). Are we building a better world with ICTs? Empirically examining this question in the domain of public health in India. *Information Technology for Development*, *22*(1), 168–176.

Scotland, J. (2012). Exploring the philosophical underpinnings of research: Relating ontology and epistemology to the methodology and methods of the scientific, interpretive, and critical research paradigms. *English Language Teaching*, *5*(9), 9–16.

Shah, T., Rabhi, F., & Ray, P. (2015). Investigating an ontology-based approach for Big Data analysis of inter-dependent medical and oral health conditions. *Cluster Computing*, *18*(1), 351–367. https://doi.org/10.1007/s10586-014-0406-8.

Sreedevi, A. G., Harshitha, T. N., Sugumaran, V., & Shankar, P. (2022). Application of cognitive computing in healthcare, cybersecurity, big data and IoT: A literature review. *Information Processing & Management, 59*(2), 102888. https://doi.org/10.1016/j.ipm.2022.102888.

Stanforth, C. (2006). Using actor-network theory to implementation in developing countries. *Information Technologies and International Development, 3*(3), 35–60.

Teles, A., & Joia, L.A. (2011). Assessment of digital inclusion via the actor-network theory: The case of the Brazilian municipality of Pirai. *Telematics and Informatics, 28*(3), 191–203. https://doi.org/10.1016/j.tele.2010.09.003.

Tresp, V., Overhage, J. M., Bundschus, M., Rabizadeh, S., Fasching, P. A., & Yu, S. (2016). Going digital: A survey on digitalization and large-scale data analytics in healthcare. *Proceedings of the IEEE, 104*(11), 2180–2206. https://doi.org/10.1109/JPROC.2016.2615052.

Van Biesen, W., Van Der Straeten, C., Sterckx, S., Steen, J., Diependaele, L., & Decruyenaere, J. (2021). The concept of justifiable healthcare and how big data can help us to achieve it. *BMC Medical Informatics and Decision Making, 21*(1), 1–17. https://doi.org/10.1186/s12911-021-01444-7.

Velpula, P., & Pamula, R. (2022). CEECP: CT-based enhanced e-clinical pathways in terms of processing time to enable big data analytics in healthcare along with cloud computing. *Computers & Industrial Engineering, 168*, 108037. https://doi.org/10.1016/j.cie.2022.108037.

Walsham, G. (1997). Actor-network theory and IS research: Current status and prospects. In: Lee, A. S., Liebenau, J., & DeGross, J. I. (eds), *Information systems and qualitative research. IFIP—The International Federation for Information Processing*. Boston, MA: Springer. https://doi.org/10.1007/978-0-387-35309-8_23.

Wyber, R., Vaillancourt, S., Perry, W., Mannava, P., Folaranmi, T., & Celi, L. A. (2015). Big data in global health: Improving health in low-and middle-income countries. *Bulletin of the World Health Organization, 93*(3), 203–208. https://doi.org/10.2471/BLT.14.139022.

11 The Implementation of Big Data Analytics for Healthcare Services

Introduction

Big data has attracted attention in all sectors, from finance to manufacturing, including governmental administrations (Cao, 2017). As with other sectors of the economy, large amounts of data from different sources (such as diagnoses and medications) and at high speed are routinely generated by healthcare facilities (hospitals and clinics) across the world. Chapter 1 provides a comprehensive introduction to the four most popular analytics: descriptive, diagnostic, predictive and prescriptive. The subsequent chapters provide a good account of the analytics tools' usefulness, including the factors that influence their use, and management for efficiency purposes. Complementary to Chapter 1, big data is described and defined as data sets with unprecedented high volume, variety and velocity characteristics that cannot be easily stored, captured, managed and analysed effectively with traditional database software and methods (Ridge, Johnston & Donovan, 2015).

Thus, by implementing big data analytics (BDA) tools (applications), organisations and healthcare facilities can derive values and insights from these voluminous and richly sourced data sets (Mehta & Pandit, 2018). The concept of BDA refers to the use of advanced analytic techniques to find and discover patterns from structured and unstructured vast data sets and associate meanings with them. Bumblauskas, Nold, Bumblauskas and Igou (2017) suggest that BDA can convert data sets into information, knowledge and ultimately action through analysis. Also, the BDA concept presents health facilities with the opportunities to analyse the increasing amount of data sets in their repositories, thereby enhancing its operations and decision-making processes, which can ultimately improve the quality of service delivery. Some of the tools that can be used are Hadoop, HDFS, MapReduce, Cassandra and PIG, to mention a few (Zakir, Seymour & Berg, 2015).

Diagnostic health analytics helps to answer why certain things happened to better understand influencing factors and operational processes, such as response time and tracking service provided (Khalifa & Zabani, 2016). Descriptive analytics helps to determine, examine and explain health-related conditions for a period. In healthcare, health facilities, particularly large hospitals, use patient data to predict epidemics and design new treatments for diseases (Sedkaoui, 2018). Thus, predictive analytics supplies organisations with future insights into health-related issues for improved decision-making. Prescriptive analytics is used to determine the course of action after processing information (Zetino & Mendoza, 2019). However, prescriptive analytics does not only predict but also provides recommendations regarding healthcare actions.

However, despite the huge and available patients' big data, some health facilities do not know how and where to begin, what type of analytics to employ to nurture the different kinds of health-related issues and what the different types of analytics mean in healthcare. Also, the nature of the sources of patients' big data can be both enabling and constraining in using analytics for health purposes (Schroeder, 2014). Attributably, the process involves revealing hidden patterns and secret correlations of huge, various health-related data (Sagiroglu & Sinanc, 2013).

The implementation of the BDA concept is confronted by various factors from both technical and non-technical perspectives. Some of the challenges are compounded by the need to integrate legacy (old and static) systems with more dynamic systems. Funding is another challenge that is encountered in attempts to implement the concept in many health facilities. Evidently, many healthcare facilities or organisations rely on donations from governments and large enterprises ((Alawode & Adewole, 2021). In some instances, the donations are either unguaranteed or delayed, disrupting plans and affecting support, sustainability and continuity (Dos Santos et al., 2021).

Also, implementing information technology (IT) solutions can be prohibitive because of the various stages and socio-technical (human and non-human) involvement. Kim, Trimi and Chung (2014) explained that due to the expensive nature of some IT solutions such as big data, implementation, support and maintenance are always threatened. Another major challenge is the scarce resource (technical expertise) in the areas of BDA, which can be attributed to the newness or emerging nature of the concept, particularly in the health environment. Big data presents challenges to health facilities because of its complex nature that require computing solutions (such as analytics and integration with other systems), which many health practitioners are not very familiar with.

Furthermore, implementing BDA tools requires stable and reliable IT infrastructure (Al Nuaimi, Al Neyadi, Mohamed & Al-Jaroodi, 2015), including components like storage, networks, databases and telecommunications capabilities (Kache & Seuring, 2017). Many health facilities worldwide, particularly the large-sized, have implemented BDA in their environments at various scales and purposes, with varying degrees of success. The general intention of the health facilities for implementing BDA tools is to improve services in the healthcare sector. While there are benefits to implementing BDA tools, some challenges of privacy and confidentiality persist (Hardy & Maurushat, 2017).

This chapter presents criteria that can guide BDA implementation by all sizes of healthcare facilities within the health sector. The criteria is based on two objectives: (1) determined how big data within the health sector is analysed; and (2) examined the factors that facilitate the implementation of BDA.

The remainder of this chapter is structured into six main sections: the first section introduces the chapter, including the focus. The second section contextualises the problem that the chapter addresses. In the third section, a review of literature is presented, covering BDA and BDA implementation in healthcare facilities. The factors that influence the implementation of BDA are holistically examined in the section that follows, and based on which, criteria are developed, presented and discussed in the fifth section. Thereafter, a summary of the chapter is presented.

Contextualising the Problem

Many healthcare organisations (facilities) have benefited from implementing BDA tools in various ways. Adrian, Abdullah, Atan and Jusoh (2018) discussed how some organisations incorporated their strategic planning to enhance organisational performance by shifting their decision-making processes to be data-driven. Also, this has a positive impact on the capabilities of IT solutions by making them sharable and integrated. However, while many healthcare facilities continue to reap the benefits of implementing BDA tools, some organisations have not been successful, particularly those in the rural areas of many countries.

Some of the challenges relate to not clearly understanding the benefits and implications of BDA implementation. However, there is a lack of expertise in BDA that leads to the problem of know-how in the selection and application of BDA to improve service delivery (Cervone, 2016; Nyikana & Iyamu, 2021). Also, the lack of know-how affects BDA implementation. Know-how is critical for innovation and exploration of traditional platforms, including IT solutions that enable and support the use of BDA, to generate meaningful information for better decision-making.

Big Data Analytics and Big Data Analytics Implementation in Healthcare

A literature review was conducted, focusing on the core aspects of the chapter, which are healthcare, healthcare BDA and implementation of BDA.

Health Services and Big Data Analytics

There is a popular view from studies that BDA can fill the growing need of healthcare practitioners (Galetsi, Katsaliaki & Kumar, 2020; Wang & Hajli, 2017). Increasingly, healthcare data continue to surge from medical practices in practitioners' attempts to improve the quality and efficiency of healthcare delivery. Diagnostic analytics can be used to diagnose a patient with a particular illness or injury based on the symptoms they are experiencing (Delen & Zolbanin, 2018). Predictive analytics aims to explain what is likely to happen in the future, which is fundamental when assessing a patient's health condition. According to Cao and Duan (2017), predictive analytics uses forecasting and predictive modelling to predict future happenings. Soltanpoor and Sellis (2016) highlight the main elements of prescriptive analytics as optimisation, simulation and evaluation methods.

Significantly, one of the challenges in leveraging BDA with healthcare services is protecting patients' personal information (Patel & Patel, 2016). Another challenge as highlighted by Kuo et al. (2014) is the integration of unstructured data. Wang, Kung, Wang and Cegielski (2018) explain that healthcare practices can be facilitated by implementing BDA. However, the challenges persist, which could be attributed to the fragmented knowledge about big data implementation in healthcare (Raghupathi & Raghupathi, 2014; Wang, Kung & Byrd, 2018).

For a health organisation to gain value from data sets, the implementation of BDA becomes a necessity. BDA are tools (applications) used to derive useful information, patterns or conclusions from big data in making purposeful and quality decisions (Adrian, Abdullah, Atan & Jusoh, 2017). Gandomi and Haider (2015) explain analytics as methods employed to examine and obtain intellect from big data. Therefore, big data analysis may be seen as a sub-process of the general process of 'insight extraction' from big data. Furthermore, BDA can empower organisations with opportunities from the perspectives of operations and effective utilisation for useful information, business processes and enhancement of analytical capabilities to derive deeper meaningful insights (Mohanty, Jagadeesh & Srivatsa, 2013).

The concept can manage volumes of incongruent data sets to permit organisations to implement BDA (Wang & Hajli, 2017). An indication that BDA has competence for improvement is shown through business value, including rapid insights, which enable the business to convert raw data into useful information. According to Batarseh, Yang and Deng (2017), BDA aims to return the intellect and attentive version of big data sets, deliver rapid insights into information and assist with conception and decision-making. The process of analysing big data employs certain methods, to gain deeper insights into the different categories of data sets: text, audio, video, and images. Hence, different BDA tools are used to retrieve insights from different kinds of data (Gandomi & Haider, 2015).

The concept of BDA is employed by healthcare facilities in various areas, such as health education, transport and logistics, to maintain patterns, reveal trends and ultimately improve services (Raghupathi & Raghupathi, 2014). This means that the concept is crucial in decision-making (Batarseh, Yang & Deng, 2017). Despite the attractive opportunities, there exist several challenges in the implementation in the health sector. According to Cheng, Zhang and Qin (2016), BDA has challenges when large-scale data needs to be analysed in a short period and with a sensibly decent performance. In addition, the rapidity of generating big data leads to a fast change of content because the content in big data changes with time, just like BDA targets (Delen & Ram, 2018; Zetino & Mendoza, 2019). BDA challenges also include data inconsistency and partial, finished, scalable, timeless and safe data (Khan et al., 2014).

In the practice of BDA, different enterprises can derive insights from their businesses to improve the performance of services with data-driven decision-making (Lee, Kweon, Kim, & Chai, 2017). This has, over the years, encouraged many enterprises to employ data-driven decision-making, which has an outcome of advancements in big data profits (Adrian, Abdullah, Atan & Jusoh, 2018). Government facilities, including healthcare, can be significantly enhanced by implementing BDA (Joseph & Johnson, 2013). Many health facilities in some countries encounter challenges regarding the factors that could influence BDA implementation in their environments.

Despite the benefits of BDA, some challenges affect the implementation within the healthcare sector. Kim, Trimi and Chung (2014) explained big data as original challenges relating to difficulty, safety and threats to confidentiality, including a necessity for modern technology equipment and human services. This information supports real-time decision-making for the health sector. Working on extracting meaningful information from big data that is generated quickly and straightforwardly is challenging. Therefore, analytics has developed to be inextricably vital to comprehend the full value of big data to advance organisations' performance and service delivery (Zakir, Seymour & Berg, 2015). According to Berg (2015), big data presents challenges to organisations because data sets are too vast, growing at a very high rate that makes it very hard to manage and difficult to analyse using traditional methods and tools.

Implementation of Big Data Analytics

Implementing BDA contains technical and non-technical factors such as procedure, error handling, competencies, capitals and big data transformation into valuable and meaningful information. 'The model is developed based on three dimensions, performing data strategy (organisation), collaborative knowledge worker (people), and executing data analytics (technology)' (Adrian, Abdullah, Atan & Jusoh, 2018, p. 23). The ability to quickly process big data and implement analytics enables an organisation to make well-informed choices in a short period compared to the competitors (Comuzzi & Patel, 2016). Furthermore, to improve service excellence, an organisation should analyse big data effectively to answer new challenges through the information retrieved from those voluminous data sets (Archenaa & Anita, 2015).

The BDA implementation can benefit long-term strategic planning to support the organisation's growth, leading to enhanced performance (Adrian, Abdullah, Atan & Jusoh, 2017). The factors that can influence BDA implementation in organisations include technology capabilities, human capability, analytics capability, organisation capability and information quality (Adrian, Abdullah, Atan & Jusoh, 2018). Archenaa and Anita (2015) discussed the advantages of implementing BDA in government enterprises, including the health sector, to improve the quality of service delivery to citizens. The Seoul government analysed big data generated from health, transport and residence and produced meaningful information by recognising the patterns and strains from the data sets, which led to improvement of services (Lim, Kim & Maglio, 2018).

Technology capability in BDA refers to IT structures and platforms that could be used to analyse data to derive insights from big data for decision-making (Adrian, Abdullah, Atan & Jusoh, 2017). Organisation capability refers to the organisation's readiness with resources to pursue BDA implementation (Chen, Preston & Swink, 2015). Human competencies are the technical IT skills and the managerial skills to coordinate the activities related to methods used to analyse big data. Information quality is the capability to make speedy decisions from predictive analytics (Adrian, Abdullah, Atan & Jusoh, 2018).

In as much as the application of BDA has benefits, it is faced with many challenges. A study by Whitelock (2018) identified some factors as culture and skillset that manifest into the implementation of analytics tools. According to Agnihotri, Mojarad, Lewkow & Essa (2016), many analytics tools are not easy to use due to the knowledge required to understand the technical details of underlying algorithms. This type of challenge begins from the implementation stage. Delen and Ram (2018) argue that analytic skills required to convert data into actionable insight are currently hard to find in the market. According to Delen and Ram (2018), many education institutions are introducing data analytics programmes to address the analytics skills gap. However, this is not specific to the healthcare environment, which is very unique. Another challenge BDA analytics faces is security and privacy concerns (Delen & Ram, 2018). Zetino and Mendoza (2019) suggest a need to protect the rights to privacy and security of individuals while accessing data for algorithms.

Big Data Analytics for Healthcare Services

This chapter aims to develop criteria that can guide the implementation of BDA health facilities. Before doing so, it is critical and essential to understand the factors that can influence the implementation of the concept within health facilities. Thus, the aim is split into two objectives. First, to gain a deeper understanding of how big data is analysed within health facilities. Second, to examine and gain better insights into the factors that can facilitate BDA implementation in healthcare environments.

How Big Data Is Analysed within Healthcare Facilities

Big data consists of a large volume of data sets. As established in the previous chapters, big data is not only all about size but also includes velocity, variety and volume often referred to as 3Vs (Miah, Camilleri & Vu, 2022). Volume: the amount or size of data sets used and managed by organisations. Variety: the different types of data sets, including images, videos, text, from various sources. Velocity: this is the frequency at which the data sets are accessed or travel between different sources. In healthcare, there are differences in some practitioners' understanding of big data. Thus, some health workers do not know whether big data exists, in their place of work. This may be caused by not having the same understanding of the big data concept.

Many health practitioners, especially those at the middle management and lower levels, see big data from an only one size perspective; it has to be huge, while some medical staff believe that for it to be named 'big data', it has to meet the characteristics, which are the 3Vs. One of the implications of the difference in understanding the concept is that data sets are inappropriately recognised, i.e. some data sets may be discarded or put in wrong categories or grouping. This affects coordinated effort, ultimately distorting big data analysis. Consequently, the meaning and usefulness of the big data are twisted and become of less value, thus inappropriately shaping services.

For big data to be useful or add value to a healthcare facility, it needs to be analysed. The method of analysing big data is through the use of analytics tools. There are different types of analytics, as explained in Chapter 1 and subsequent chapters of this book. This book focuses on the four most commonly used analytics: diagnostic, descriptive, predictive and prescriptive. Diagnostic analytics focuses on the present and perforates into the why certain things happened, which helps to diagnose events and circumstances. Descriptive analytics tools are used to describe the past 'what has happened?' by analysing data sets. Predictive analytics tools are used to analyse data sets to predict the future. Prescriptive tools go beyond the description of what has happened and make some recommendations going into the future. However, without a proper grouping of the data sets, these analytics are highly likely to produce results that may not add value to service delivery but instead add complexity to the functions and services of health practitioners. Through analysis, irregularities are corrected, situations are enhanced and processes are improved.

Currently, in many countries' healthcare facilities, not much analytics occurs because of two main factors. First, it is because the concept of big data in healthcare is still new. Second, because of the newness of the concept, understanding among health practitioners is generally at a low rate. According to Batarseh, Yang and Deng (2017), some enterprises are beginning to understand the benefits of BDA and how it can improve service delivery, and enhance operations and well-informed decision-making. Many health professionals cannot differentiate between data and big data.

For now, IT units drive the concept in many health facilities, which is another challenge to analysing patients' big data from three straining perspectives. First, there is a lack of, or limited buy-in from the healthcare practitioners. Second, there is bound to be restricted access to the data sets owing to the lack of understanding. Third, the IT specialists have a limited understanding of the health operations, activities and diagnoses; therefore, they have no full knowledge of what is supposed to be analysed. Thus, the analytics may be limited to the IT aspect of healthcare big data, which has neither addressed the challenges identified nor contributed to improving service delivery.

Furthermore, IT units are usually divided into subunits or teams, focusing on different aspects in enabling and supporting the implementation of BDA for healthcare purposes, meaning that these smaller groupings also have distinctive deliverables. For example, exclusively, a group applies BDA to provide service delivery to its system's users. The objective entails analysing log calls or incidences that were reported. This is different from analysing diagnoses and medical history, which apparently do not benefit from analysing 'logged calls'.

The Factors that Can Facilitate the Implementation of Big Data Analytics

Primarily, the implementation of BDA for healthcare purposes is based on three vital components: organisation (facility), people and technology (IT solutions). Berry (2021) explains how Healthcare is increasingly embracing and implementing big data, to improve performance and efficiency. The organisation formulates a data strategy. People include specialists from both health and IT units that exercise their expertise in big data and BDA. The technology enables both big data and BDA, which consists of the platforms and integrated (middleware) solutions. Adrian, Abdullah, Atan and Jusoh (2018) described BDA implementation as procedures of handling BDA capabilities, capitals, and transforming big data valuable information.

Different factors contribute to the successful implementation of BDA. Some of these factors are knowledgeability (Van Biesen et al., 2021), skills, experience, management support and access to data sets (He, Nazir & Hussain, 2021). Understanding the BDA concept is one of the most crucial parts in that the specialists need to know how to select the analytics tools, and how to implement the tools and other IT solutions associated with them, including the techniques used.

When it comes to experience, the personnel that implements BDA must have a background in working with various databases and using analytics tools. This includes managers who provide technical and management support for implementing and practising the concepts in their environments. Also, the managers need to understand the techniques used for BDA in their environments to increase the usefulness and gain appropriate benefits.

The success of BDA implementation is measured by its benefits to a healthcare facility, by helping to make better decisions and improve service delivery. For a health facility to reduce complexity and reap the benefits of BDA, it must conduct a readiness assessment that will help identify potential risks, technology needs and necessary human capital, which ultimately are the main influencing factors. Thus, the facility must invest in these factors to increase the chances of implementation success, return on investment and most importantly improve the quality of services provided to the community.

Criteria for the Implementation of Big Data Analytics

From examining the objectives discussed above, four criteria are the most crucial for BDA implementation. These are Knowledge, Process, Differentiation and Skillset.

Subject Knowledge

Knowledge is explained as facts, information and skills. It can be gained by an individual's experience of being educated about the subject. In many health facilities worldwide, the understanding is different in knowledge about big data and BDA because the concepts are generally new in the healthcare environment. Also, many healthcare practitioners are embracing the concepts but not yet where they can take full ownership and accountability. The challenge is that for a healthcare facility to implement BDA, it needs to have good understanding of what it entails, including the factors that influence it, from selection to management and support (Nyikana & Iyamu, 2022).

Patients' big data must be analysed to make absolute sense to the users. Only then the users can gain better insights into its usefulness, value and necessity. What is termed full (or good) understanding is deep insights, including the attributes, factors of influence, intended use and potential benefits of big data. In the health sector, BDA is very critical in delivering quality service to patients. The success of BDA implementation is measured by gaining its benefits. The benefits of BDA include being able to make data-driven decisions from the analysis using analytics tools. Additionally, the benefits cover being able to predict the future about diseases or a patient's medical condition.

Process Leading to Action

Process constitutes a series of planned actions taken to achieve desired results. For uniformity and consistency, procedures must be followed. Procedures help keep orderliness and shape understandings towards mutual direction based on which common techniques are applied, leading to the selection and practice of the BDA. Also, process helps to understand the flow of events from one stage to the other. This can manifest in the categorisation of big data for analysis purposes. Without process, analysis can be skewed and consequently affect the results, which can be detrimental to patient's health.

Process must be followed in selecting, implementing and using BDA to ensure that the analytics tools are integrated with other systems, such as finance, for administrative purposes. A health facility can have a better understanding of patients' growing size, response time and services through integrated systems by identifying relationships among various variables in the data set. The analytics tools for analysing big data in healthcare help in many ways that were ordinarily complex, such as to enhance drug development and find the most appropriate patients for clinical trials. However, prescriptive analytics tools are complex, which slows or affects their deployment in the healthcare sector.

Differentiation between Big Data and Data

Differentiation is being able to distinguish between two or more subjects or concepts. It is crucial, to differentiate between big data and small data, and between big data and data sets. If the organisation does not understand the difference, an analysis might also be skewed and the implications can negatively affect services. Importantly, this is because data and big data are analysed differently, using different tools, especially when analytics such as predictive and prescriptive are required. Predictive analytics is about the subsequent step in data reduction. It helps to set realistic long- and short-term goals and objectives. Through the goals and objectives, effective planning and restraining expectations in the processes and activities relating to health services are made. Substantially, in prescriptive analytics, health-related activities and events can be made into actions through metrics.

Data is only about volume. The high quantity of data generated by an organisation and stored in its databases does not make it big data. For 'data' to be categorised as big data, it has to meet the basic 3Vs at least: volume, variety and velocity. This takes us back to the knowledge of big data being a critical factor in BDA implementation. Understanding what makes data to be called big data entails having a full understanding of the characteristics of big data, called the 3Vs: volume, velocity and variety. This can help an organisation, in differentiating between small data and big data.

Required BDA Skillset

Skillset is an individual's range of abilities. It is not easy to find highly skilled people that focus on the concept of BDA. The newness of the concepts makes it necessary to find healthcare practitioners skilled in big data and BDA. The skillset needed in BDA implementation includes knowledge and experience about the concept. The skills are crucial because it requires specialisation and experience to implement any of the BDA tools. In addition, the specialists must make sense of the results produced using the analytics tools to gain the desired value of the health facility.

BDA skills are highly practical on strategic and operational bases, primarily because big data functions are unique and require specialised skills. For example, the skill enables the personnel to detect and analyse actionable data from hidden trends and patterns. Also, the skill necessitates versatility because there are components of IT and health from the perspectives of data processes. Thus, the skilled persons can operationalise analytics tools and formulate strategic analytics for healthcare service delivery.

The Criteria Model

As discussed above, four factors, Knowledge; Process; Differentiation and Skillset, influence the implementation and practice of BDA tools within healthcare facilities. The criteria mean expressing clear and transparent requirements based on which the services provided are assessed against the BDA used in the process. The clarity of evaluation helps determine the ease and readiness with which stakeholders can select, use and manage BDA for health-related strategic and operational activities, to improve quality services.

The criteria that can be used in the practice of the analytics tools are depicted in Table 11.1. The weights are associated with values: 5 as the highest, and 1, the lowest. The weights are briefly defined in the table.

To use the tools to improve the usefulness and purposefulness of BDA, the health facility must have achieved a certain level. This is to help ascertain benefits and gain results from the analysis of patients' big data. The different levels are defined by the factors that influence the use of the tools, revealed from examining BDA for healthcare services in this chapter. The influencing factors and key indicators determine the differences.

Key Indicator

The key indicator quantifies the measure of the criteria within requirements and timeframe, based on which BDA is implemented in a facility. Thus, outcomes are put in context and perspective to assess the value of BDA in delivering healthcare services. The key indicator is used to calculate the weights associated with the factors that influence the implementation of the tools. The indications are divided into three categories, Advance, Intermediary and Foundation, as shown in Table 11.2.

How to employ the criteria:

1 The organisation assesses or evaluates itself in accordance with the set of criteria.
2 The weight is added and the total score is reached.
3 The total score is aligned with the key indicator as described above.
4 Based on the alignment, a decision is reached.

The criteria for the implementation provide standards and principles for assessing the implementation of the tools. Criteria constitute the requirements based on which evaluation of implementation is based. Thus, the implementation metrics provides a sound knowledge of logic for risk analysis and assessment. Also, the criteria encourage and promote fundamental ingredients of success, such as reliability, flexibility, validity and accuracy.

Table 11.1 Criteria for big data analytics tools

Weight	5	4	3	2	1
Knowledge	Understand BDA tools and able to use the tools	Understand how the BDA tools work but not use them	Understand a few BDA tools and know how to use the tools	Have a basic understanding of the tools but do not know how to apply them	Do not understand the concept of BDA
Process	There is a procedure for selecting tools. It describes the goal and criteria for organisational purposes.	The goal is described with no criteria put in place in selecting BDA tools.	There is no procedure followed in selecting BDA tools. Make use of available BDA tools	Described the goal but did not know how to select the suitable BDA tools	There is no procedure and no BDA tools used
Differentiation	Understand the difference between data and Big Data.	Understand the characteristics of big data.	Have an average understanding of big data.	Have a little understanding of big data.	Do not understand the difference.
Skillset	Understand BDA tools. Have experience in using BDA tools.	Understand BDA tools with only basic experience.	Understands BDA tools with no experience.	Have little understanding of BDA tools with no experience.	Do not understand BDA tools.
Total	20	16	12	8	4

Table 11.2 Key indicator for the use of big data analytics tools

Score	Level	Description
16–20	Above average	Advanced in understanding BDA tools and implementation. Minimal or error-free implementation.
10–15	Average	A good understanding of BDA tools. Errors and challenges are easily detected and resolved.
0–9	Below average	Have little or no understanding of the BDA tools. Errors and challenges take long or are hardly resolved.

Summary

This chapter explores an area vital to the healthcare sector in striving to improve the quality of services they provide to patients. Through the influencing factors revealed and discussed in this chapter, health facilities can learn and add value to their processes and activities by selecting the most appropriate BDA tools. Also, the chapter provides a guide on how practitioners can manage and justify the practice of BDA for their services. To be more specific, the influencing factors and the criteria presented in this chapter can help health practitioners and IT specialists gain a deeper understanding of the challenges they are faced with in their attempts to employ BDA. Also, the chapter can assist data scientists in designing and formulating policies and standards to ensure the appropriate use of BDA tools in their organisations. In addition, IT managers can be guided in developing employees' retention strategies while using BDA tools for healthcare purposes. In addition, IT specialists can gain better insights about criteria in their quest for support and enablement of big data tools. Another significant contribution is that health practitioners and IT and health informatics students can draw references from the chapter.

References

Adrian, C., Abdullah, R., Atan, R., & Jusoh, Y. Y. (2017). Factors influencing to the implementation success of big data analytics: A systematic literature review. In: *International conference on research and innovation in information systems (ICRIIS)*, 16–17 July, Langkawi, Malaysia. https://doi.org/10.1109/ICRIIS.2017.8002536

Adrian, C., Abdullah, R., Atan, R., & Jusoh, Y. Y. (2018). Conceptual model development of big data analytics implementation assessment effect on decision-making. *International Journal of Interactive Multimedia and Artificial Intelligence*, 5(1), 101–106.

Agnihotri, L., Mojarad, S., Lewkow, N., & Essa, A. (2016). Educational data mining with Python and Apache spark: A hands-on tutorial. In: *Proceedings of the sixth international conference on learning analytics & knowledge* (pp. 507–508). Edinburgh United Kingdom: ACM. https://doi.org/10.1145/2883851.2883857.

Al Nuaimi, E., Al Neyadi, H., Mohamed, N., & Al-Jaroodi, J. (2015). Applications of big data to smart cities. *Journal of Internet Services and Applications, 6*(1), 1–15. https://doi.org/10.1186/s13174-015-0041-5.

Archenaa, J., & Anita, E. M. (2015). A survey of big data analytics in healthcare and government. *Procedia Computer Science, 50,* 408–413. https://doi.org/10.1016/j.procs.2015.04.021.

Berry, D. (2021). Application of big data in healthcare: Examination of the military experience. *Health and Technology, 11*(2), 251-256. https://doi.org/10.1007/s12553-020-00513-7

Batarseh, F. A., Yang, R., & Deng, L. (2017). A comprehensive model for management and validation of federal big data analytical systems. *Big Data Analytics, 2*(1), 1–22. https://doi.org/10.1186/s41044-016-0017-x.

Bumblauskas, D., Nold, H., Bumblauskas, P., & Igou, A. (2017). Big data analytics: Transforming data to action. *Business Process Management Journal, 23*(3), 703–720. https://doi.org/10.1108/BPMJ-03-2016-0056.

Cao, L. (2017). Data science: A comprehensive overview. *ACM Computing Surveys, 50*(3), 1–42. https://doi.org/10.1145/3076253.

Cao, G., & Duan, Y. (2017). How do top- and bottom-performing companies differ in using business analytics? *Journal of Enterprise Information Management, 30*(6), 874–892. https://doi.org/10.1108/JEIM-04-2016-0080.

Cervone, H. F. (2016). Organisational considerations initiating a big data and analytics implementation. *Digital Library Perspectives, 32*(3), 137–141. https://doi.org/10.1108/DLP-05-2016-0013.

Chen, D. Q., Preston, D. S., & Swink, M. (2005). How the use of big data analytics affects value creation in supply chain management. *Journal of Management Information Systems, 32*(4), 4–39. https://doi.org/10.1080/07421222.2015.1138364.

Cheng, S., Zhang, Q., & Qin, Q. (2016). Big data analytics with swarm intelligence. *Industrial Management & Data Systems, 116*(4), 646–666. https://doi.org/10.1108/IMDS-06-2015-0222.

Comuzzi, M., & Patel, A. (2016). How organisations leverage big data: A maturity model. *Industrial Management & Data Systems, 116*(8), 1468–1492. https://doi.org/10.1108/IMDS-12-2015-0495.

Delen, D., & Ram, S. (2018). Research challenges and opportunities in business analytics. *Journal of Business Analytics, 1*(1), 2–12. https://doi.org/10.1080/2573234X.2018.1507324.

Delen, D., & Zolbanin, H. M. (2018). The analytics paradigm in business research. *Journal of Business Research, 90,* 186–195. https://doi.org/10.1016/j.jbusres.2018.05.013.

Dos Santos, R. G., Bouso, J. C., Rocha, J. M., Rossi, G. N., & Hallak, J. E. (2021). The use of classic hallucinogens/psychedelics in a therapeutic context: Healthcare policy opportunities and challenges. *Risk Management and Healthcare Policy, 14,* 901-910. https://doi.org/10.2147/RMHP.S300656

He, W., Nazir, S., & Hussain, Z. (2021). Big data insights and comprehensions in industrial healthcare: an overview. *Mobile Information Systems, 2021.* https://doi.org/10.1155/2021/6628739.

Galetsi, P., Katsaliaki, K., & Kumar, S. (2020). Big data analytics in health sector: Theoretical framework, techniques and prospects. *International Journal of Information Management, 50,* 206–216. https://doi.org/10.1016/j.ijinfomgt.2019.05.003.

Gandomi, A., & Haider, M. (2015). Beyond the hype: Big data concepts, methods, and analytics. *International Journal of Information Management, 35*(2), 137–144. https://doi.org/10.1016/j.ijinfomgt.2014.10.007.

Hardy, K., & Maurushat, A. (2017). Opening up government data for Big Data analysis and public benefit. *Computer Law & Security Review, 33*(1), 30–37. https://doi.org/10.1016/j.clsr.2016.11.003.

Joseph, R. C., & Johnson, N. A. (2013). Big data and transformational government. *IT Professional, 15*(6), 43–48. https://doi.org/10.1109/MITP.2013.61.

Kache, F., & Seuring, S. (2017). Challenges and opportunities of digital information at the intersection of Big Data analytics and supply chain management. *International Journal of Operations & Production Management, 37*(1), 10–36. https://doi.org/10.1108/IJOPM-02-2015-0078.

Khalifa, M., & Zabani, I. (2016). Utilizing health analytics in improving the performance of healthcare services: A case study on a tertiary care hospital. *Journal of Infection and Public Health, 9*(6), 757–765. https://doi.org/10.1016/j.jiph.2016.08.016.

Khan, N., Yaqoob, I., Hashem, I. A. T., Inayat, Z., Ali, M., Kamaleldin, W., Alam, M., Shiraz, M., & Gani, A. (2014). Big data: Survey, technologies, opportunities, and challenges. *The Scientific World Journal, 2014,* 712826. https://doi.org/10.1155/2014/712826.

Kim, G. H., Trimi, S., & Chung, J. H. (2014). Big-data applications in the government sector. *Communications of the ACM, 57*(3), 78–85. https://doi.org/10.1145/2500873.

Kuo, M. H., Sahama, T., Kushniruk, A. W., Borycki, E. M., & Grunwell, D. K. (2014). Health big data analytics: Current perspectives, challenges and potential solutions. *International Journal of Big Data Intelligence, 1*(1–2), 114–126.

Lim, C., Kim, K. J., & Maglio, P. P. (2018). Smart cities with big data: Reference models, challenges, and considerations. *Cities, 82,* 86–99. https://doi.org/10.1016/j.cities.2018.04.011.

Lee, H., Kweon, E., Kim, M., & Chai, S. (2017). Does implementation of big data analytics improve firms' market value? Investors' reaction in stock market. *Sustainability, 9*(6), 1–17. https://doi.org/10.3390/su9060978.

Mehta, N., & Pandit, A. (2018). Concurrence of big data analytics and healthcare: A systematic review. *International Journal of Medical Informatics, 114,* 57–65. https://doi.org/10.1016/j.ijmedinf.2018.03.013.

Miah, S. J., Camilleri, E., & Vu, H. Q. (2022). Big Data in healthcare research: a survey study. *Journal of Computer Information Systems, 62*(3), 480-492. https://doi.org/10.1080/08874417.2020.1858727

Mohanty, S., Jagadeesh, M., & Srivatsa, H. (2013). *Big data imperatives: Enterprise 'Big Data' warehouse, BI implementations and analytics.* Berkeley, CA, USA: Apress.

Nyikana, W., & Iyamu, T. (2022, January). A Guide for selecting big data analytics tools in an organisation. In *Proceedings of the 55th Hawaii International Conference on System Sciences HICSS* (pp. 5451–5461). January 3–7, Maui, HI. DOI: 10.24251/HICSS.2022.664

Okpechi, I. G., Bello, A. K., Luyckx, V. A., Wearne, N., Swanepoel, C. R., & Jha, V. (2021). Building optimal and sustainable kidney care in low resource settings: The role of healthcare systems. *Nephrology, 26*(12), 948–960. https://doi.org/10.1111/nep.13935

Patel, S., & Patel, A. (2016). Abig data revolution in health care sector: Opportunities, challenges and technological advancements. *International Journal of Information*, 6(1/2), 155–162. https://doi.org/10.5121/ijist.2016.6216.
Raghupathi, W., and Raghupathi, V. (2014). Big data analytics in healthcare: Promise and potential. *Health Information Science and Systems*, 2(1), 1–10. https://doi.org/10.1186/2047-2501-2-3.
Ridge, M., Johnston, K. A., & Donovan, B. (2015). The use of big data analytics in the retail industries in South Africa. *African Journal of Business Management*, 9(19), 688–703. https://doi.org/10.5897/AJBM2015.7827.
Sagiroglu, S., & Sinanc, D. (2013, May). Big data: A review. In: *2013 international conference on collaboration technologies and systems (CTS)* (pp. 42–47). IEEE. https://doi.org/10.1109/CTS.2013.6567202
Schroeder, R. (2014). Big Data and the brave new world of social media research. *Big Data & Society*, 1(2), 1–11. https://doi.org/10.1177/2053951714563194.
Sedkaoui, S. (2018). How data analytics is changing entrepreneurial opportunities? *International Journal of Innovation Science*, 10(2), 274–294. https://doi.org/10.1108/IJIS-09-2017-0092.
Soltanpoor, R., & Sellis, T. (2016). Prescriptive analytics for big data. In: Cheema, M., Zhang, W., & Chang, L. (eds), *Databases theory and applications* (pp. 245–256). Lecture Notes in Computer Science, Vol. 9877. Cham: Springer. https://doi.org/10.1007/978-3-319-46922-5_19.
Van Biesen, W., Van Der Straeten, C., Sterckx, S., Steen, J., Diependaele, L., & Decruyenaere, J. (2021). The concept of justifiable healthcare and how big data can help us to achieve it. *BMC Medical Informatics and Decision Making*, 21(1), 1–17. https://doi.org/10.1186/s12911-021-01444-7
Wang, Y., & Hajli, N. (2017). Exploring the path to big data analytics success in healthcare. *Journal of Business Research*, 70, 287–299. https://doi.org/10.1016/j.jbusres.2016.08.002.
Wang, Y., Kung, L., & Byrd, T. A. (2018). Big data analytics: Understanding its capabilities and potential benefits for healthcare organisations. *Technological Forecasting and Social Change*, 126, 3–13. https://doi.org/10.1016/j.techfore.2015.12.019.
Wang, Y., Kung, L., Wang, W. Y. C., & Cegielski, C. G. (2018). An integrated big data analytics-enabled transformation model: Application to health care. *Information & Management*, 55(1), 64–79. https://doi.org/10.1016/j.im.2017.04.001.
Whitelock, V. (2018). Business analytics and firm performance: Role of structured financial statement data. *Journal of Business Analytics*, 1(1), 81–92. https://doi.org/10.1080/2573234X.2018.1557020.
Zakir, J., Seymour, T., & Berg, K. (2015). Big data analytics. *Issues in Information Systems*, 16(2), 81–90.
Zetino, J., & Mendoza, N. (2019). Big data and its utility in social work: Learning from the big data revolution in business and healthcare, social work in public health. *Social Work in Public Health*, 34(5), 409–417. https://doi.org/10.1080/19371918.2019.1614508.

12 The Evaluation of Big Data Analytics Tools for Healthcare Services

Introduction

Big data is an information technology (IT) solution used to enable and support organisations (healthcare facilities included) for services that lead to sustainability, advancement and competitiveness, including assessing well-being and health conditions. it has been well explained in Chapter 11, that big data is not about data size but is characterised by three main dimensions: variety, volume and velocity (Gandomi & Haider, 2015). Big data is processed by computerised software or applications, referred to as big data analytics (BDA). The most common BDA, diagnostic, descriptive, predictive and prescriptive, are introduced in Chapter 1 and discussed in subsequent Chapters. Briefly, descriptive analytics is about what happened; diagnostic analytics draws on the rationale of what happens; predictive analytics focuses on the future and prescriptive analytics centres on the response to potential future events. There are thin lines between where one analytics stops, and another begins. Thus, selection of the tools is always going to be difficult and confusing. Hence, evaluation is crucial to avoid or reduce overlapping and duplications.

Also, the use of BDA is not straightforward and cannot be considered a one-size-fits-all approach. Thus, human intervention is essential to determine and identify the type of analytics that can be leveraged to benefit an environment, optimally. BDA can help health practitioners, to follow and understand patients' conditions, grow a patient base and offer a much more accurate and higher quality of service. The four dominant types of analytics – diagnostic, descriptive, predictive and prescriptive – are inter-related solutions to increasing the usefulness of big data for healthcare services. These analytics types are also discussed in Chapter 11. Despite the inter-relationship between the analytics tools, each offers different insights and can be used for deliverables, distinctive, to improve strategic and operational capabilities. Thus, evaluation is necessary.

Although the focus of this chapter is not on the detailed level of analytics products, it is necessary to highlight that some of the common ones are Hadoop, Apache Spark MapReduce, Tableau and RapidMiner (Bonthu & Bindu, 2017; Katal, Wazid & Goudar, 2013). There is increasing interest

DOI: 10.4324/9781003251064-12

in the use of BDA from both academia and industry (Ghazal et al., 2013; Hofacker, Malthouse, & Sultan, 2016), which can be attributed to the premise that the concept brings a positive change to an environment that deploys it (Demchenko, De Laat & Membrey, 2014; He, Nazir & Hussain, 2021). Velpula and Pamula (2022) suggest that the use of BDA in healthcare helps to predict diseases.

Some healthcare facilities adopt the big data concept to get some insights into using the data to predict the future. This is critical for patient care primarily because most health-related matters are unprecedented. Also, many healthcare facilities employ big data to improve activities and events such as analysing patients' response and future predictions. In the process of optimising the benefits of BDA, some healthcare facilities divide it into two sections: management, which is the extraction, retrieval and storage of data sets for transformation and decision-making purposes; and as information technology (IT) solution for analysing big data.

Despite the benefits that BDA seem to present, there are challenges with the concept, including the violation of privacy, security, data quality, slowness in query processing, scalability problems, integration complexities and scarcity of big data skills (Gandomi & Haider, 2015; Suthaharan, 2014; Veiga et al., 2016). Some of the challenges persist because there has been a lack of research, theoretical constructs and academic rigour from a management perspective in big data and BDA (Sivarajah et al., 2017). There has also been a lack of research studies or books that comprehensively address the key challenges of BDA or investigate opportunities for new theories or emerging practices. Some of the challenges contribute to why evaluation of BDA has been few and slow (George, Haas & Pentland, 2014; Nyikana & Iyamu, 2022).

The main challenge is that there seems to be no available evaluation models or methods to assess BDA tools, and neither research nor books have focused on this aspect. Because of the variation of the BDA tools, some organisations have a challenge in selecting the most appropriate application for analysis (Barton & Court, 2012; Nyikana & Iyamu, 2022). In the field of information systems (IS), many of models only focus on evaluating solutions such as software and business requirements (Andargoli, Scheepers, Rajendran & Sohal, 2017; Delone & McLean, 2003). As at the time of writing this chapter, the only study that seem to focus on evaluating BDA tools, Hadoop, Spark and Flink, was from a performance perspective (Agostinho et al., 2016). This means that the gap remains, which this chapter aimed to address by proposing a solution through a model. The model can be used for evaluation, to ensure the most appropriate BDA is selected, for healthcare purposes.

Based on the aim, two fundamental questions are formulated: (1) what factors (technical or non-technical) influence the selection of big data analytics in a healthcare facility; and (2) what criteria can be used to determine the appropriateness of BDA tools in a healthcare facility? The chapter reveals that the role of criteria, business and IT alignment, governance and skillsets as critical factors. In the context of this chapter and book, healthcare activities are also considered as business. Primarily because the activities are services provided to patients. Based on the factors, a model is proposed, which can be used as a building block through which BDA tools are evaluated in a healthcare facility.

The remainder of this chapter is divided into five main sections and sequentially arranged to ease understanding. The first section introduces the chapter including the aim. In the second section a review of literature covering three main aspects of the chapter: BDA, value of BDA, and evaluation models and techniques is presented. This is followed by answering the fundamental questions in the chapter: What factors influence the selection of BDA in healthcare facilities? What criteria can be used to determine the appropriateness of BDA tools in a healthcare facility? In the fourth section, the evaluation model is presented and discussed, and finally, a conclusion is summarised.

Big Data Analytics and Evaluation Model

The literature review is focuses on the three main areas of the chapter: BDA, the value of big data in organisations and evaluation techniques.

Big Data Analytics

The BDA approaches include predictive, descriptive and prescriptive. The approaches focus on analysing unstructured, semi-structured and structured data sets, images, audio or text (Gandomi & Haider, 2015). BDA involves machine learning applications or software like Hadoop, MapReduce, Apache and many more (Katal, Wazid & Goudar, 2013).

Predictive analytics focuses on historical data to predict the future. The analysis uses machine learning algorithms and statistical models to assess historical data sets for future predictions (Davenport & Dyché, 2013). Descriptive analytics concentrate on the current state of present data sets (Daniel, 2015). It uses historical data sets to identify patterns that can be reported or compared to current trends. Prescriptive analytics assesses the current situation to decide (Gandomi & Haider, 2015). It combines both descriptive and predictive analytics in finding new ways to achieve positive outcomes for organisations.

The efficiency of BDA is one of the reasons why healthcare facilities adopt and use the concept as a solution to decision-making (Van Biesen). According to Berry (2021), the concept of BDA is primarily to assess and improve performance and efficiency It is argued that BDA is used to deliver predictive insights into operations, drive real-time decision-making and redesign business processes in achieving results for organisational goals and objectives (Wolfert, Ge, Verdouw & Bogaardt, 2017). Despite the consistent argument that BDA has a lot to offer to organisations (healthcare facilities included), many challenges have been identified in the use of the concept (Katal, Wazid

& Goudar, 2013; Zijing, Yuchuan, Zhiping & Tengfei, 2021), including data validation, data cleansing, scalability of algorithms and parallel data processing (Najafabadi et al., 2015).

Value of Big Data Analytics in Healthcare

In recent years, there has been an increase in the use of BDA tools, which can be attributed to the values associated with the concept. The concept of BDA can be used to promote productivity and decision-making, which brings forth to organisations (Grover, Chiang, Liang & Zhang, 2018). Wang, Kung and Byrd (2018) suggest that the BDA is helps in the analytical capability for patterns of care, for managerial and strategic purposes. Two socio-technical features, convenience and interconnectivity, are identified as the factors that influence the value of BDA in many organisations (Günther, Mehrizi, Huysman & Feldberg, 2017). In some quarters, personnel are fascinated with the BDA's capabilities in that it enables the integration of data types from different perspectives such as size and variety (Grover, Chiang, Liang & Zhang, 2018).

In healthcare facilities, the value of BDA is viewed from different perspectives. One viewpoint on the value of BDA is about collecting, storing and gaining insights to enhance performance (Erevelles, Fukawa & Swayne, 2016). From another angle, the ability to integrate, accessibility and response time are the values of the BDA, to many stakeholders (Ji-fan Ren et al., 2017). However, the BDA tools do not operate themselves, which is another challenge associated with the concept and influences the value obtained. The emerging nature of the BDA makes skillsets scarce (Alharthi, Krotov & Bowman, 2017; Wang, Kung & Byrd, 2018).

Evaluation Models and Techniques

In IS, software evaluation is critical due to increasing reliance on it as a solution in organisations. Another rationale for evaluating software is ensuring awareness and detecting deficiency (Pearlson, Saunders & Galletta, 2016). Thus, many computer systems undergo an evaluation process (Andargoli et al., 2017). Within the computing environment, there are various models and techniques for evaluating software and approaches. One of the techniques is that the evaluation begins with evaluating technology functionalities, to align with requirements and needs.

There are numerous types of evaluation models and techniques. One of the evaluation techniques is a Holistic Framework on IS evaluation which consists of five evaluation factors: Strategic value, Profitability, Risk, Successful Development and Procurement, and Successful Use and Operations (Hallikainen & Chen, 2006). Another rationale for evaluation in the IS field is to mitigate against risk in projects and assess the effectiveness of systems in an organisation. Also, there is no limit to an evaluation in that there will always be new factors to evaluate (Irani & Love, 2002).

The similarities among the BDA ease and, at the same time, complicate the evaluation of the tools. Thus, it is difficult to apply any of the existing IS models in the evaluation process of BDA. Otherwise, it increases the challenges and complexity encountered in evaluating an IT solution (Irani & Love, 2002; Pearlson, Saunders & Galletta, 2016). Also, big data, particularly in the healthcare environment, is unique. Therefore, generic IS models are not suitable. Marthandan and Meng Tang (2010) explained a lack of understanding on 'why', 'how' and 'when' to evaluate specific IS solutions, which is a persistent challenge in the field.

Factors Influencing Appropriateness of Big Data

The focuses are from two main angles: (1) the relationships between humans and big data within the healthcare environment; and (2) the interactions that often happen between humans on the one hand, and between humans and big data on the other. By understanding the relationships and interactions between human-to-human and human-to-big data, the questions are answered, and the aim of the chapter is achieved.

This is to gain deeper understanding of the relationships and interactions that exist between human-to-human, human-to-big data and big data-to-big data in answering the questions the chapter seeks to answer. In answering the questions, the focus is on: (1) to determine the factors influencing the selection of BDA in organisations; and (2) to establish criteria for appropriate BDA tools in an organisation.

What Are the Factors Influencing the Selection of Big Data Analytics in Healthcare?

Big data is not all about volume but is defined by its characteristics, including the Vs, volume, velocity, veracity, variety and value. The tools employed in the analyses of big data are referred to as analytics tools. Some BDA tools/software have the capabilities to process data sets that organisations employ for various purposes. There are different BDA tools: diagnostic, descriptive, predictive and prescriptive (Mgudlwa & Iyamu, 2021). Using BDA tools, healthcare facilities can make effective and appropriate strategic decisions.

BDA is sophisticated. The same sophistication makes it complex. Thus, many people, including healthcare practitioners and enablers of health-related processes and activities, are sometimes confused about the purposes and types of BDA. The selection and use of Pentaho data integrator and Pentaho business analytics are examples; many users and managers get confused between the two tools.

The BDA topic appears to be an overwhelming subject in many healthcare facilities. This could be because some stakeholders focus on the bigger picture in terms of the terminology that comes with the tools. In some healthcare facilities, processes are followed in the selection of BDA tools. However, the processes are not always sequential, meaning the steps do not necessarily depend on each other. Primarily, the components of the process should include an understanding and formulating of needs, exploring available analytics tools and evaluating the relevance of the tools within context. In the evaluation, the components should be viewed from the aspects of technical and non-technical factors.

Organisational goals and objectives are a guide to choosing tools that suit its needs. The selection of analytics tools depends not only on the goals but also on humans' involvement, particularly in the decision-making aspect and consideration of the users. Individuals such as managers of health facilities and patients' data seem to influence the decision to select BDA tools. Nonetheless, in many healthcare facilities, it appears to be the persons leading the IT units that agree and take ownership of selecting the tools employed. However, the tool that is selected must be aligned with the objectives of the facility. Thus, the facility's requirements should ultimately determine the selection of the tools. This limits the challenges in formulating technical requirements of the tools to enable integration, compatibility and co-existence.

In some health facilities, the input of employees using BDA influences the selection of the tools. Despite the business requirements, the staff consider and evaluate the technical and non-technical factors of the tools because they know how they work. In this circumstance, roles and responsibilities lag and confusion reigns, including a lack of understanding of the various BDA tools. This manifests in selecting the tools as some managers claim that a visualisation tool is not the same as a data analytics tool. Significantly, this usually impacts the selection of appropriate tools for healthcare purposes. One of the implications is that it restricts the scope and functions where such tools are applied.

Despite numerous BDA tools, many health facilities, especially the small-sized ones, do not select and use the tools. Some facilities do not consider any of the tools suitable, which can be linked to a lack of know-how. In a health facility, evaluation should comprise different phases, consisting of health-related and technology requirements, from which the factors that influence selection should be understood. Usually, a facility aims to have a tool that can improve healthcare service delivery and increase its strategic and operational progress. It is also to get BDA tools that are flexible and scalable to advance sustainability and manageability of processes and activities of healthcare.

The diagnostic analysis relationship between different attributes is explored using data visualisation methods, which help trace and connect heterogeneity in patients' big data. Descriptive analytics are based on standard aggregated functions to gain insights into what happened. In descriptive analytics, the data can be real-time or historical. Predominantly, it assists in shaping the future. Predictive analytics helps predict the likelihood of certain health conditions or diseases reoccurring using various statistical and machine learning algorithms. Scientifically or socially, the accuracy of predictions cannot be 100%, primarily because it is based on probabilities. Healthcare makes use of prescriptive analytics to arrive at the most appropriate outcomes and make better decisions.

What Are the Criteria that Determine Appropriateness of Big Data Analytics in Healthcare?

Criteria are a set of standards and principles that guide decision-making and measure the scope and boundaries of actions in an activity or environment. The standards and principles are embedded with factors (Etzioni, 1967). In health facilities, criteria should be formulated and used for selecting BDA tools. The criteria should consist of factors, such as cost, supportability, features and skills required to use and support the tools. Despite a set of criteria, familiarity with a tool is also important. Managers of health facilities or patients' big data should understand that cost, knowledge and skills are some of the factors required to evaluate tools. The cost is about maintenance for continuity purposes. Essentially, skillsets enable useability and technical support of the tool, thereby ensuring continuity.

In a health facility, criteria should be used as guidelines in selecting a tool intended to benefit health-related processes and activities from a quality service delivery point of view. This means that the criteria also act as principles, which guide the employees in their focus and actions, and should not allow the easy move from one tool to another. In addition, a complementarity of requirements of both health and IT should be the determining factor. This is purposely because the product owners and sales vendors market some tools very well. As a result, without requirements, there is a high possibility of selecting inappropriate tools.

Two requirements, business and IT units, formed the criteria, enabled by communication. The criteria were defined through communication between the units, including the management team. The management of both IT and business units of the organisation was involved in gathering the requirements used to formulate the criteria primarily because they knew better about the current and future states of the organisation. However, there usually no substantiative explanations why specific BDA tools were selected from the involved employees. This is attributed to the organisation's management taking ownership of the process and the selected tool.

Despite the strengths of some of the tools employed in healthcare facilities, there are challenges highlighted in different studies (Daniel, 2015; Najafabadi et al., 2015; Sivarajah et al., 2017). The main challenge that some healthcare facilities seem to be facing with the currently employed tools is the scarcity of skilled personnel to use and provide technical support. In achieving a facility's objectives of improving service delivery, the tools require special skills, a person or persons with an understanding of the functionalities and operationalisation of the tools. This ensures know-how, granularity and continuity, which foster the stability, viability and quality needed to deliver healthcare services.

Looking for a tool that would cater for everything is almost impossible. A healthcare facility highlights challenges while selecting the appropriate tool from the limitless tools/applications available in the market. Without properly defined requirements and criteria formulation, there will always be challenges in selecting BDA tools. Also, some healthcare facilities would change the tools frequently as they get influenced by excitable new functions that some of the tools present.

Changing the tools from one BDA tool to another takes much effort and can be costly. Some healthcare facilities seem to have a strategy to accommodate such a situation but hardly implemented and evaluated. The change is accepted only when a tool offers better features than the one currently used in the organisation. Also, organisational change leans towards goals and objectives.

Evaluation Model for Healthcare Big Data

From the above sections, four factors are considered critical in shaping and influencing the selection of BDA tools in healthcare facilities. The factors are based on the understanding from subjective reasoning. As shown in Figure 12.1, the factors are the role of criteria, business/IT alignment, governance and skillsets. The factors are based on organisational vision. The factors are, therefore, a set of building blocks, as discussed below.

The purpose of the evaluation criteria is primarily to support consistent, improved quality because it helps assess specific interventions, especially in a sensitive environment such as the health sector. Also, the criteria make it clear and transparent that healthcare practitioners, enablers (IT specialists) and patients understand the processes involved in providing services, including awareness about individual roles and responsibilities.

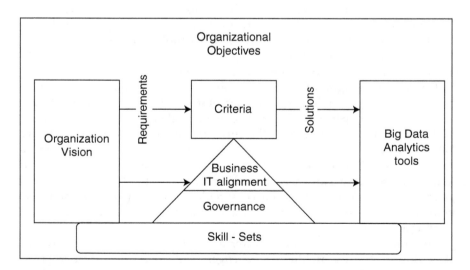

Figure 12.1 Building blocks

The Role of Criteria

Criteria are a set of guidelines built on principles and standards that can evaluate the BDA tools for organisations (Cai & Zhu, 2015). In this chapter, criteria consist of two main components: the business (healthcare activities) requirements and IT requirements. Business requirements are mostly connected with the goals, mission and objective, based on the organisational vision. Business requirements work towards paving and setting what the business seeks to achieve. The IT requirements are based on technology types, co-existence and compatibility, capacity and flexibility of technologies. The IT requirements seek to enable and support the business requirements towards achieving the objectives of the healthcare facility. Also, this means IT solutions can be a constraint in that deficiency within IT will negatively impact the business requirements.

Based on business and IT requirements, the criteria can be used as a control mechanism for selecting the most appropriate BDA tools for organisational purposes. The vital role of the criteria is that the healthcare facilities have a rich understanding of what they want to do and what will fit their needs. This also means that there is an evaluation process undertaken in the selection of the tools. Another significant factor in creating criteria is that it minimises the chances of duplicating analytics tools for the same or similar purpose and mitigates risks.

Business and IT Alignment

The concept of business and IT alignment is not new. It has been explored or applied in various ways. Also, it has been expressed in several terms, such as linkage, integration and agreement. However, alignment does not refer to being aligned or not aligned. Rather, the relationship needs to be adjusted based on unforeseen business events (Luftman, Lyytinen & Zvi, 2017). Communication and uniformity are among the most crucial contributors identified in the alignment between business and IT in selecting BDA tools. Communication plays a significant role between the business and IT units in decision-making. In addition, the uniformity of how things are done, following processes and policies of an organisation, is important.

Lack of alignment between the business and IT units can cause chaos in selecting BDA tools. As a result, the working environment can become unstable, leading to deploying applications that cannot serve the organisational purpose. Lack of alignment between business and IT units has huge implications, such as prohibitive cost and technology compatibility risks for an organisation in selecting BDA tools.

Governance

Governance consists of standards, principles and policies (Shaanika & Iyamu, 2018). It gives a structural guide to specialists and managers in decision-making. It is also procedural, which gives power to the relevant authority to make decisions (Bennett, Bradbury & Prangnell, 2006). Thus, governance can be used to guide the selection of appropriate BDA tools in an organisation. This means that the selected BDA tools adhere to the standards and principles of the facility.

Selecting the analytics tools is one thing. Using it is another. The use of the BDA tools is as critical as the selection, which therefore also requires guidance. Governance can guide the use and management of the tools to avoid technology conflicts and abnormalities. Lack of governance principles in facilities promotes poor product quality. Also, it allows employees to avoid or shift accountability and responsibility as they deem.

Big Data Analytics Skillset

BDA is an emerging concept, particularly in developing countries. As a result, there is a scarcity of BDA skillset, which affects the slow deployment of the concept in healthcare facilities, in many developing countries. Skillset plays a very critical role in the deployment and use of BDA (Ahmed et al., 2017). The noticeable reasons of the complexity of BDA require data scientists to perform. The machine learning applications designed to analyse big data require the skills of data scientists.

Although it is crucial to have the skillset, what is even more important is the retention of the personnel. Retention allows a health facility to keep their trained and skilled personnel if possible. This saves the cost of upskilling, which can be very prohibitive and affect the return on investment. Lack of skills leads to incorrect data and operations falling apart, influencing decision-making, and ultimately negatively affecting business goals.

Summary

This chapter is to assist healthcare facilities that wish to deploy and those that have already deployed BDA tools evaluate them to get the tools that suit a health facility's goal. From this chapter, healthcare facilities can better understand how to select appropriate tools guided by the set criteria. Also, this chapter can be useful to healthcare facilities that seek to understand the value of having criteria to evaluate available BDA tools. The chapter is limited to evaluating BDA tools meaning that it excludes other activities such as deployment and readiness and the applications connected to BDA tools for health-related purposes.

References

Agostinho, C., Ducq, Y., Zacharewicz, G., Sarraipa, J., Lampathaki, F., Poler, R., & Jardim-Goncalves, R. (2016). Towards a sustainable interoperability in networked enterprise information systems: Trends of knowledge and model-driven technology. *Computers in Industry, 79,* 64–76. https://doi.org/10.1016/j.compind.2015.07.001.

Ahmed, E., Ibrar, Y., Ibrahim, A., Targio, H., Imran, K., Abdelmuttlib, I., Abdalla, A., Muhammad, I., & Athanasios, V. (2017). The role of big data analytics in Internet of Things. *Computer Networks, 129*(2), 459–471. https://doi.org/10.1016/j.comnet.2017.06.013.

Alharthi, A., Krotov, V., & Bowman, M. (2017). Addressing barriers to big data. *Business Horizons, 60*(3), 285–292. https://doi.org/10.1016/j.bushor.2017.01.002.

Andargoli, A. E., Scheepers, H., Rajendran, D., & Sohal, A. (2017). Health information systems evaluation frameworks: A systematic review. *International Journal of Medical Informatics, 97*, 195–209. https://doi.org/10.1016/j.ijmedinf.2016.10.008.

Barton, D., & Court, D. (2012). Making advanced analytics work for you. *Harvard Business Review, 90*(10), 78–83.

Bennett, B., Bradbury, M., & Prangnell, H. (2006). Rules, principles and judgments in accounting standards. *Abacus, 42*(2), 189–204. https://doi.org/10.1111/j.1467-6281.2006.00197.x.

Bonthu, S., & Bindu, K. H. (2017). Review of leading data analytics tools. *International Journal of Engineering & Technology, 7*(3.31), 10–15.

Cai, L., & Zhu, Y. (2015). The challenges of data quality and data quality assessment in the big data era. *Data Science Journal, 14*(2), 1–10. http://doi.org/10.5334/dsj-2015-002.

Daniel, B. (2015). Big Data and analytics in higher education: Opportunities and challenges. *British Journal of Educational Technology, 46*(5), 904–920. https://doi.org/10.1111/bjet.12230.

Davenport, T. H., & Dyché, J. (2013). Big data in big companies. *International Institute for Analytics, 3*, 1–31.

Delone, W. H., & McLean, E. R. (2003). The DeLone & McLean model of information systems success: A ten-year update. *Journal of Management Information Systems, 19*(4), 9–30. https://doi.org/10.1080/07421222.2003.11045748.

Demchenko, Y., De Laat, C., & Membrey, P. (2014). Defining architecture components of the Big Data ecosystem. In: *Proceedings of the international conference on collaboration technologies and systems (CTS)* (pp. 104–112), 19–23 May, Minneapolis, MN, USA. IEEE. https://doi.org/10.1109/CTS.2014.6867550.

Erevelles, S., Fukawa, N., & Swayne, L. (2016). Big Data consumer analytics and the transformation of marketing. *Journal of Business Research, 69*(2), 897–904. https://doi.org/10.1016/j.jbusres.2015.07.001.

Etzioni, A. (1967). Mixed-scanning: A "third" approach to decision-making. *Public Administration Review, 27*, 385–392. https://doi.org/10.2307/973394.

Gandomi, A., & Haider, M. (2015). Beyond the hype: Big data concepts, methods, and analytics. *International Journal of Information Management, 35*(2), 137–144. https://doi.org/10.1016/j.ijinfomgt.2014.10.007.

George, G., Haas, M. R., & Pentland, A. (2014). Big data and management. *Academy of Management Journal, 57*(2), 321–326. https://doi.org/10.5465/amj.2014.4002.

Ghazal, A., Rabl, T., Hu, M., Raab, F., Poess, M., Crolotte, A., & Jacobsen, H. A. (2013). BigBench: Towards an industry standard benchmark for big data analytics. In: *Proceedings of the 2013 ACM SIGMOD international conference on Management of data* (pp. 1197–1208). ACM. https://doi.org/10.1145/2463676.2463712.

Grover, V., Chiang, R. H., Liang, T. P., & Zhang, D. (2018). Creating strategic business value from big data analytics: A research framework. *Journal of Management Information Systems, 35*(2), 388–423. https://doi.org/10.1080/07421222.2018.1451951

Günther, W. A., Mehrizi, M. H. R., Huysman, M., & Feldberg, F. (2017). Debating big data: A literature review on realizing value from big data. *The Journal of Strategic Information Systems, 26*(3), 191–209. https://doi.org/10.1016/j.jsis.2017.07.003.

Hallikainen, P., & Chen, L. (2006). A holistic framework on information systems evaluation with a case analysis. *Lead. Issues Information and Communication Technology Evaluation, 9*, 57–64.

He, W., Nazir, S., & Hussain, Z. (2021). Big data insights and comprehensions in industrial healthcare: an overview. *Mobile Information Systems, 2021*. https://doi.org/10.1155/2021/6628739.

Hofacker, C. F., Malthouse, E. C., & Sultan, F. (2016). Big data and consumer behavior: Imminent opportunities. *Journal of Consumer Marketing, 33*(2), 89–97. https://doi.org/10.1108/JCM-04-2015-1399.

Irani, Z., & Love, P. E. (2002). Developing a frame of reference for ex-ante IT/IS investment evaluation. *European Journal of Information Systems, 11*(1), 74–82. https://doi.org/10.1057/palgrave.ejis.3000411.

Ji-fan Ren, S., Fosso Wamba, S., Akter, S., Dubey, R., & Childe, S. J. (2017). Modelling quality dynamics, business value and firm performance in a big data analytics environment. *International Journal of Production Research, 55*(17), 5011–5026. https://doi.org/10.1080/00207543.2016.1154209

Katal, A., Wazid, M., & Goudar, R. H. (2013). Big data: Issues, challenges, tools and good practices. In: *Proceedings of the international conference on contemporary computing (IC3)* (pp. 404–409), 8–10 August, Noida, India. IEEE. https://doi.org/10.1109/IC3.2013.6612229.

Luftman, J., Lyytinen, K., & Zvi, T. B. (2017). Enhancing the measurement of information technology (IT) business alignment and its influence on company performance. *Journal of Information Technology, 32*(1), 26–46. https://doi.org/10.1057/jit.2015.23.

Marthandan, G., & Meng Tang, C. (2010). Information technology evaluation: Issues and challenges. *Journal of Systems and Information Technology, 12*(1), 37–55. https://doi.org/10.1108/13287261011032643.

Mgudlwa, S., & Iyamu, T. (2021). A framework for accessing patient big data: ANT view of a South African health facility. *The African Journal of Information Systems, 13*(2), 225–240.

Najafabadi, M. M., Villanustre, F., Khoshgoftaar, T. M., Seliya, N., Wald, R., & Muharemagic, E. (2015). Deep learning applications and challenges in big data analytics. *Journal of Big Data, 2*(1), 1–21. https://doi.org/10.1186/s40537-014-0007-7.

Pearlson, K. E., Saunders, C. S., & Galletta, D. F. (2016). *Managing and using information systems, binder ready version: A strategic approach*. New York: John Wiley & Sons.

Shaanika, I., & Iyamu, T. (2018). Developing the enterprise architecture for the Namibian government. *The Electronic Journal of Information Systems in Developing Countries, 84*(3), e12028. https://doi.org/10.1002/isd2.12028.

Sivarajah, U., Kamal, M. M., Irani, Z., & Weerakkody, V. (2017). Critical analysis of Big Data challenges and analytical methods. *Journal of Business Research, 70*, 263–286. https://doi.org/10.1016/j.jbusres.2016.08.001.

Suthaharan, S. (2014). Big data classification: Problems and challenges in network intrusion prediction with machine learning. *Performance Evaluation Review, 41*(4), 70–73. https://doi.org/10.1145/2627534.2627557.

Van Biesen, W., Van Der Straeten, C., Sterckx, S., Steen, J., Diependaele, L., & Decruyenaere, J. (2021). The concept of justifiable healthcare and how big data can help us to achieve it. *BMC Medical Informatics and Decision Making, 21*(1), 1–17. https://doi.org/10.1186/s12911-021-01444-7

Velpula, P., & Pamula, R. (2022). CEECP: CT-based enhanced e-clinical pathways in terms of processing time to enable big data analytics in healthcare along with cloud computing. *Computers & Industrial Engineering, 168*, 108037. https://doi.org/10.1016/j.cie.2022.108037.

Veiga, J., Expósito, R. R., Pardo, X. C., Taboada, G. L., & Tourifio, J. (2016). Performance evaluation of big data frameworks for large-scale data analytics. In: *Proceedings of the international conference on Big Data* (pp. 424–431), 5–8 December, Washington, DC, USA. IEEE. https://doi.org/10.1109/BigData.2016.7840633.

Wang, Y., Kung, L., & Byrd, T. A. (2018). Big data analytics: Understanding its capabilities and potential benefits for healthcare organisations. *Technological Forecasting and Social Change, 126*, 3–13. https://doi.org/10.1016/j.techfore.2015.12.019.

Wolfert, S., Ge, L., Verdouw, C., & Bogaardt, M. J. (2017). Big data in smart farming—A review. *Agricultural Systems, 153*, 69–80. https://doi.org/10.1016/j.agsy.2017.01.023.

Zijing, G. U. O., Yuchuan, L. U. O., Zhiping, C. A. I., & Tengfei, Z. H. E. N. G. (2021). Overview of privacy protection technology of big data in healthcare. *Journal of Frontiers of Computer Science & Technology, 15*(3), 389.

Index

Note: **Bold** page numbers refer to tables and *italic* page numbers refer to figures.

Abdel-Fattah, M. A. 75
Abdullah, R. 161, 166
Abkenar, S. B. 129
accountability 62, 126
Acharjya, D. P. 74
actor-network theory (ANT) 3, 8–10, *9*, 75, 90, 99, 100, 102, 107, 142; actors 145–146; data set 151–152; data set integrity 154–155; enrolment 148–149; external healthcare organisations 152–153; formation 100; framework for 150–151; healthcare big data 109–112, 143–144; interessement 147–148; language semantics 153–154; medical apparatus 152; mobilisation 149–150; problematisation 144, 146–147; socio-technical theory 144; translate big data 111
actors: actor-network theory 145–146; enrolment of 116–117; human actors 109–110; non-human actors 66, 109–110; and relationship 100–101
administrative 146–147
administrators 145
Adrian, C. 161, 166
agency 22–23
agents 22, 24–25
Agnihotri, L. 164
Ahmed, K. 74
Akter, S. 77, 81
alarm systems 133
algorithm adaption 79
Al-Jaroodi, J. 49, 53, 80
AlShamsi, A. 49, 53
ambulance services 22
Al Ameen, M. 137

analysis 1; actor-network theory 9; advanced method of 2; interpretivism 8–9
Anita, E. M. 164
Ansari, M. D. 53
Apostolou, D. 7
Archenaa, J. 164
Armour, F. 75
artificial intelligence (AI) 33
Asur, S. 127
Atan, R. 161, 166
Aurum, A. 77
availability, cloud-hosted data 54

Barrett, A. K. 54
Bashir, S. 150
Batarseh, F. A. 162, 165
Begoli, E. 62
Belhadi, A. 8
Belle, A. 58, 68
Bendre, M. R. 6
Berg, K. 163
Berry, D. 166, 177
Bhardwaj, R. 62
big data 2; challenges of 5–6; characteristics of 89, 126; complexity of 96; concept of 102, 128; data analytics tools 58; epistemology of 102; filtration of 80; and healthcare **60**; for healthcare services 59–61; heterogeneity 58; heterogeneity of 100, *101*; holistic demystification of 90; literature review 62–63; multi-level analysis of 98; transformation of 78
big data analysis: analytics method for 76; current approach of 90

Index

big data analytics (BDA) 2, 3, 4, 5, 8, 46, 90–92, 101–102, 106, 129, 159; analytics, levels of 96; analytics tools 68; categories of 4; challenges and opportunities 59; complementarity of 95–96; decision-making 10; definition of 74; descriptive analytics 6–7; diagnostic analytics 6; evaluation model 177–178; framework for 65, 65–66; and healthcare 5, **61,** 63–64; for healthcare services 66; heterogeneous data set 96–97; implementation of 163; influencing factors 66–67; integration of 64; and interpretivist approach 76, 81; medical information 62; organisations 91–93; paper-based approach 4; for patients' data 60; practice, implication of 69; predictive analytics 7; prescriptive analytics 7–8; source of 67; technology capability 164; type of 67–68; understanding 94–95; validation, framework 68–69
Bleakley, A. 97, 144, 145
Bogers, M. 31
Boone, C. A. 81, 92
Boswell, W. R. 97
Bottles, K. 62
bottom-up approach 65
Bousdekis, A. 7
Bowman, M. 33, 35
Breckels, L. M. 97
Brodie, J. 39
Bryson, J. K. 99
Bryson, J. M. 99
Bu, F. F. 82
building theory 92
Bulgacov, S. 116
Bullinger, A. C. 32, 36
Bumblauskas, D. 159
Bumblauskas, P. 159
business and IT alignment 182
business requirements 183
Byrd, T. A. 76, 98, 178

Callon, M. 119
Canary, H.E. 15
Cao, G. 162
Cardon, P. 75
Carr, C.T. 129
Castiglione, A. C. 16, 106
Cegielski, C. G. 162
Chang, C. L. 20

Chawla, N.V. 141
Chen, D. Q. 77
Cheng, S. 162
Chen, Y.Y. 82
Cherrafi, A. 8
Chesbrough, H.W. 33
Chisalita, C. M. 19
Choi, B. K. 48
Chung, J. H. 160, 163
Clement, M. 33, 35
clinical decision-making 143
closed-circuit television (CCTV) 64
cloud computing solutions 53–54; algorithm adaption 79; big data, filtration of 80; communication 48; facilitate contradiction 79; healthcare practitioners 50; hermeneutic circle technique 79; integration 80–81; interaction and information sharing 51–53; literature review 47–48; security and privacy 50
commercialisation approach 33
communications 18, 48, 118, 133; interaction and information sharing 51–53; mobile healthcare systems 49–51
communicative tools 54
competitiveness 89
complement analytics methods 75
comprehensive healthcare 2
confidentiality 126
connectivity, social media 132
Costello, K. 117
cost implication perspective 31
Counts, S. 131, 133
COVID-19 pandemic 16
Cresswell, K. M. 9
Criscuolo, P. 39
criteria model 169, **170**
Crosby, B. C. 99
cultural affiliation 36

data: analysis framework 151; availability 54; vs. big data 168; innovation-based management 34; management 16; storage capacity 31
database systems 74, 81
Data Protection Act 40
data set 151–152
data set integrity 154–155
Daviaud, E. 143
Davies, G. H. 32, 33, 35
Davis, D. A. 141

De Choudhury, M. 131, 133
decision-making process 6, 7, 14, 46, 74, 96, 120, 134, 141, 153, 177, 180; analytics tools for 116; healthcare facilities 20; mechanisms and tools 76; patient's health condition 153; strategic activities 16
decomposition approach 119–120
Delen, D. 164
Dellavalle, R. P. 131
Deng, L. 162, 165
Dery, K. 100, 109
descriptive analytics 6–7, 91–92
Devarakonda, M.V. 49, 50, 54
developing countries 46; healthcare service delivery 30
diagnostic health analytics 6, 8, 63, 159, 162
Dilla, T. 108, 143
Dix, A. 19
3D medical images 17
duality dimension 18, 18–19
duality of structure 21
Duan, Y. 162
Durepo, G. 109

Eaton, C. 89
e-health 48
electronic communication tools 50
electronic healthcare records (EHRs) 74, 137
employ: innovative technologies 47; structure 15; traditional analysis methods 66
employees 146
employment responsibility 31
Englund, H. 20
Enkel, E. 33
enquiry 113
enrolment 148–149
epistemology 111
Espinosa, J. A. 75
Esposito, C. 106, 143
Essa, A. 164
Eswari, T. 62
evaluation model: big data analytics 177–178; business and IT alignment 183; criteria, role of 183; governance 183–184; healthcare big data 182; skillset, big data analytics 184; and techniques 178–179; value, big data analytics 178
Evans, J. R. 97

evidence-based care 132
external healthcare organisations 152–153
extra care 22
Ezell, J. D. 81, 92

facilitate contradiction 79
facility 23–24
Fahrenwald, N. 127
Fascia, M. 39
fashion complex queries 102
Fawcett, S. E. 99
Feldman, B. 134
Fenwick, T. J. 97, 100, 102
Ficco, M. 106
Fico, G. 106
financial implications 31
Fontenot, R. 75
Fortin, M. 116
Fouweather, I. 16
Fraunholz, B. 100
Friedrich, C. 127

Galetsi, P. 47
Galuba, W. 127
Gamon, M. 131, 133
Gandomi, A. 162
Gao, G. 109
Gao, P. 99
Garcia, L. 150
Gassmann, O. 33
Gautam, P. 53
Gebremeskel, G. 16
generalisability 68
general practitioners (GP) 145
geographical boundaries lack 133
Georgakopoulos, D. 102
Georgiou, D. 54
Gerdin, J. 20
Ghazal, A. 89
Ghazisaeedi, M. 49, 50, 54
Giannakos, M. 78
Giddens, A. 15, 16, 17, 75
Gillela, K. 127
Goudar, R. H. 74, 77, 95
Goudos, S. K. 48
governance 183–184
Govrdhan, A. 17
Grama, A. 89
Greenhalgh, T. 9
Gregory, I. 16
Groen, A. J. 30
Gurtner, S. 32

Haghighi, M. S. 49, 50, 54
Hahn, J. 109
Haider, M. 162
Haile, D. 16
Hall, R. 100, 109
Hayes, R. A. 129
Hazen, B. T. 81, 92
healthcare: activities 115–117; and big data perspectives 4; challenges of 5; concept of 1; facilities 164–165; innovation in 31; mobilisation of 118; professionals 22; requirements 98; service delivery 17; supply chain 17
healthcare big data 2, 4, 108–109, 109–112, 114, 143–144, 182; actor-network theory 109–112; decomposition of 119–120; healthcare activities 113–114; interactive scheme 120–121; interessement 114–115; interpretive analysis 120; practice, implications for 121; problematisation 112–113; subjective, criticality of 120; translation, moments of 109–111; translation of 118–119
healthcare data 16–17; agency 22–23; agent 24–25; conceptual framework 20–22; criticality of 17; facility 23–24; healthcare stakeholders 16; patients' data 17; privacy of 23; sensitivity of 24; structuration theory 17–19; structure interacts 22; theoretical framework 19–20
healthcare environment 179; challenge for 49
healthcare information systems (HISs) 137
healthcare services: conceptual framework for 20–21, 21; delivery 15, 23, 30; facility 23; to patients 21; provision 16; well-being and safety 24
healthcare stakeholders 16, 17; poor data quality 17
healthcare vs health care 1
healthcare workers 21, 22
health economy 36, 39
health environment: data-intensive nature of 47
health facility 150
health monitoring systems 49
Health Professional Council 21
health systems: and big data analytics 161–162; data challenges in 143; innovation of 36
Henderson, A. 81
hermeneutic circle technique 79

heterogeneity 58, 64
heterogeneous data set 96–97
He, Z. 16
high-quality health 49
Hilbert, M. 143
Hirschheim, R. A. 8
Holistic Framework on IS evaluation 178
Horvitz, E. 131, 133
Hose, R. 14
Howe, W. 131
Hsu, C. L. 137
Huberman, B. A. 127
human actors 109–110
human-centric approach 31
human immunodeficiency virus (HIV) 35
human knowledge 120
humans vs. big data 179
human-to-big data interactions 179
human-to-human interactions 179
Hunter, P. 14
Huxtable-Thomas, L. 32

Iahad, N. A. 111
Igou, A. 159
inbound knowledge 36
Indeje, W. 15, 18
information security 36
information systems (IS) 1, 14, 143, 176
information technology (IT) 1, 14, 46, 58, 74, 106, 127, 143, 160, 175
information useability 53
inseparability 109
insight extraction 162
integration 5, 80–81
intellectual property (IP) 41
interaction and information sharing: cloud solution 53–54; communicative tools 54; data availability 54
interactive scheme 120–121
interessement 114–115, 147–148
Internet of Things 74
interpretive analysis 120
interpretive approach 2
interpretive schemes 18
interpretivism 8–9
interpretivist approach 81, 82
Iqbal, R. 74
Irani, Z. 6
IT requirements 183
Iyamu, T. 9, 30, 34, 37, 40, 47, 48, 76, 100, 110

Jadhav, A. 108
Jagadish, H. V. 58, 141
Jameii, S. M. 129

Jee, K. 17
Jones-Farmer, L. A. 81, 92
Joynt, K. E. 63, 68, 109
Jusoh, Y.Y. 161, 166

Kaisler, S. 75
Kamal, M. M. 6
Kambatla, K. 89
Kankanhalli, A. 109
Kashani, M. H. 129
Katal, A. 74, 77, 95
Katsaliaki, K. 47
Kaul, A. 17
Kaul, C. 17
Kaur, K. 14
Kayyali, B. 132–134
key indicator, big data analytics 169–171, **171**
Khanal, R. C. 81
Kim, G. H. 17, 160, 163
Kim, Y. S. 48
Kitchin, R. 135
Klein, H. K. 79
Knott, D. 132–134
knowledgeability 39, 166
Kollias, G. 89
Koppius, O. R. 92, 99
Krogstie, J. 78
Kumar, H. 64
Kumar, S. 47
Kumar, V. 89
Kung, L. 76, 98, 162, 178
Kuo, M. H. 141, 162
Kwak, K. 137
Kwon, L. S. 48
Kwon, O. 62
Kyriazakos, S. 48

Labrinidis, A. 58, 141
Lambrinoudakis, C. 54
language 147, 150
language semantics 153–154
Latour, B. 99
LaValle, S. 75, 76
Lavanya, S. 62
Law, J. 64
Lee, C. H. 64
Lee, M. R. 137
Lee, N. 62
Leon, N. 143
Lepenioti, K. 7
Lewkow, N. 164
Lindner, C. H. 97
Linton, J. D. 30
Liu, J. 137

Lukka, K. 75
Lundberg, N. 35, 36

macro-transformative processes 97
Maddox, T. M. 63, 68, 109
Mahdipour, E. 129
Marshall, B. 75
Marthandan, G. 179
Martin, E. M. 134
Marx, V. 129
Mashilo, M. 30, 34, 37, 40
Mathew, P.S. 68
Mathur, K. 143
Matthias, O. 16
McCormack, L. A. 127
McPhee, R.D. 15
medical aid professionals 22
medical apparatus 152
medical associations 22
medical information 62
medical practitioners 145
medical unit 146
Mehta, N. 5, 8
Memos, V. A. 48
Mendoza, N. 164
Meng Tang, C. 179
Mentzas, G. 7
Meshram, C. 48
Mgudlwa, S. 9
Micheni, E. M. 63
micro-transformative processes 97
Mikalef, P. 78
Mills, A. J. 109
mission-critical data 54
Mittal, A. 48
mobile systems 46, 47; care, quality of 48; healthcare facility 47; in health service delivery 48; patients' data 47
mobilisation stage 110, 112, 117, 118, 149–150
Mohamed, N. 49, 53, 80
Mojarad, S. 164
Money, W. 75
Montenegro, L. M. 116
Muhammad, I. 112
multi-level analysis: actor-network theory 93–94, 100; actors and relationship 100–101; big data analysis 97–98; big data analytics 91–93, 101–102; big data, micro and macro levels 90; healthcare requirements 98; operational level 99; single analysis method 89; strategic level 99–100
Murphy, S. 33
Myers, M. D. 75, 79

Nachtmann, H. 17
Najafabadi, M. M. 77, 79, 96
Nambiar, R. 62
National Health Systems (NHS) 39
Naz, S. 129
network heterogeneity 90
Nguyen, L. 100
Nold, H. 159
non-government organisations 22
non-human actors 66, 109–110
non-technical agents 18, 20, 24, 63
Al Nuaimi, N. 49, 53

obligatory passage point (OPP) 118
Ojha, M. 143
ontology 111
open technology innovation (OTI): awareness of 32; benefits of 41–42; challenges of 42; cultural affiliation 38; factors influencing 36; for healthcare service 34–36; health economy 39; implications of 40–41; information security 39–40; literature review 32–34; perspectives 30; social context 36–37; technology solution 37–38
organisational performance 161

Palmieri, F. 106
Pamula, R. 176
Panahiazar, M. 108
Pandit, A. 5, 8
Pappas, I. O. 78
Park, Y. T. 48
Passiante, G. 37, 41
Pathak, J. 108
patients 17; availability of 54; big data privacy 134; data for communication 50; delivering service 145; education programmes 24; electronic healthcare records 137; health assessment 147; health condition 112; information 30; information type 50; management of 21
Perera, C. 102
Personal Data Protection Act (PDPA) 40
personal data, sensitivity 7
Personally Controlled Electronic Health Record (PCEHR) 112
pharmaceutical companies 22
Pillai, A.S. 68
Poddar, A. 75
Pohl, E. 17
policymakers 50, 52

Pollack, J. 117
practice, implications of 82–84, **83**
predictive analytics 7, 92, 98, 162, 177
prescriptive analytics 7–8, 92, 160
Preston, D. S. 77
Privacy and Personal Information Protection Act (PPIPA) 40
problematisation 3–4, 100, 111, 112–113, 144, 146–147
process constitutes 167–168
Protection of Personal Information Act (PoPIA) 40
Psannis, K. E. 48
public health policy 23

Qin, Q. 162
quality healthcare 2, 130
Quek, F. 150
Qureshi, J. A. 150

radiology network system 144–145
Raghupathi, V. 63, 68
Raghupathi, W. 63, 68
Ram, S. 164
Rani, K. 17
Rani, R. 14
Razzak, I. 129
realism 107, 143
reality sense-making 111
real-time access 132
real-time situations 89
Rehman, A. 129
Reinhardt, R. 32
reliability 126
reproductive system 17, 19
research & development (R&D) 33
Robert, J. 145
Roderick, S. 32
Romero, D. M. 127
Ronan, G. 33, 35
Roode, D. 76, 100, 110
Rumsfeld, J. S. 63, 68, 109
Russom, P. 102

Sacristan, J. A. 109, 143
Saedi, A. 111
Sagiroglu, S. 128
Saldžiūnas, K. 80
Salter, A. 39
Sampath, P. 63
Sankaran, S. 117
scalability 107
Schiuma, G. 37, 41

Schneider, H. 143
Secundo, G. 37, 41
security/privacy 5, 48, 134
Sellis, T. 162
sense-making 49
service delivery 90
Sethi, A. 63
Shaanika, I. 47, 48
Sha'ri, M.Y. 8
Sharma, S. K. 53, 90
Sheikh, A. 9
Shek, D.T. 82
Shin, B. 62
Shmueli, G. 92, 99
Siegel, E. 7
Şimşek, K. 39
Sinanc, D. 128
Singh, N. 64
single analysis method 89
Sivarajah, U. 6
skill and specialisation factors 50
skillset, big data analytics 168, 184
Skotnes, T. 134
Skyrius, R. 80
Smith, B. 17
Smithson, S. C. 8
social context 36
social media 4, 74, 126; benefits and challenges 130; big data 128, 133–134; connectivity 132; ethical risk 128; healthcare environment 133; healthcare purposes 130; influence, factors of *130*; integration of 134, 137; IT integration of *135*; and IT solutions 136, 137; flexibility and compatibility 136; limitation, lack of 131; privacy 136–137; roles and effects 131–133; security/privacy 134; size and velocity 127
social systems 15, 18
social theory 17, 18
socio-cultural differences 147
socio-technical framework 110
socio-technical levels 106
socio-technical theory, 2, 9, 76, 109
Soltanpoor, R. 162
Specker, B. 127
Srinivas, K. 17
stakeholders 147
Standing, C. 9
Stockdale, R. 9
Stones, R. 9
structuration theory (ST) 2, 15, 17–19
structure interacts 22

subjective criticality 120
subjectivism 82, 150
subject knowledge 167
Su, C. H. 137
supportability 181
sustainability 89, 90
Swink, M. 77
Syed, A. 127
Syed, S. 150

Tan, S. 109
Taslimitehrani, V. 108
Tatnall, A. 100
technical agents 18
technology innovations 30
Teoh, S.Y. 112
Ter Wal, A. L. 39
Thanh, N. C. 80
Thanh, T. T. 80
Thool, V. R. 6
Toma, A. 37, 41
transformation 133–134
translate big data 111
translation 109–111, 118–119
Tresp, V. 143
Trimi, S. 160, 163
Troshani, I. 120
Twitter 129

unethical act 24
units-based analysis 119
Unnithan, C. 100

validation process 23
value, big data analytics 178
Vance, K. 131
Van Kuiken, S. 132–134
Vargheese, R. 63
Velpula, P. 176
Venugopal, C. 127
Verma, S. 17
Vernon, A. 16
Viceconti, M. 14
Vimarlund, V. 32
volume, velocity and variety (3Vs) 58, 165, 168, 179
vulnerability 31, 48
Vyas, D. 19

Wailes, N. 100, 109
Waller, M. A. 99
Walsham, G. 19, 75, 144
Wamba, S. F. 81

Wang, W. Y. C. 162
Wang, Y. 76, 98, 162, 178
Wass, S. 32
Watson, H. J. 6, 82
Wazid, M. 74, 77, 95
Weerakkody, V. 6
Whitehouse, D. E. 8
Whitelock, V. 164
Wiblen, S. 100, 109
Wickramasinghe, N. 112, 120
Wohlin, C. 77
Worley, B. 63
Worth, A. 9
Wright, P. M. 97
Wyber, R. 109, 143

Xu, B. 48

Yang, R. 162, 165
Yi, C. 16
Yin, J. 129
Yıldırım, N. 39
Yoon, H. J. 64

Zaman, I. 64
Zandesh, Z. 49, 50, 54
Zaslavsky, A. 102
Zetino, J. 164
Zheng, Q. 15, 18, 162
Zikopoulos, P. 89
Zkik, K. 8

Printed in the USA
CPSIA information can be obtained
at www.ICGtesting.com
LVHW021735041124
795688LV00040B/1253